Lecture Notes in Artificial Intelligence   12175

Subseries of Lecture Notes in Computer Science

Series Editors

Randy Goebel
University of Alberta, Edmonton, Canada
Yuzuru Tanaka
Hokkaido University, Sapporo, Japan
Wolfgang Wahlster
DFKI and Saarland University, Saarbrücken, Germany

Founding Editor

Jörg Siekmann
DFKI and Saarland University, Saarbrücken, Germany

More information about this series at http://www.springer.com/series/1244

Davide Calvaresi · Amro Najjar ·
Michael Winikoff · Kary Främling (Eds.)

Explainable, Transparent Autonomous Agents and Multi-Agent Systems

Second International Workshop, EXTRAAMAS 2020
Auckland, New Zealand, May 9–13, 2020
Revised Selected Papers

 Springer

Editors
Davide Calvaresi 🆔
University of Applied Sciences Western
Switzerland
Sierre, Switzerland

Amro Najjar 🆔
University of Luxembourg
Esch-sur-Alzette, Luxembourg

Michael Winikoff 🆔
Victoria University of Wellington
Wellington, New Zealand

Kary Främling 🆔
Umeå University
Umeå, Sweden

ISSN 0302-9743   ISSN 1611-3349 (electronic)
Lecture Notes in Artificial Intelligence
ISBN 978-3-030-51923-0   ISBN 978-3-030-51924-7 (eBook)
https://doi.org/10.1007/978-3-030-51924-7

LNCS Sublibrary: SL7 – Artificial Intelligence

This Springer imprint is published by the registered company Springer Nature Switzerland AG
The registered company address is: Gewerbestrasse 11, 6330 Cham, Switzerland

Preface

The domain of eXplainable Artificial Intelligence (XAI) emerged to explain the often-opaque decision mechanisms of machine learning algorithms and autonomous systems. In particular, as intelligent agents and robots get more complex and more involved in the daily lives of millions of users, making agents and robots decision-making processes explainable is a chief priority to enhance their acceptability, avoid failures, and comply with national and international relevant regulations.

The 2020 edition of the EXplainable TRansparent Autonomous Agents and Multi-Agent Systems (EXTRAAMAS 2020) built on the successful track of workshops initiated last year in 2019 in Montreal. In particular, EXTRAAMAS 2020 set the following aims:

1. To strengthen the common ground for the study and development of explainable and understandable autonomous agents, robots, and Multi-Agent Systems (MAS)
2. To investigate the potential of agent-based systems in the development of personalized user-aware explainable AI
3. To assess the impact of transparent and explained solutions on the user/agents behaviors
4. To discuss motivating examples and concrete applications in which the lack of explainability leads to problems, which would be resolved by explainability
5. To assess and discuss the first demonstrators and proof of concepts paving the way for the next generation systems

EXTRAAMAS 2020 received 20 submissions. Each submission underwent a rigorous peer-review process (at least three reviewers per paper). At the end of the review process, nine papers were accepted (eight full papers and one demo) – contained in this volume.

Unfortunately, due to COVID-19 travel restrictions, the workshop (and the AAMAS[1] conference) were held online, rather than in Auckland, New Zealand. For each paper, the authors pre-recorded a video presentation, which is available on the EXTRAAMAS website.[2] Participants also had access to a Slack workspace, where discussion took place. The keynote by Professor Miller was presented live using Zoom, and a recording of the talk was subsequently made available online.

---

[1] International Conference on Autonomous Agents and Multi-Agent Systems.
[2] https://extraamas.ehealth.hevs.ch/program.html.

We would like to thank the publicity chairs and Program Committee for their valuable work. We also thank the authors, presenters, participants, and Tim Miller for his fantastic keynote.

May 2020

Davide Calvaresi
Amro Najjar
Michael Winikoff
Kary Främling

Organization

General Chairs

Davide Calvaresi — University of Applied Sciences Western Switzerland, Switzerland
Amro Najjar — University of Luxembourg, Luxembourg
Michael Winikoff — Victoria University of Wellington, New Zealand
Kary Främling — Umeå University, Sweden

Publicity Chairs

Timotheus Kampik — Umeå University, Sweden
Giovanni Ciatto — University of Bologna, Italy

Advisory Board

Tim Miller — The University of Melbourne, Australia
Michael Schumacher — University of Applied Sciences Western Switzerland, Switzerland
Virginia Dignum — Umeå University, Sweden
Leon van der Torre — University of Luxembourg, Luxembourg

Program Committee

Andrea Omicini — Università di Bologna, Italy
Ofra Amir — Technion IE&M, Israel
Olivier Boissier — ENS-MINES Saint-Étienne, France
J. Carlos N. Sanchez — Umeå University, Sweden
Tathagata Chakraborti — IBM Research AI, USA
Salima Hassas — Université Lyon 1, France
Gauthier Picard — ENS-MINES Saint-Étienne, France
Jean-Guy Mailly — Laboratoire d'Informatique Paris Descartes, France
Aldo F. Dragoni — Università Politecnica delle Marche, Italy
Patrick Reignier — LIG, France
Stephane Galland — UTBM, France
Grégory Bonnet — University of Caen, France
Jean-Paul Calbimonte — University of Applied Sciences Western Switzerland, Switzerland
Sarath Sreedharan — Arizona State University, USA
Laëtitia Matignon — Université Lyon 1, France
Daniele Magazzeni — King's College London, UK
Cesar A. Tacla — UTFPR Curitiba, Brazil

Avleen Malhi   Thapar Institute of Engineering & Technology, India
Stefano Bromuri   Open University of the Netherlands, The Netherlands
Rob Wortham   University of Bath, UK
Suna Bensch   Umeå University, Sweden
Timotheus Kampik,   Umeå University, Sweden
RyazanYazan Mualla   UTBM, France
Nicola Falcionelli   Università Politecnica delle Marche, Italy
Önder Gürcan   CEA, France
Stefan Sarkadi   King's College London, UK
Silvia Tulli   INESC-ID, Portugal
Jérémie Dauphin   University of Luxembourg, Luxembourg
Francisco J. Rodríguez Lera   University of León, Spain
Julian Alfredo Mendez   Umeå University, Sweden
Prashan Mathugama   The University of Melbourne, Australia
   Babun Apuhamilage
Sviatlana Höhn   University of Luxembourg, Luxembourg
Isaac Lage   Harvard University, USA

Contents

Demos

Explainable Agents

Agent-Based Explanations in AI: Towards an Abstract Framework

Giovanni Ciatto[1]([✉]) [iD], Michael I. Schumacher[2] [iD], Andrea Omicini[1] [iD],
and Davide Calvaresi[2] [iD]

[1] University of Bologna, 47521 Cesena, FC, Italy
{giovanni.ciatto,andrea.omicini}@unibo.it
[2] HES-SO Valais, 3960 Sierre, Switzerland
{michael.schumacher,davide.calvaresi}@hevs.ch

Abstract. Recently, the eXplainable AI (XAI) research community has
focused on developing methods making Machine Learning (ML) predictors more *interpretable* and *explainable*. Unfortunately, researchers are
struggling to converge towards an unambiguous definition of notions such
as *interpretation*, or, *explanation*—which are often (and mistakenly) used
interchangeably. Furthermore, despite the sound metaphors that Multi-
Agent System (MAS) could easily provide to address such a challenge,
and agent-oriented perspective on the topic is still missing. Thus, this
paper proposes an abstract and formal framework for XAI-based MAS,
reconciling notions, and results from the literature.

Keywords: Explainable artificial intelligence · Multi-agent systems ·
Understandability · Explainability · Interpretability

1 Introduction

The adoption of intelligent systems (IS) in modern society is booming: the trend
is mostly due to the recent momentum gained by Machine Learning (ML). In the
past decades, disruptive results from ML dictated several waves of temporary
yet massive adoption of AI systems, in both academia and industry. Therefore,
some authors refer to the current era as the third *spring of AI*—stressing that
AI has already lived two *winters*.

As in the previous springs of AI, the expectations are being inflated by the
promising predictive capabilities showed by ML-based IS. Besides the remarkable
computational capability characterising this era, the vast availability of data is
the second key aspect enabling the new spring. However, also modern researchers
and stakeholders are experiencing problems stemming from the *opacity* of ML-
based solutions.

The opacity of numeric predictors (i.e., the outcome of ML techniques applied
on data) is a broadly acknowledged issue, which has been studied even before

This paper is the full version of the extended abstract [9] soon to be appearing on the
AAMAS '20 Proceedings.

© Springer Nature Switzerland AG 2020
D. Calvaresi et al. (Eds.): EXTRAAMAS 2020, LNAI 12175, pp. 3–20, 2020.
https://doi.org/10.1007/978-3-030-51924-7_1

the current spring of AI. However, mostly due to the unprecedented pace and extent of ML adoption in several, often critical domains (e.g., finance, health-care, and law), the need for addressing such opacity issues is more compelling than ever [2].

The opaqueness of ML-based solutions is an unacceptable condition in a world where ML is involved in many (safety-)critical activities. Indeed, perform-ing automatic, good predictions (resp. provide useful decisions) is essential as much as letting the humans involved in those contexts *understand* why and how such predictions (resp. decisions) have been obtained. When humans can-not understand the outcome or the behaviour of ML predictors involved in some business processes, bad consequences can follow. This is because, in the current society, the liability of decisions/actions is still mainly associated with human beings (even if the outcomes have been obtained via IS). To make the picture even more complicated, modern regulations recognise citizens right to receive meaningful explanations when automatic decisions may affect their lives [12]. For all the above reasons, the problem of understanding ML results is rapidly gaining momentum in recent AI research [5].

The topic of understandability in AI is nowadays the main concern of the eXplainable AI community (XAI henceforth), whose name is due to a successful project of DARPA [24]. There, the authors review the main approaches to make AI more understandable to human beings. However, as further discussed in this paper, we argue that studies in this field are flawed by a fundamental issue—namely, they lack an unambiguous definition for the concept of *explanation* and, consequently, a clear understanding of what X in XAI actually means. Indeed, the notion of *explanation* is not clearly established in the literature, nor is there a consensus on what the property named "explainability" should imply. This is especially true for ML-based solutions, where knowledge is represented in a *sub-symbolic*, unintelligible way.

Similar issues exist as far as the notion of *interpretation* is concerned. The two terms are sometimes used interchangeably in the literature, whereas other times they carry different meanings. To face such issues, we argue that since multi-agent systems (MAS) offer a coherent yet expressive set of abstractions, promoting *conceptual integrity* in the engineering of complex software systems [18] – and of socio-technical systems (STS) in particular –, they can be exploited to define a sound and unambiguous reference framework for XAI.

In this paper, we propose an abstract framework for XAI relying on notions and results from the MAS literature. The framework is mostly targeting sub-symbolic AI and ML-based intelligent systems. In particular, our framework introduces a clear distinction among two orthogonal, yet interrelated, activities – i.e., *interpretation* and *explanation* – which can be performed on sub-symbolic predictors to make them more understandable in the eyes of human beings. Thus, it provides a formal definition for such activities in the MAS perspective, thus stressing the *objective* nature of explanation, other than the *subjective* nature of interpretation.

Accordingly, the paper is structured as follows. In Sect. 2 we provide an overview of the XAI research domain. In Sect. 3 we present our abstract framework. Then, Sect. 4 assesses our framework by showing how it can help in unambiguously defining the main problems in XAI. Conversely, Sect. 5 speculates on some future directions. Finally, Sect. 6 concludes the paper.

2 Background

Most IS today leverage on *sub-symbolic* predictive models that are trained from data through ML. The reason for such wide adoption is easy to understand. We live in an era where the availability of data is unprecedented, and ML algorithms make it possible to detect useful statistical information hidden into such data semi-automatically. Information, in turn, supports decision making, monitoring, planning, and forecasting in virtually any human activity where data is available.

However, ML is not the silver bullet. Despite the increased predictive power, ML comes with some well-known drawbacks which make it perform poorly in some use cases. One blatant example is algorithmic *opacity*—that is, essentially, the difficulty of the human mind in *understanding* how ML-based IS function or compute their outputs. This represents a serious issue in all those contexts where human beings are liable for their decision, or, when they are expected to provide some sort of *explanation* for it—even if the decision has been supported by some IS. For instance, think about a doctor willing to motivate a serious, computer-aided diagnosis, or, a bank employee in need of explaining to a customer why his/her profile is inadequate for a loan. In all contexts, ML is at the same time an enabling – as it aids the decision process by automating it – and a limiting factor—as opacity prevents human awareness of *how* the decision process works.

Opacity is why ML predictors are also referred to as *black boxes* into the literature. The "black box" expression refers to models where knowledge is not explicitly represented [15]. The lack of some explicit, symbolic representation of knowledge is what makes it hard for humans to *understand* the functioning of black boxes, and why they led to suggest or undertake a given decision. Clearly, troubles in understanding black-box content and functioning prevent people from fully trusting – therefore accepting – them. To make the picture even more complex, current regulations such as the GDPR [25] are starting to recognise the citizens' *right to explanation* [12]—which implicitly requires IS to eventually become *understandable*. Indeed, understanding IS is essential to guarantee algorithmic fairness, to identify potential bias/problems in the training data, and to ensure that IS perform as designed and expected.

Unfortunately, the notion of understandability is neither standardised nor systematically assessed, yet. At the same time, there is no consensus on what exactly providing an *explanation* should mean when decisions are supported by a black box. However, several authors agree that not all black boxes are equally *interpretable*—meaning that some black boxes are more susceptible to understand than others for our minds. For example, Fig. 1 is a common way to illustrate the differences in black-box interpretability.

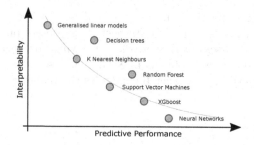

Fig. 1. Interpretability/performance trade-off for some common sorts of black-box predictors

Even though informal – as pointed on in [22], given the lack of ways to measure "interpretability" – Fig. 1 effectively expresses why more research is need on understandability. In fact, the image essentially states how the better performing black boxes are also the less interpretable ones. This is a problem in practice since only rarely predictive performances can be sacrificed in favour of a higher degree of interpretability.

To tackle such issues, the XAI research field has recently emerged. Among the many authors and organisations involved in the topic, DARPA has proposed a comprehensive research road map [24], which reviews the main approaches to make black boxes more understandable. There, DARPA categorises the many currently available techniques aimed at building meaningful interpretations or explanations for black-box models, it summarises the open problems and challenges, and it provides a successful reference framework for the researchers interested in the field. Unfortunately, despite the great effort in defining terms, objects, and methods for the research line, a clear definition of fundamental notions such as *interpretation* and *explanation* is still missing.

2.1 Related Work

Notions such as explanation, interpretation, and transparency are mentioned, introduced, or informally defined in several works. However, a coherent framework has not yet emerged. This subsection recalls some significant contributions from the literature discussing concepts of explanation and interpretation – or any variant of theirs. Our goal here is to highlight the current lack of consensus on the meaning of such terms, for which we propose a possible, unambiguous alternative in the next sections.

Similarly to what we do here, Lipton [15] starts his discussion by recognising how most definitions of ML interpretability are often inconsistent and underspecified. In his clarification effort, Lipton essentially maps interpretability on the notion of *transparency*, and explanation on the notion of *post-hoc* interpretation. Then, he enumerates and describes the several possible variants of transparency, that are *(i)* simulatability – i.e., the *practical* possibility, for a human being, to "contemplate the entire model at once" and simulate its functioning on some data – which characterises, for instance, generalised linear models; *(ii)* decomposability – i.e., the possibility, for the model to be decomposed in elementary parts whose functioning is intuitively understandable for humans and helpful in understanding the whole model – which characterises, for instance, decision trees; and *(iii)* algorithmic transparency – i.e., the possibility, for a human being, to intuitively understand how a given learning algorithm, or the predictors it produces, operate – which characterises, for instance, k-nearest-neighbors techniques. Similarly, *post-hoc* interpretability is defined as an approach where some information is extracted from a black box in order to ease its understanding. Such information have not necessarily to expose the internal functioning of the black box. As stated in the paper: "examples of post-hoc interpretations include the verbal explanations produced by people or the saliency maps used to analyze deep neural networks".

Conversely, Besold et al. [3] discuss the notion of explanation at a fundamental level. There, the authors provide a philosophical overview on such topic, concluding that "explanation is an epistemological activity and explanations are an epistemological accomplishment—they satisfy a sort of epistemic longing, a desire to know something more than we currently know. Besides satisfying this desire to know, they also provide the explanation-seeker a direction of action that they did not previously have". Then they discuss the topic of explanation in AI from a historical perspective. In particular, when focussing on ML, they introduce the following classification of IS systems: *(i)* opaque systems – i.e., black boxes acting as oracles where the logic behind predictions is not observable or understandable –, *(ii)* interpretable systems – i.e., white boxes whose functioning is understandable to humans, also thanks to the expertise, resources, or tools –, and *(iii)* comprehensible systems—i.e., "systems which emit *symbols* along with their outputs, allowing the user to relate properties of the input to the output". According to this classification, while interpretable systems can be inspected to be understood – thus letting observer draw their explanations by themselves–comprehensible systems must explicitly provide a symbolic explanation of their functioning. The focus is thus on *who* produces explanations, rather than *how*.

In [10], the interpretability of ML systems is defined as "the ability to explain or to present in understandable terms to a human". Interpretations and explanations are therefore collapsed in this work, as confirmed by the authors using the two terms interchangeably. The remainder of that paper focuses *(i)* on identifying under which circumstances interpretability is needed in ML, and *(ii)* how to assess the quality of some explanation.

The survey by Guidotti et al. [13] is a nice entry point to explainable ML. It consists of an exhaustive and recent survey overviewing the main notions, goals, problems, and (sub-)categories in this field, and it encompasses a taxonomy of existing approaches for "opening the black box"—which may vary a lot depending on the sort of data and the family of predictors at hand. There, the authors define the verb to interpret as the act of "providing some meaning of explaining and presenting in understandable terms some concepts", borrowing such a definition from the Merriam-Webster[1] dictionary. Consequently, they define interpretability as "the ability to explain or to provide the meaning in understandable terms to a human"— a definition they again borrow from [10]. So, in this case as well the notions of *interpretation* and *explanations* are collapsed.

In [22], Rudin does not explicitly define explainability or interpretability, and she refers to interpretable or explainable ML almost interchangeably. However, she states some interesting properties of *interpretability*, which influenced our work. In particular, she acknowledges that "interpretability is a domain-specific notion". Furthermore, she links interpretability of information with its complexity – and, in particular, its *sparsity* –, as the amount of cognitive entities the human mind can handle at once is minimal ($\sim 7 \pm 2$ according to [16]). As far as explainability is concerned, apparently, Rudin adopts a *post-hoc* perspective similar to the one in [15], as she writes, "an explanation is a separate model that is supposed to replicate most of the behaviour of a black box". In the remainder of that paper, the author argues how the path towards interpretable ML steps through broader adoption of inherently interpretable predictors – such as generalised linear models or decision trees – rather than relying on *post-hoc* explanations which do not reveal what is inside black boxes—thus preventing their full understanding.

Finally, the recent article by Rosenfeld et al. [21] is similar in its intents to our current work. There, the authors attempt to formally define what explanation and interpretation respectively are in the case of ML-based classification. However, their work differs from ours in several ways. In particular, they define interpretation and explanation differently from what we do. In fact, according to the authors, "interpretation" is a function mapping data, data schemes, and predictors to some representation of the predictors internal logic, whereas "explanation" is defined as "the human-centric objective for the user to understand" a predictor using the aforementioned interpretation function. Other notions are formally defined into the paper, such as for instance, *(i)* explicitness, *(ii)* fairness, *(iii)* faithfulness, *(iv)* justification, and *(v)* transparency. Such concepts are formally defined in terms of the aforementioned interpretation and explanation functions. The reminder of that paper then re-interprets the field of XAI in terms of all the notions mentioned so far.

3   Explanation *vs.* Interpretation

This section introduces the preliminary notions, intuitions, and notations we leverage upon in Sect. 3.1 and subsequent sections, in order to formalise our abstract framework for agent-based explanations. We start by providing an intuition for the notion of *interpretation*, and, consequently, for the *act* of interpreting something. Accordingly, we provide an intuition for the property of "being interpretable" as well, stressing its comparative nature. Analogously to what we did with *interpretation*, we then provide intuitions for terms such as *explanation* and its derivatives.

---

[1] https://www.merriam-webster.com/dictionary/interpret.

About Interpretation. Taking inspiration from the field of Logics, we define the *act* of "interpreting" some object X as the activity performed by an agent A – either human or software – assigning a *subjective* meaning to X. Such meaning is what we call *interpretation*. Roughly speaking, an object X is said to be *interpretable* for an agent A if it is *easy* for A to draw an interpretation for X—where "easy" means A requires a low *computational* (or *cognitive*) effort to understand X. For instance, consider the case of road signs, which contain symbols instead of scripts to be easily, quickly, and intuitively interpretable.

We model such intuition through a function $I_A(X) \mapsto [0, 1]$ providing a *degree of interpretability* – or simply interpretability, for short – for X, in the eyes of A. The value $I_A(X)$ is not required to be directly observable or measurable in practice, since agents' mind may be inaccessible in most cases. This is far from being an issue, since we are not actually interested in the absolute value of $I_A(X)$, for some object X, but rather we are interested in being able to order different objects w.r.t. their subjective interpretability. For instance, we write $I_A(X) > I_A(Y)$, for two objects X and Y, meaning that the former is more interpretable than the latter, according to A. For example, consider the case of a neural network and a decision tree, both trained on the same examples to solve the same problem with similar predictive performances. Both objects may be represented as graphs. However, it is likely for a human observer to see the decision tree as more interpretable—as their nodes bring semantically meaningful, high-level information.

Summarising, we stress the subjective nature of interpretations, as agents assign them to objects according to their State of Mind (SoM) [19] and background knowledge, and they need not be formally defined any further.

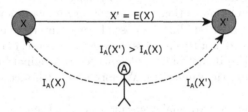

Fig. 2. Explanation vs. Interpretation: a simple framework

About Explanation. We define "explaining" as the activity of producing a more interpretable object X' out of a less interpretable one, namely X, performed by agent A. More formally, we define *explanation* as a function $E(X) \mapsto X'$ mapping objects into other objects, possibly, in such a way that $I_A(X') > I_A(X)$, for some agent A. The simple framework described so far is summarised in Fig. 2.

Notice that human beings tend to collapse into the concept of "explanation" the whole sequence of steps actually involving both explaining and interpreting, according to our framework. This happens because, if the explained object X' is as interpretable for the listening agent B as it is for the explaining agent A, then both A and B are likely to be satisfied with X'. Conversely, it may also happen the explanation E adopted by A produces an object X', which is more interpretable than X for A but not for B. Similarly to how two persons would handle such an unpleasant situation, we envision that interaction and communication may be adopted to break such *impasses* in multi-agent systems.

In the following sections, we develop such an idea, describing how our simple framework could be extended to support ML-based intelligent systems.

3.1   A Conceptual Framework for XAI

In AI several tasks can be reduced to a functional model $M : X \to Y$ mapping some input data $X \subseteq \mathcal{X}$ from an input domain $\mathcal{X}$ into some output data $Y \subseteq \mathcal{Y}$ from an output domain $\mathcal{Y}$.

In the following, we denote as $\mathcal{M}$ the set of all *analogous* models $M' : X \to \mathcal{Y}$, which attempts to solve the same problem on the same input data—usually, in (possibly slightly) different ways. For instance, according to this definition, a decision tree and a neural network, both trained on the same data-set to solve the same classification problem with similar accuracies, are analogous—even if they belong to different families of predictors.

At a very high abstraction level, many tasks in AI may be devoted to compute, for instance:

- the best $M^* \in \mathcal{M}$, given $X \subseteq \mathcal{X}$ and $Y \subseteq \mathcal{Y}$ (e.g. supervised ML),
- the best M^* and Y, given X (e.g. unsupervised ML),
- the best Y^*, given X and M (e.g. informed/uninformed search),
- the best X^*, given Y and M (e.g. abduction, most likely explanation), etc.

according to some goodness criterion which is specific for the task at hand.

In the reminder of this section, we discuss how explanation may be defined as a function searching or building a – possibly more interpretable – model w.r.t. the one to be explained. For this process to even make sense, of course, we require the resulting model to be not only analogous to the original but also similar in the way it behaves on the same data. We formalise such a concept through the notion of *fidelity*.

Let $M, M' \in \mathcal{M}$ be two analogous models. We then say M has a *locally good fidelity* w.r.t. M' and Z if and only if $\Delta f(M(Z), M'(Z)) < \delta$ for some arbitrarily small threshold $\delta \geq 0$ and for some subset of the input data $Z \subset X$. There, $\Delta f : 2^{\mathcal{Y}} \times 2^{\mathcal{Y}} \to \mathbb{R}_{\geq 0}$ is a function measuring the performance *difference* among two analogous models.

Local Interpretations. When an observer agent A is *interpreting* a model M behaviour w.r.t. some input data $Z \subseteq X$, it is actually trying to assign a subjective interpretability value $I_A(R)$ to some representation $R = r(M, Z)$ of choice, aimed at highlighting the behaviour of M w.r.t. the data in Z. There, $r : \mathcal{M} \times 2^{\mathcal{X}} \to \mathcal{R}$ is *representation means*, i.e., a function mapping models into *local* representations w.r.t. a particular subset of the input domain, whereas $\mathcal{R}$ is the set of model representations. For instance, in the case M is a classifier, R may

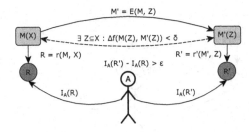

Fig. 3. Local explanation and interpretation of model M

be a graphical representation of (a portion of) the decision boundary/surface for a couple of input features.

There may be more or less interpretable *representations* of a particular model for the same observer A. Furthermore, representations may be either global or local as well, depending on whether they represent the behaviour of the model for the whole input space, or for just a portion of it. For example, consider the case of a plot showing the decision boundary of a neural network classifier. This representation is likely far more interpretable to the human observer than a graph representation showing the network structure, as it synthesise the global behaviour of the network concisely and intuitively. Similarly, saliency maps are an interpretable way to *locally* represent the behaviour of a network w.r.t. some particular input image. So, a way for easing interpretation for a given model behaviour w.r.t. a particular sort of inputs is about looking for the right representation in the eyes of the observer.

Local Explanations. Conversely, when an observer A is *explaining* a model M w.r.t. some input data $Z \subseteq X$, it is actually trying to produce a model $M' = E(M, Z)$ through some function $E : \mathcal{M} \times 2^{\mathcal{X}} \to \mathcal{M}$. In this case, we say M' is a *local explanation* for M w.r.t. to Z. We also say that M' is produced through the explanation strategy E.

Furthermore, we define an explanation M' as *admissible* if it has a valid fidelity w.r.t. the original model M and the data in Z—where Z is the same subset of the input data used by the explanation strategy. More precisely, we say M' is δ-admissible in Z w.r.t. M if $\Delta f(M(Z), M'(Z)) < \delta$.

Finally, we define an explanation M' as *clear* for A, in Z, and w.r.t. the original model M, if there exists some representation $R' = r(M', Z)$ which is more interpretable than the original model representation R. More precisely, we say M' is ε-clear for A, in Z, and w.r.t M if $I_A(R') - I_A(R) > \varepsilon$ for some arbitrarily big threshold $\varepsilon > 0$.

Several *explanations* may actually be produced for the same model M. For each explanation, there may be again more or less interpretable *representations*. Of course, explanations are useful if they ease the seek for more interpretable representations. Thus, providing an explanation for a given model behaviour w.r.t. a particular class of inputs is about creating *ad-hoc* metaphors aimed at easing the observer's understanding.

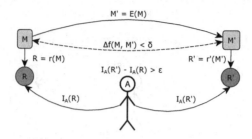

Fig. 4. Global explanation and interpretation of model

Global/Local Explanations. The theoretical framework described so far – which is graphically synthesised in Fig. 3 – is aimed at modelling *local* interpretations and explanations, that are, the two means an explanator agent may exploit in order to make AI tasks' *outcomes* more understandable in the eyes of some explanee.

Conversely, when the goal is not to understand some model outcome, but the model itself, from a *global* perspective – or, equivalently, when the goal is to understand the model outcome w.r.t the whole set of input data X –, the theoretical framework described so far is simplified as shown in Fig. 4, where the dependency on the input data is omitted from functions E, Δf, and r. This is possible because we consider the global case as a particular case of the local one, where $Z \equiv X$.

Finally, we remark that the case where a model M is to be understood on a single input-output pair, say x and $y = M(x)$, is simply captured by the aforementioned local model, through the constraint $Z = \{x\}$ and $M(Z) = \{y\}$.

3.2   Discussion

Our framework is deliberately abstract in order to capture a number of features we believe to be essential in XAI. First of all, our framework acknowledges – and properly captures – the orthogonality of interpretability w.r.t. explainability. This is quite new, indeed, considering that most authors tend to use the two concepts as if they were equivalent or interchangeable.

Furthermore, our framework explicitly recognises the *subjective* nature of interpretation, as well as the subtly *objective* nature of explanation. Indeed, interpretation is a subjective activity directly related to agents' perception and SoM, whereas explanation is an epistemic, computational action which aims at producing a high-fidelity model. The last step is objective in the sense that it does not depend on the agent's perceptions and SoM, thus being reproducible in principle. Of course, the *effectives* of an explanation is again a subjective aspect. Indeed, a clear explanation (for some agent) is a more interpretable variant of some given model—thus, the subjective activity of interpretation is again implicitly involved.

The proposed framework also captures the importance of representations. This is yet another degree of freedom that agents may exploit in their seek for a wider understandability of a given model. While other frameworks consider interpretability as an intrinsic property of AI models, we stress the fact that a given model may be represented in several ways, and each representation may be interpreted differently by different agents. As further discussed in the remainder of this paper, this is far from being an issue. This subjectivity is deliberate, and it is the starting point of some interesting discussions.

Finally, our framework acknowledges the global/local duality of both explanation and interpretation, thus enabling AI models to be understood either general or with respect to a particular input/output pair.

3.3 Practical Remarks

The ultimate goal of our framework is to provide a general, flexible, yet minimal framework describing the many aspects concerning AI understandability in the eyes of a *single* agent. We here illustrate several practical issues affecting our framework in practice, and further constraining it.

According to our conceptual framework, a *rational* agent seeking to understand some model M (or make it understandable) may either choose to elaborate on the *interpretation axis* – thus looking for a (better) representation R of M – or it can elaborate on the *explainability axis*—thus producing a novel, high fidelity model M', coming with a representation R' which is more interpretable than the original one (i.e., R).

Notice that, in practice, the nature of the model constrains the set of admissible representations. This means that a rational agent is likely to exploit both the explanation and interpretation axes in the general case—because novel representations may become available through an explanation. we argue and assume that each family of AI models comes with just a few *natural* representations. Because of this practical remark, we expect that, in real-world scenarios, an agent seeking for understandability is likely to "work" on both the interpretation and the explanation axes.

For instance, consider decision trees, which come with a natural representation as a tree of subsequent choices leading to a decision. Conversely, neural networks can either be represented as graphs or as algebraic combinations of tensors. In any case, neural network models are commonly considered less interpretable than other models. In such situation, a rational agent willing to make a neural network more understandable may choose to combine decision trees extraction (explanation) – possibly focusing on methods from the literature [1,4] – to produce a decision tree whose tree-like structure (representation) could be presented to the human observer to ease his/her interpretation. The decision-tree like representation is not ordinarily available for neural networks, but it may become available provided that an explanation step is performed.

Another interesting trait of our framework concerns the semantics of clear explanations. The current definition requires explanation strategies to consume a model M with a given representation R and to produce a high-fidelity model M' for which a representation R' exists, which is more interpretable than R. Several semantics may fit this definition. This is deliberate, since different semantics may come with different computational requirements, properties, and guarantees. For instance, one agent may be interested in finding the *best* explanation—that is, the one for which *each* representation is more interpretable than the most interpretable representation of the original model. Similarly, in some cases, it may be sufficient – other than more feasible – to find an *admissible* explanation—that is, a high-fidelity model for which *some* representation exists that is more interpretable than *some* representation of the original model. However, the inspection of the possible semantics and their properties falls outside the scope of this paper and is going to be considered as a future research direction.

4   Assessment of the Framework

The abstraction level of the presented framework has also been conceived in order to capture most of the current state of the art. Along this line, this section aims at validating the fitting of the existing contributions w.r.t. the framework presented in Sect. 3.1: if our framework is expressive enough, it should allow most (if not all) existing approaches to be uniformly framed, to be easily understood and compared. To this end, we leverage on the work by Guidotti et al. [13], where the authors perform a detailed and extensive survey on the state-of-the-art methods for XAI, by categorising the surveyed methods according to an elegant taxonomy. Thus, hereafter, we adopt their taxonomy as a reference for assessing our framework.

The taxonomy proposed by Guidotti et al. essentially discriminates among two main categories of XAI methods. These are the "transparent box design" and the "black-box explanation" categories. While the former category is not further decomposed, the latter comes with three more sub-categories, such as "model explanation", the "outcome explanation", and the "model inspection". Notice that, despite the authors' definition of "explanation" does not precisely match the one proposed in this paper, we maintained the original categorisation.

The remainder of this section navigates such a taxonomy accordingly, by describing how each (sub-)category – along with the methods therein located – fits our abstract framework.

4.1   Model Explanation

The mapping of the methods classified as part of the "model explanation" sub-category into our framework is seamless. Hence, it can be defined as follows:

Let M be a sub-symbolic classifier whose internal functioning representation R is poorly interpretable in the eyes of some explanee A, and let $E(\cdot)$ be some *global* explanation strategy. Then, the model explanation problem consists of computing some *global* explanation $M' = E(M)$ which is δ-admissible and ε-clear w.r.t. to A, for some $\delta, \varepsilon > 0$.

For instance, according to Guidotti et al., possible sub-symbolic classifiers are neural (possibly deep) networks, support vector machines, and random forests.

Conversely, explanation strategies may consist of algorithms aimed at *(i)* extracting decision trees/rules out of sub-symbolic predictors and the data they have been trained upon, *(ii)* compute feature importance vectors, *(iii)* detecting saliency masks, *(iv)* detecting partial dependency plots, etc.

In our framework, all the algorithms mentioned above can be described as *explanation strategies*. Such mapping is plausible given their ability to compute an admissible, and possibly more explicit models out of black boxes and the data they have been trained upon. However, it is worth to highlight that the clarity gain produced by such explanation strategies mostly relies on the implicit assumption that their output models come with a natural representation which is intuitively interpretable to the human mind.

4.2   Outcome Explanation

Methods classified as part of the "outcome explanation" sub-category can be very naturally described in our framework as well. In fact, it can be defined as follows:

> Let M be some sub-symbolic classifier whose internal functioning representation $R = r(M, Z)$ in some subset $Z \subset \mathcal{X}$ of the input domain is poorly interpretable to some explanee A, and let $E(\cdot, \cdot)$ be some *local* explanation strategy. Then, the outcome explanation problem consists of computing some *local* explanation $M' = E(M, Z)$ which is δ-admissible and ε-clear w.r.t. to A, for some $\delta, \varepsilon > 0$.

Summarising, while input black boxes may still be classifiers of any sort, explanation, and explanation strategies differ from the "model explanation" case. In particular, explanation strategies in this sub-category may rely on techniques leveraging on attention models, decision trees/rules extraction, or well-established algorithms such as LIME [20], and its extensions—which are essentially aimed at estimating the contribution of every input feature of the input domain to the particular outcome of the black box to be explained.

Notice that the explanation strategies in this category are only required to be admissible and clear in the portion of the input space surrounding the input data under study. Such a portion is implicitly assumed to be relatively small in most cases. Furthermore, the explanation strategy is less constrained than in the global case, as it is not required to produce explanations elsewhere.

4.3   Model Inspection

Methods classified as part of the "model inspection" sub-category can be naturally defined as follows:

> Let M be a sub-symbolic classifier whose available *global* representation $R = r(M)$ is poorly interpretable to some explanee A, and let $r(\cdot), r'(\cdot)$ be two different representation means. Then, the model inspection problem consists of computing some representation $R' = r'(M)$ such that $I_A(R') > I_A(R)$.

Of course, solutions to the model inspection problem vary a lot depending on which specific representation means $r(\cdot)$ is exploited by the explanator, other than the nature of the data the black box is trained upon. Guidotti et al. also provide a nice overview of the several sorts of representations means which may be useful to tackle the model inspection problem, like, for instance, sensitivity analysis, partial dependency plots, activation maximization images, tree visualisation, etc.

It is worth pointing out the capability of our framework to reveal the actual nature of the inspection problem. Indeed, it clearly shows how this is the first problem among the ones presented so far, which only relies on the interpretation axis alone to provide understandability.

4.4   Transparent Box Design

Finally, methods classified as part of the "transparent box design" sub-category can be naturally defined as follows:

> Let $X \subseteq \mathcal{X}$ be a dataset from some input domain $\mathcal{X}$, let $r(\cdot)$ be a representation means, and let A be the explanee agent. Then the transparent box design problem consists of computing a classifier M for which a global representation $R = r(M, X)$ exists such that $I_A(R) > 1 - \delta$, for some $\delta > 0$.

Although very simple, the transparent-box design is of paramount importance in XAI systems as it is the basic brick of most general explanation strategies. Indeed, it may be implicit in the functioning of some explanation strategy E to be adopted in some other model or outcome explanation problem.

For instance, consider the case of a local explanation strategy $E(M, X) \mapsto M'$. In the general case, to compute M', it relies on some input data X and the internal of the to-be-explained model M. However, there may be cases where the actual internal of M are not considered by the particular logic adopted by E. Instead, in such cases, E may only rely on X and the outcomes of M, which are $Y = M(X)$. In this case, the explanation strategy E is said *pedagogical*—whereas in the general case it is said *decompositional* (cf. [1]).

In other words, as made evident by our framework, the pedagogical methods exploited to deal with the model or outcome explanation problems must internally solve the transparent box design problem, as they must build an interpretable model out of some sampled data-set and nothing more.

5   Towards the Social Dimension of Explainability

In previous sections, we mostly focus on understandability from the single-agent perspective. Conversely, in this section we move from the *intra*-agent perspective – relying on the framework presented in Sect. 3.1 – to the *inter*-agent one—where two or more interacting agents are involved [8].

Our discussion stems from the observation that the agent extracting/eliciting information In other words, no agent explains something to itself. Furthermore, in a multi-agent setup, it is plausible to have agents characterised by heteroge-neous (potentially exclusive) capabilities and knowledge bases. In this situation, transferring knowledge and demanding for explanations may not even be possible without a *social* connotation. Indeed, the social, interactive dimension of under-standability is well recognised (e.g., in the social sciences), and some authors are already suggesting the XAI research community should take it into account [17]. Accordingly, we argue that our framework should be extended in this direction.

In particular, we envision two main actors

explanator—formulating and sharing an explanation, and the
explanee—consuming and possibly demanding the explanation

needing to establish a *mutual-understanding*. The explanator and the explanee can be a software agent, a human, or a grouped combination of them.

The possible social scenarios to share explanations can be generalised in 1-to-1, 1-to-n, and m-to-n. Thus, the framework presented in Sect. 3.1 – which mostly focuses on the single-agent perspective – needs further extensions to tackle the challenge of understandability in a multi-agent scenario.

Mutual understanding is not just an algorithm, nor is it some cognitive activ-ity that an agent can perform by itself; it is instead a formalised protocol involv-ing two or more parties. Therefore, aiming at scaling our framework to the MAS setup, we envision the following behaviours to be modelled.

As the interpretation function is subjective by construction, a piece of given information can be considered interpretable by agent A but not by another agent B. Consequently, if agent A is willing to make a model X understandable by another agent B, a joint *agreement* about the representation of the explanation has to be established. We define *mutual understanding* as a request-response protocol involving at least one agent acting as *explanator* and one agent acting as *explanee*—both either virtual or humans. Such an agreement may involve the establishment of a common taxonomy and knowledge reconciliation [14,23].

The protocol can begin with the explanator taking the initiative to share an explanation or with an explanee requiring it. The object of the explanation is the desire to understand the behaviour of a given model M w.r.t some data X—which is naturally represented through $R = r(M, X)$. Assuming that the explanator can rely on a wider dataset $X' \supseteq X$ than the one the explanee is relying upon (i.e., X), it may respond in several ways:

– it may produce an alternative representation $R' = r'(M, X')$ of M on some data $X' \supseteq X$, expecting that R' may result more interpretable than R in the eyes of the explanee
– it may produce an explanation for M in X' by leveraging on some internal strategy E, hoping that the natural representation $R'' = r''(E(M), X')$ of $E(M)$ in X' may result more interpretable than R in the eyes of the explanee

In turn, the explanee may provide feedback based on its subjective interpreta-tion of the proposed representation. The protocol may thus go through one or more request-response rounds. The object of the further iteration(s) can be *(i)* a specific component of the explanation – possibly demanding for a new level of granularity of the explanation – or *(ii)* the entire explanation that might need a complete rehearsal to be eventually understood. To prevent possible endless *(diverging)* explanations, we have to discriminate their underlying scenario. E.g.:

1-to-1—Once reached the most granular representation of an information, the agent say "no more additional information are available" concluding the iterations and declaring the *failure* of the explanation;

1-to-n—In case of misalignment on the understanding of a given explanation, techniques from defeasible reasoning [11] might be exploited to avoid the failure of the explanation;

m-to-n—Likewise the previous scenario, it is envisioned to possibly implement defeasible reasoning. Moreover, mechanisms enabling explanation-support among the n explanator might be developed to overcome the *failure* for lack of specification.

Another factor raising the complexity of the *mutual-understanding* is the possible heterogeneous composition of the explanator(s) or explanee(s) (e.g., a composition of both virtual and humans actors). A possible solution might be to generate clusters (e.g., sub-pools of explanators and explainees) and generate reconciled and personalised explanations. Including the human factor in the social explainability demands to consider elements such as *expectations, trust, State of Mind* (SoM), *emotions* and multi-modal *formats* of the explanation (e.g., natural language and graphical).

Finally, it is worth to be mentioned that the idea of leveraging on interaction to reach mutual understanding shares some similarities with several works from the planning literature, such as [6,7], For instance, in [7], agents support humans' understanding via *model reconciliation*, that is, a corpus of methods aimed at letting a human receive explanations w.r.t. the sequence of actions computed by a planning agent. In particular, such methods *(i)* define explanation in a planning-specific way, and *(ii)* involve interaction among the human (explanee) and the agent (explanator). However, despite some common insights, we argue our framework is original w.r.t the area of explainable planning. Indeed, whereas works in this area mostly focus on planning – which is an important subset of *symbolic* AI – our work mostly focuses on *sub-symbolic* AI—a difference which heavily affects how understandability is defined and pursued. Furthermore, while other works target scenarios involving both humans and software agents, we explicitly target both this case and the agents-only one.

6   Conclusion

Despite the many efforts of the XAI community in addressing *opacity* issues in ML-based intelligent systems, most works in this area still rely on natural-language-based definitions of fundamental concepts such as *explanation* and *interpretation*. Accordingly, in this work, we firstly explore the inconsistencies still affecting the definitions of interpretability and explainability in some recent impactful papers. Then, to overcome the limitations of natural language definitions, we propose an abstract framework for XAI deeply rooted in the MAS mindset—which is the main contribution of this paper. To assess the proposed framework, we compare it against existing studies in the field of XAI, showing how it can naturally and unambiguously provide clear definitions for the main sorts of tasks laying under the XAI umbrella. Finally, we propose some ways to scale the intra-agent to the inter-agent explainability and elaborate on the potential social implications characterising the dynamics among the agents.

References

1. Andrews, R., Diederich, J., Tickle, A.B.: Survey and critique of techniques for extracting rules from trained artificial neural networks. Knowl.-Based Syst. **8**(6), 373–389 (1995). https://doi.org/10.1016/0950-7051(96)81920-4
2. Anjomshoae, S., Najjar, A., Calvaresi, D., Främling, K.: Explainable agents and robots: results from a systematic literature review. In: Proceedings of the 18th International Conference on Autonomous Agents and Multi-Agent Systems, pp. 1078–1088. International Foundation for Autonomous Agents and Multiagent Systems (2019)
3. Besold, T.R., Uckelman, S.L.: The what, the why, and the how of artificial explanations in automated decision-making, pp. 1–20. CoRR abs/1808.07074 (2018)
4. Calegari, R., Ciatto, G., Dellaluce, J., Omicini, A.: Interpretable narrative explanation for ML predictors with LP: a case study for XAI. In: Bergenti, F., Monica, S. (eds.) WOA 2019–20th Workshop "From Objects to Agents", CEUR Workshop Proceedings, vol. 2404, pp. 105–112. Sun SITE Central Europe, RWTH Aachen University, Parma, 26–28 June 2019. http://ceur-ws.org/Vol-2404/paper16.pdf
5. Calvaresi, D., Najjar, A., Schumacher, M., Främling, K. (eds.): EXTRAAMAS 2019. LNCS (LNAI), vol. 11763. Springer, Cham (2019). https://doi.org/10.1007/978-3-030-30391-4
6. Chakraborti, T., Sreedharan, S., Kambhampati, S.: Balancing explicability and explanation in human-aware planning (2017). https://arxiv.org/abs/1708.00543
7. Chakraborti, T., Sreedharan, S., Zhang, Y., Kambhampati, S.: Plan explanations as model reconciliation: moving beyond explanation as soliloquy. In: 26th International Joint Conference on Artificial Intelligence (IJCAI 2017), pp. 156–163. AAAI Press, Melbourne (2017). https://doi.org/10.24963/ijcai.2017/23
8. Ciatto, G., Calegari, R., Omicini, A., Calvaresi, D.: Towards XMAS: eXplainability through multi-agent systems. In: Savaglio, C., Fortino, G., Ciatto, G., Omicini, A. (eds.) AI&IoT 2019 - Artificial Intelligence and Internet of Things 2019. CEUR Workshop Proceedings, vol. 2502, pp. 40–53. Sun SITE Central Europe, RWTH Aachen University, November 2019
9. Ciatto, G., Calvaresi, D., Schumacher, M.I., Omicini, A.: An abstract framework for agent-based explanations in AI. In: 19th Interational Conference on Autonomous Agents and Multi-Agent Systems (AAMAS 2020). IFAAMAS, Auckland (2020)
10. Doshi-Velez, F., Kim, B.: Towards a rigorous science of interpretable machine learning. CoRR abs/1702.08608 (2017)
11. García, A.J., Simari, G.R.: Defeasible logic programming: an argumentative approach. Theor. Pract. Log. Prog. **4**(2), 95–138 (2004). https://doi.org/10.1017/S1471068403001674

12. Goodman, B., Flaxman, S.: European Union regulations on algorithmic decision-making and a "right to explanation". AI Mag. **38**(3), 50–57 (2017). https://doi.org/10.1609/aimag.v38i3.2741
13. Guidotti, R., Monreale, A., Turini, F., Pedreschi, D., Giannotti, F.: A survey of methods for explaining black box models. ACM Comput. Surv. **51**(5), 1–42 (2019). https://doi.org/10.1145/3236009
14. Katarzyniak, R.P., Nguyen, N.T.: Reconciling inconsistent profiles of agents' knowledge states in distributed multiagent systems using consensus methods. Syst. Sci. **26**(4), 93–119 (2000)
15. Lipton, Z.C.: The mythos of model interpretability. Commun. ACM **61**(10), 36–43 (2018). https://doi.org/10.1145/3233231
16. Miller, G.A.: The magical number seven, plus or minus two: some limits on our capacity for processing information. Psychol. Rev. **63**(2), 81–97 (1956). https://doi.org/10.1037/h0043158
17. Miller, T.: Explanation in artificial intelligence: insights from the social sciences. Artif. Intell. **267**, 1–38 (2019). https://doi.org/10.1016/j.artint.2018.07.007
18. Omicini, A., Zambonelli, F.: MAS as complex systems: a view on the role of declarative approaches. In: Leite, J., Omicini, A., Sterling, L., Torroni, P. (eds.) DALT 2003. LNCS (LNAI), vol. 2990, pp. 1–16. Springer, Heidelberg (2004). https://doi.org/10.1007/978-3-540-25932-9_1
19. Premack, D., Woodruff, G.: Does the chimpanzee have a theory of mind? Behav. Brain Sci. **1**(4), 515–526 (1978). https://doi.org/10.1017/S0140525X00076512
20. Ribeiro, M.T., Singh, S., Guestrin, C.: "Why should I trust you?": explaining the predictions of any classifier. In: 22nd ACM SIGKDD International Conference on Knowledge Discovery and Data Mining (KDD 2016), pp. 1135–1144. ACM Press, San Francisco, 22–26 August 2016. https://doi.org/10.1145/2939672.2939778
21. Rosenfeld, A., Richardson, A.: Explainability in human–agent systems. Auton. Agent. Multi-Agent Syst. **33**(6), 673–705 (2019). https://doi.org/10.1007/s10458-019-09408-y
22. Rudin, C.: Stop explaining black box machine learning models for high stakes decisions and use interpretable models instead. Nat. Mach. Intell. **1**(5), 206–215 (2019). https://doi.org/10.1038/s42256-019-0048-x
23. Tamma, V., Bench-Capon, T.: A conceptual model to facilitate knowledge sharing in multi-agent systems. In: Ontologies in Agent Systems (OAS 2001). CEUR Workshop Proceedings, vol. 52, pp. 69–76 (2001). http://ceur-ws.org/Vol-52/oas01-tamma.pdf
24. Turek, M.: Explainable artificial intelligence (XAI). Funding Program DARPA-BAA-16-53, Defense Advanced Research Projects Agency (DARPA) (2016). http://www.darpa.mil/program/explainable-artificial-intelligence
25. Voigt, P., von dem Bussche, A.: The EU General Data Protection Regulation (GDPR). LNCS (LNAI). Springer, Cham (2017). https://doi.org/10.1007/978-3-319-57959-7

Agent EXPRI: Licence to Explain

Francesca Mosca[✉], Ştefan Sarkadi, Jose M. Such, and Peter McBurney

Department of Informatics, King's College London, London, UK
{francesca.mosca,stefan.sarkadi,jose.such,peter.mcburney}@kcl.ac.uk

Abstract. Online social networks are known to lack adequate multi-user privacy support. In this paper we present EXPRI, an agent architecture that aims to assist users in managing multi-user privacy conflicts. By considering the personal utility of sharing content and the individually preferred moral values of each user involved in the conflict, EXPRI identifies the best collaborative solution by applying practical reasoning techniques. Such techniques provide the agent with the cognitive process that is necessary for explainability. Furthermore, the knowledge gathered during the practical reasoning process allows EXPRI to engage in contrastive explanations.

Keywords: Multi-user privacy · Practical reasoning · Explainable AI

1 *"EXPRI, Agent EXPRI"*: Introduction

Online collaborative platforms have recently generated an increasing concern for individual privacy. One specific privacy problem is that, whenever the content to be shared involves more than a person, the privacy policies should be understood and approved by all the users involved. If this does not happen, a *multi-user privacy conflict* (MPC) is likely to occur. Among other platforms, online social networks (OSNs) have proved to be particularly unsuitable to manage access control in a satisfying way for the users [6,12,36]. A common example of MPC in the literature is the case of a picture representing a group of friends, where each of them would assign different degrees of publicity/privacy to the picture on the OSN. Currently, most platforms lack built-in mechanisms that allow the users to discuss and agree on a policy in advance [42], and the responsibility of selecting a policy is generally left solely to the uploader. The other involved users, if unhappy with the uploader's choice, can only resort to unsatisfying reparative solutions, such as untagging or asking for the content to be removed.

MPCs happen frequently, with a majority of users having experienced at least one MPC [37]. However, generally users have collaborative attitudes, e.g. in a recent study [37] most uploaders wished to have known in advance the consequences of their decisions in order to tackle the conflicts before they occurr.

Previously, in [21], we have outlined an agent architecture to assist users during MPCs. In this paper we define further this agent architecture, that we now name EXPRI, especially in regard of its explainable component. EXPRI is

© Springer Nature Switzerland AG 2020
D. Calvaresi et al. (Eds.): EXTRAAMAS 2020, LNAI 12175, pp. 21–38, 2020.
https://doi.org/10.1007/978-3-030-51924-7_2

an agent that aims to help users solve MPCs in OSNs by computing the optimal sharing policy for all the involved users. Optimality is considered in terms of (i) the utility that each user gains from sharing the content with a particular audience, and (ii) the promotion of moral values, i.e. the degree of coherency with the individual morality of choosing each possible policy. Several previous studies pointed out the necessity for autonomous systems to fully support users in privacy decisions (and not only), they need to be transparent and explainable [23,34]. We show how EXPRI, which follows practical reasoning techniques to identify the optimal action, is fully equipped with the necessary information to provide a justification for the optimal action to the end-user; then we present a collection of starting points to inspire the development of the social process of EXPRI, e.g. how to best convey a justification to the end-user.

2 *"For Your Eyes only"*: Related Work in Privacy

In recent years, models for better supporting users to collaboratively deal with MPCs have been proposed in the related literature. We refer the interested reader to more comprehensive surveys like [12,23,36] for further details on multiuser privacy management. Researchers focused on the achievement of desirable properties [21], such as role-agnosticism, adaptability, explainability, and value- and utility-orientation. Given the aim of this paper, we particularly focus on what previous works have achieved in terms of explainability.

The ability of a system to be able to explain itself and justify its outputs is generally considered crucial for fostering the users' trust towards autonomous systems [23,34]. Of course, this is also valid in the context of multiuser privacy. The running hypothesis is that, by interacting with explainable systems, users will find it easier to understand the received recommendations and, consequently, to endorse them, notably reducing the occurrence of MPCs.

The approaches suggested for this type of application range from game theoretical solutions [27,32], to agent-based ones [22,35,38], to learning models [10,40], and more technical, fine-grained systems [13]. Despite the abundance of efforts, none of these approaches can be considered fully explainable. However, some solution-concepts, like argumentation-based models, make it easier than others to meet the explainability requirement. In [14] each user of the OSN is represented by an agent that captures its user's privacy constraints through ontologies and semantic rules. When MPCs occur, the agents interact in persuasion dialogues to defend their privacy preferences. The arguments generated in the dialogue can be reported to the users as a justification of the output, even though the best way to do so is not investigated by the authors. In [9], the authors design a recommendation system, where the prediction of the optimal collective sharing policy is based on the scenario's context, the users' preferences, and their arguments about those preferences. A limited set of arguments is considered, leaving unclear their efficacy in convincing the users, but providing the first steps towards an explanation of the system's decision.

Our work differs from the literature because it presents a design that is explicitly oriented towards the provision of an explanation. We consider the transparency of the process as the main feature of our model, where the provided explanation is crucial and not just an accessory of the model.

3 "A View to an EXPRI": The Agent Architecture

In this section we detail the components of our agent architecture, EXPRI. We instantiate an agent EXPRI for each user registered to the OSN: each agent supports a user while taking decisions on multiuser privacy. In order to do so, the agent needs to be aligned with the user's preference, in terms of (i) *utility* and (ii) *moral values*. In fact, users are reported to share content online for personal advantage [15], but they may also consider the consequences of their decisions and transcend their own benefit to accommodate others' preferences [37].

3.1 Utility-Driven Component of EXPRI

We represent a OSN as a graph $G = (Ag, R)$, where Ag is the set of all the registered agents/users a_k, and R is the set of all their relationships (a_k, a_j, i_{kj}), with i_{kj} being the *intimacy* of the relationship between the users a_k and a_j. We consider *intimacy* as defined in [11], where the authors present also a way to elicit it automatically.

We assume that every user has an individual preference in terms of publicity/privacy for sharing content, that can be elicited automatically for each item or a collection of them [20,33]. We define the concepts below for each individual content x, even though for simplifying the notation we do not always report x.

Definition 1. *The user a_k defines the **sharing policy** $sp_k = \langle d, i \rangle$ for the item x, meaning that a_k wants to allow access to x to any other user who is distant at most d and intimate at least i.*

Definition 2. *The **individual audience** for the user a_k is the set $aud_{sp,k}$ of users who satisfy the conditions set by a sharing policy sp for the content x.*

Definition 3. *The **collective audience** is the set $aud_{sp} = \bigcap_{k \in Ag} aud_{sp,k}$, that is the intersection of the individual audiences of all the involved users generated by the sharing policy sp for the content x.*

A multi-user privacy conflict (MPC) occurs whenever two or more users, who are involved in the same content, have contrasting preferred sharing policies, i.e. their preferred individual audiences do not coincide.

As discussed in [15], we believe that users perceive some type of benefit when sharing an appealing photo online, but they can also experience some discomfort whenever a picture is seen by undesired people. We refer to this advantage and disadvantage in terms of gain or loss of *utility*. Furthermore, in order to find a compromise to solve the MPC, users may be more inclined to overshare or undershare, that is to make the content available to a broader or smaller audience than the preferred one.

Definition 4. *The function* **appreciation** *determines whether the user prefers to overshare ($app_k(x) = 1$) or undershare ($app_k(x) = -1$) the item x.*

Definition 5. *Given the preferred audience aud_k and a sharing policy sp, if sharing with the collective audience aud_{sp}, the individual* **utility** *of user a_k varies according to:*

$$u_{aud_{sp},k} = \sum_{j \in allDesAud} \frac{i_j}{d_j} - \sum_{j \in excDesAud} \frac{i_j}{d_j} + app_k(x) \sum_{j \in allExtAud} \frac{i_j}{d_j}, \quad (1)$$

where allDesAud (allowed desired audience) is the set of users who a_k desires to grant access to x and that are part of aud_{sp}; excDesAud (excluded desired audience) is the set of users who a_k desires to grant access to but that are excluded by aud_{sp}; allExtAud (allowed extra audience) is the set of users who a_k desires to forbid access from but that are part of aud_{sp}.

Users perceive a gain in utility whenever approved people access the content, but they can lose utility if undesired people access the content (if *appreciation* is negative) or desired people are excluded. Also, these effects get amplified with people that are closer and more intimate, as reported in recent user studies [37].

Example. Let us consider the simplified OSN in Fig. 1. Alice, Bob and Charlie appear together in the picture x. Their preferred sharing policies are respectively $sp_A = \langle 2, 2 \rangle$, $sp_B = \langle 1, 3 \rangle$ and $sp_C = \langle 3, 4 \rangle$, and generate the following preferred individual audiences: $aud_A = \{A, B, C, D, E, F, G, I, L\}$, $aud_B = \{A, B, C, D, G\}$ and $aud_C = \{A, B, C, G, I\}$. A conflict occurs, because the three preferred individual audiences do not coincide. The collective audiences resulting from the intersection of the individual ones generated by each policy are $aud_{sp_A} = \{A, B, C, D, E, G, I, L\}$, $aud_{sp_B} = \{A, B, C\}$ and $aud_{sp_C} = \{A, B, C, G, I\}$. Furthermore, Alice and Bob have a positive appreciation for x ($app_A(x) = app_B(x) = 1$), while for Charlie it is negative ($app_C(x) = -1$).

Let us consider $sp' = \langle 2, 3 \rangle$ as a possible sharing policy for x: the collective audience generated by sp' is $aud_{sp'} = \{A, B, C, D, G, I\}$ (that we rename as aud' for brevity). Then, Alice, Bob and Charlie would perceive the following variation in utility:

$$u_{aud',A} = \sum_{j \in \{B,C,D,G,I\}} \frac{i_j}{d_j} - \sum_{j \in \{E,F,L\}} \frac{i_j}{d_j} = \frac{5}{1} + \frac{4}{1} + \frac{3}{1} + \frac{10}{2} + \frac{9}{2} - \frac{2}{1} - \frac{6}{2} - \frac{2}{1} = 14.5$$

$$u_{aud',B} = \sum_{j \in \{A,C,D,G\}} \frac{i_j}{d_j} + \sum_{j \in \{I\}} \frac{i_j}{d_j} = \frac{5}{1} + \frac{3}{1} + \frac{3}{1} + \frac{5}{1} + \frac{8}{2} = 20$$

$$u_{aud',C} = \sum_{j \in \{A,B,G,I\}} \frac{i_j}{d_j} - 1 \cdot \sum_{j \in \{D\}} \frac{i_j}{d_j} = \frac{4}{1} + \frac{3}{1} + \frac{8}{2} + \frac{5}{1} - \frac{7}{2} = 12.5$$

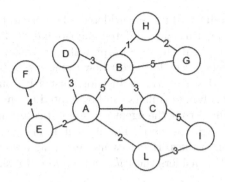

Fig. 1. The simplified online social network discussed in the example.

Table 1. Interpretation of the Schwartz values in the multi-user application and details of their promotion and demotion for a user, comparing different sharing options with own preference.

Value	Interpretation	Condition
OTC	Appreciate compromises which differ from anyone's initial preference	+ If sharing with no one's initial preference
		− If sharing with another user's preference
CO	Preserve individual and social security	+ If sharing with a smaller audience
		− If sharing with a bigger audience
ST	Do what is good for the other people	+ If sharing with the other's preference
		+ If compromising with the other user
		− If ignoring the other user's preference
		− If rejecting an offer
SE	Maintain or increase one's own utility	+ If sharing with own preference
		+ If gaining a better utility
		− If gaining a worse utility

3.2   Value-Aligned Component of EXPRI

We base the moral component of EXPRI on the Schwartz Theory of Basic Values [30]. This is the most well-known and established theory of human values and combines a complete theoretical architecture with a strong empirical validation.

Values are socially desirable concepts representing the mental goals which drive human behaviour [30], influencing any decision. In particular, the Schwartz theory presents ten main values, organised along four directions (which we refer to as $\mathcal{V}$) that pull apart. On one axis, *openness to change* (OTC) is opposed to *conservation* (CO), representing dynamic and independent ways of acting versus conservatory and self-restraining attitudes. On the other axis, *self-transcendence* (ST) reflects tolerant and altruistic behaviours in opposition to *self-enhancement* (SE), which characterises authoritarian and image-conscious conducts. The individual preference over these values, which is considered relatively stable over time [5], can be elicited from the users through validated questionnaires [30].

Given the MPC application, we interpret the Schwartz value-directions as described in Table 1, where we also report how the user's behaviour can promote or demote the values. However, this is just for illustrative purpose, because our agent architecture for solving conflicts can be adapted to any other value theory or application. We believe that the agent can suggest solutions to the MPC that are more compatible with the user's morale if it is informed about the user's preferred order over the values. Hence, while reasoning about possible solutions to the conflict, EXPRI considers the *value promotion* of a sharing policy.

Definition 6. *Given a user a_k and her preferred order o_k over $\mathcal{V}$, the **value promotion** of an audience aud for the user a_k is given by*

$$v_{aud,k} = \sum_{i=1}^{|\mathcal{V}|} (I - i) \cdot prom_{aud}(o_i), \tag{2}$$

where $I = |\mathcal{V}| + 1$, and $prom(o_i) = 1$ if the i-th preferred value is promoted by selecting aud, $prom(o_i) = -1$ if the i-th preferred value is demoted, and $prom(o_i) = 0$ otherwise.

Running Example. Alice, Bob and Charlie's preferred orders over the values $\mathcal{V}$ are, respectively:

$$OTC \prec_A SE \prec_A CO \prec_A ST$$
$$CO \prec_B OTC \prec_B ST \prec_B SE$$
$$ST \prec_C CO \prec_C OTC \prec_C SE$$

The selection of $aud' = aud_{sp'} = \{A, B, C, D, G, I\}$ generates the following individual value promotions:

$$v_{aud',A} = +4 - 3 + 2 + 1 = 4$$
$$v_{aud',B} = -4 + 3 + 2 + 1 = 2$$
$$v_{aud',C} = +4 - 3 + 2 - 1 = 2$$

Alice promotes every value but SE, Bob promotes every value but CO, and Charlie promotes only ST and OTC.

3.3   Resolution of MPCs

Each EXPRI agent can cover two roles in the resolution of a MPC: *uploader*, when the user wants to share some content online, and *co-owner*, when the user is involved in some content that another user wants to share. Let us recall that we consider a non-adversarial setting: therefore, we assume that the agents cooperate in order to identify a collectively satisfying solution to the MPC. In fact, empirical studies showed how users are frequently willing to find acceptable compromises; in particular, uploaders reported to wish to have known in advance the preferences of the co-owners, to avoid conflicts before their occurrence [37].

For each conflict involving n users, a set $\mathcal{A}$ of at most $n + 1$ audiences are considered as possible solutions: the collective audiences aud_{sp_k} generated by each individually preferred sharing policy sp_k, and aud', generated in such a way that $aud' \neq aud_{sp_k} \forall k$.

Independently of the role, all agents compute an *individual score* for each possible solution, expressing their appreciation of the option in terms of both utility and value promotion:

$$s_{aud,k} = \begin{cases} +|u_{aud,k}| \cdot |v_{aud,k}| & \text{if } u_{aud,k} > 0 \wedge v_{aud,k} > 0, \\ -|u_{aud,k}| \cdot |v_{aud,k}| & \text{otherwise.} \end{cases} \tag{3}$$

Then, each EXPRI-coowner shares with EXPRI-uploader its individual scores: in this way, each agent collaborates without directly disclosing its potential gain in terms of neither utility nor value promotion. Then, EXPRI-uploader aggregates all the individual scores into a *collective score* for each possible solution:

$$s_{aud} = \sum_{k \in Ag} s_{k,aud}. \tag{4}$$

Finally, EXPRI-uploader identifies the most desirable solution, through the process we describe in the next section, and suggests it to the EXPRI-coowners. The EXPRI-coowners also perform a similar reasoning process to decide whether to accept or reject the offer. At the end of the deliberations, the outcomes can be reported to the users: we discuss possible guidelines to do this in Sect. 5.

Running Example. Table 2 reports the individual utilities and value promotions for each agent and each possible audience. The details of the computations are reported, for instance regarding the utilities and the value promotions for sp', in the previous examples.

Table 2. Individual and collective metrics for the scenario in the example.

Agents	aud_{sp_A}			aud_{sp_B}			aud_{sp_C}			$aud_{sp'}$		
	u	v	s	u	v	s	u	v	s	u	v	s
A	22.5	0	0	−10.5	−4	−42	8.5	−4	−34	14.5	+4	58
B	27	−4	−108	0	0	0	14	−4	−56	20	+2	40
C	6.5	−2	−13	2	+4	8	16	−5	−64	12.5	+2	25
Collective			−121			−34			−154			123

4 *"From Practical Reasoning with Love"*: Design of the Cognitive Process

As Miller discusses in [19], an *explanation* is composed by a *cognitive process*, i.e. the process of abductive inference determining the causal attribution for a given event, and a *social process*, i.e. the interactive process of transferring knowledge between the explainer and the explainee. In this section we describe how techniques from computational argumentation can be applied in order to provide EXPRI with a cognitive process that allows the agent to gather the necessary information in order to justify to the user the selection of the optimal solution to the MPC.

We start by considering that an argument scheme (AS) and its associated critical questions can enable an agent to propose, attack and defend justifications for a given action [3]. In the following we adapt the AS, that was introduced by Atkinson, to EXPRI-uploader (AS-U) and EXPRI-coowners (AS-C). For AS-U, this would take the form of *"Given the current conflict, I should offer the audience aud, that will be accepted by the co-owners and therefore will solve the conflict, that will provide the score s_{aud} and that will promote my values V"*. Symmetrically, AS-C results to be: *"Given the current conflict, I should accept the audience aud and solve the conflict, to get the score s_{aud} and to promote my values V"* [1]. An agent who does not accept this presumptive argument, can challenge it by presenting *critical questions* (CQs), formally described in [3]. Unfavourable answers to the CQs provide attacks to the original argument. Attacks can be directed to different elements of the argument, i.e. to the different stages of the *practical reasoning* (PR) which led to such conclusion. In line with [2,3], in the remaining part of this section we present the three stages of the practical reasoning (PR) process for the agent EXPRI, namely (i) the *problem formulation*, (ii) the *epistemic stage*, and (iii) the *choice of action*.

Table 3. Detail of the joint actions J_{Ag}, for each $aud_i \in \mathcal{A}$, and the partial transition function τ when $n = 3$ in a MPC scenario.

J_{Ag}	τ
$j_{1-4} = \langle \text{offer}_{aud_i}, \text{reject}_{2,aud_i}, \text{reject}_{3,aud_i} \rangle$	$\tau(\text{conflict}, j_{1-4}) = \text{conflict}$
$j_{5-8} = \langle \text{offer}_{aud_i}, \text{accept}_{2,aud_i}, \text{reject}_{3,aud_i} \rangle$	$\tau(\text{conflict}, j_{5-8}) = \text{conflict}$
$j_{9-12} = \langle \text{offer}_{aud_i}, \text{reject}_{2,aud_i}, \text{accept}_{3,aud_i} \rangle$	$\tau(\text{conflict}, j_{9-12}) = \text{conflict}$
$j_{13-16} = \langle \text{offer}_{aud_i}, \text{accept}_{2,aud_i}, \text{accept}_{3,aud_i} \rangle$	$\tau(\text{conflict}, j_{13-16}) = \text{agreement}_{aud_i}$

4.1 Problem Formulation

The first step of PR consists of representing the relevant elements of the situation (i.e. conflict occurrence, possible solutions, involved users' preferences, etc.). We perform this task by building an Action-Based Alternating Transition Systems with Values (AATS+V) [3]. This structure provides the underlying semantics that we use to describe the world and formulate the arguments about action, in particular when the outcome of an individual action (e.g. for the uploader to

---

[1] Note that the definition of "values" in [3] is based on [26], which is different from that of Schwartz [31] that we use in this paper.

offer some particular solution) depends on what the other agents decide to do (e.g. whether the co-owners accept or reject the uploader's offer). We refer to this case as *joint actions* (J_{Ag}), i.e. actions that are performed at the same time[2] by a set of agents. For clarity, in Table 3 we show the possible joint actions in the MPC scenario with $n = 3$ agents involved: we reported all the combinations of individual actions that are available to each agent, i.e. $offer_{aud_i}$ for the uploader, and $accept_{aud_i}$ and $reject_{aud_i}$ for the co-owners, referring to all the possible audiences $aud_i \in \mathcal{A}$. We adapt for the MPC scenario the definition of AATS+V given in [3].

Definition 7. *In the context of a MPC among n users, an **AATS+V** is a $2n + 8$ tuple $\Sigma = \langle Q, q_0, Ag, Ac_1, ..., Ac_n, \rho, \tau, S, \mathcal{V}, Av_1, ..., Av_n, \delta \rangle$, where:*

- $Q = \{conflict, agreement_{aud} \quad \forall aud \in \mathcal{A}\}$ *is a finite, non-empty set of states;*
- $q_0 = conflict$ *is the initial state;*
- $Ag = \{up_1, co_2, ..., co_n\}$ *is the set of agents involved in the MPC, with the roles of uploader or co-owners;*
- $Ac_1 = \{offer_{aud} \quad \forall aud \in \mathcal{A}\}$ *are the actions available to the agent up_1;*
- $Ac_k = \{accept_{k,aud}, reject_{k,aud} \quad \forall aud \in \mathcal{A}\}$ *are the actions available to the agent co_k, for $k = 2...n$;*
- $\rho : Ac_{Ag} \rightarrow 2^Q$ *is the action-precondition function, which defines the set of states from which an action $ac \in Ac_{Ag}$ can be executed: $\rho(offer_{aud}) = \rho(accept_{aud}) = \rho(reject_{aud}) = conflict$;*
- $\tau : Q \times J_{Ag} \rightarrow Q$ *is the partial system transition function, which defines what state results from performing the joint action j in the state q, where possible (see the case with $n = 3$ in Table 3);*
- $S = \{0, s_{aud} \quad \forall aud \in \mathcal{A}\}$ *is the set of collective scores characterising each state, where $s_{conflict} = 0$;*
- $\mathcal{V} = \{SE, ST, CO, OTC\}$ *is the set of values considered by each agent;*
- $Av_k = o_k(\mathcal{V})$ *is the preferred total order of the agent Ag_k over the values $\mathcal{V}$;*
- $\delta : Q \times Q \times Av_{Ag} \rightarrow \{+, -, =\}$ *is the valuation function, which defines the effect of a transition over each value of each agent (see Table 1).*

Running Example. Considering the scenario described in the previous examples and Table 3, the first step of the reasoning process for EXPRI-uploader, that represents Alice, consists of the problem formulation given by the AATS+V in Fig. 2. Note that each agent knows only its own value preference (therefore the evaluation of δ); however, in the figure we represent all the promoted and demoted values for completeness: δ_A is in red, δ_B in blue, and δ_C in green.

4.2 Epistemic Stage

The epistemic stage consists of determining what the agent believes about the current situation, given the previous problem formulation. Let us recall our

---

[2] Similarly to [4], we assume the offer and the response to be a "simultaneous" action, despite its sequentiality.

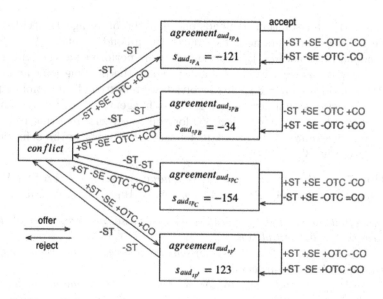

Fig. 2. Problem formulation through AATS+V for the scenario in example. (Color figure online)

assumption, based on empirical evidence [37], that the EXPRI agents have a collaborative and non-adversarial behaviour. From this underlying assumption we can further imply other two fundamental epistemic assumptions:

– EA1 (for all the agents): all agents interpret the world in a similar manner: hence, all the agents have the same knowledge regarding all the components of the AATS+V, the only exception being Av_k. In fact, in order to preserve even further the privacy of the users involved in the MPC, we assume that each agent k only knows its own preferred order Av_k over the values and is uninformed about any other Av_j for $j \neq k$.
– EA2 (for EXPRI-uploader): the co-owners are believed to accept an offer in two situations, i.e. when the offered audience guarantees either (i) the maximum score for the co-owner itself ($s_{k,aud'} = \max_A s_{k,aud}$), or (ii) the maximum collective score ($s_{aud'} = \max_A s_{aud}$).

With reference to the CQs in [3], because of EA1, we are not interested in the CQs that are related to the problem formulation (CQ2-4 and CQ12-16) and its truthfulness (CQ1). Because of EA2, we are able to evaluate appropriately CQ17 when instantiated for each possible argument.

4.3   Choice of Action

The last step of the PR is the choice of action, that is the development of a value-based argumentation framework (VAF), which instantiates an appropriate argumentation scheme, and the consequent evaluation of the arguments according to the preference of values.

We focus in particular on AS-U and AS-C, and the critical questions which contest the optimality of the identified action, i.e. to offer *aud* for the EXPRI-uploader, and to accept or reject *aud* for the EXPRI-coowners. We refer to the questions CQ5-CQ11 from [3]: CQ5, CQ6 and CQ7 offer alternative actions that realise the same consequence, goal and value promotion; CQ8, CQ9 and CQ10 consider unacknowledged side effects, such as demotion of desired values or promotion of other values; and, finally, CQ11 wonders whether there is any other action that is more desirable in terms of values promotion.

The collection of negative answers to these CQs provides the justification for action. We argue that this abductive reasoning is sufficient to define the causal attribution of the recommended event and, therefore, the practical reasoning process can be equivalent to the cognitive process required for providing an explanation.

Running Example. Let us analyse the process of choosing an action for the agent EXPRI acting on behalf of Alice, the uploader. Given the assumption of cooperative behaviour and the common goal of solving the MPC by reaching an agreement, EXPRI-uploader discards immediately the joint actions j_{1-12}: in fact, if at least one of the co-owners does not accept the offer, the conflict is guaranteed to persist. The uploader needs to identify the optimal audience to offer, i.e. the one that, if accepted by the co-owners like in j_{13-16} provides the best agreement. In order to do this, with reference to Fig. 2, the uploader examines one by one its possibilities and checks whether they get challenged by any CQ. Note that we do not report a graphical representation of the VAF that would be generated in this process because of the high number of considered arguments; however, we detail the main arguments and all the attacks provided by the CQs (we leave implicit any supporting relationship).

– AS-U for j_{13}: "Given the current conflict, I should offer aud_{sp_A}, that will be accepted by the co-owners, to solve the conflict, to obtain the score $s_{A,aud_{sp_A}}$ and to promote SE and CO."
  - obj13.1: a better score can be achieved by performing alternative actions (CQ5): *successful*, e.g. in j_{14} and j_{16};
  - obj13.2: the agreement is reached also with alternative actions (CQ6): *successful*, e.g. in j_{14}, j_{15} and j_{16};
  - obj13.3: CO is promoted also with alternative actions (CQ7): *successful*, e.g. in j_{14}, j_{15} and j_{16};
  - obj13.4: ST is demoted (CQ9): *rejected*, because Alice cares more about SE and CO (here promoted) than ST;
  - obj13.5: OTC is demoted (CQ9): *successful*, OTC is the most preferred value for Alice;
  - obj13.6: other values can be promoted by performing alternative actions (CQ11): *successful*, e.g. +OTC in j_{16}, which Alice prefers to SE and CO;
  - obj13.7: EXPRI-Bob will not accept the offer (CQ17): *successful*, because $s_{B,aud_{sp_A}} \neq \max_A s_{B,aud}$ and $s_{aud_{sp_A}} \neq \max_A s_{aud}$;
  - obj13.8: EXPRI-Charlie will not accept the offer (CQ17): *successful*, because $s_{C,aud_{sp_A}} \neq \max_A s_{C,aud}$ and $s_{aud_{sp_A}} \neq \max_A s_{aud}$.

- AS-U for j_{14}: "Given the current conflict, I should offer aud_{sp_B}, that will be accepted by the co-owners, to solve the conflict, to obtain the score $s_{A,aud_{sp_B}}$ and to promote ST and CO."
  - obj14.1: a better score can be achieved by performing alternative actions (CQ5): *successful*, e.g. j_{16};
  - obj14.2: the agreement is reached also with alternative actions (CQ6): *successful*, e.g. in j_{13}, j_{15} and j_{16};
  - obj14.3: CO is promoted also with alternative actions (CQ7): *successful*, e.g. in j_{13}, j_{15} and j_{16};
  - obj14.4: ST is promoted also with alternative actions (CQ7): *successful*, e.g. in j_{15} and j_{16};
  - obj14.5: SE is demoted (CQ9): *successful*, SE is the second most preferred value for Alice;
  - obj14.6: OTC is demoted (CQ9): *successful*, OTC is the most preferred value for Alice;
  - obj14.7: other values can be promoted by performing alternative actions (CQ11): *successful*, e.g. +OTC in j_{16}, which Alice prefers to ST and CO;
  - obj14.8: EXPRI-Bob will not accept the offer (CQ17): *successful*, because $s_{B,aud_{sp_B}} \neq \max_A s_{B,aud}$ and $s_{aud_{sp_B}} \neq \max_A s_{aud}$;
  - obj14.9: EXPRI-Charlie will not accept the offer (CQ17): *successful*, because $s_{C,aud_{sp_B}} \neq \max_A s_{C,aud}$ and $s_{aud_{sp_B}} \neq \max_A s_{aud}$.
- AS-U for j_{15}: "Given the current conflict, I should offer aud_{sp_C}, that will be accepted by the co-owners, to solve the conflict, to obtain the score $s_{A,aud_{sp_C}}$ and to promote ST and CO."
  - obj15.1: a better score can be achieved by performing alternative actions (CQ5): *successful*, e.g. j_{16};
  - obj15.2: the agreement is reached also with alternative actions (CQ6): *successful*, e.g. in j_{13}, j_{14} and j_{16};
  - obj15.3: CO is promoted also with alternative actions (CQ7): *successful*, e.g. in j_{13}, j_{14} and j_{16};
  - obj15.4: ST is promoted also with alternative actions (CQ7): *successful*, e.g. in j_{14} and j_{16};
  - obj15.5: SE is demoted (CQ9): *successful*, SE is the second most preferred value for Alice;
  - obj15.6: OTC is demoted (CQ9): *successful*, OTC is the most preferred value for Alice;
  - obj15.7: other values can be promoted by performing alternative actions (CQ11): *successful*, e.g. +OTC in j_{16}, which Alice prefers to ST and CO;
  - obj15.8: EXPRI-Bob will not accept the offer (CQ17): *successful*, because $s_{B,aud_{sp_C}} \neq \max_A s_{B,aud}$ and $s_{aud_{sp_C}} \neq \max_A s_{aud}$;
  - obj15.9: EXPRI-Charlie will not accept the offer (CQ17): *successful*, because $s_{C,aud_{sp_C}} \neq \max_A s_{C,aud}$ and $s_{aud_{sp_C}} \neq \max_A s_{aud}$.
- AS-U for j_{16}: "Given the current conflict, I should offer $aud_{sp'}$, that will be accepted by the co-owners, to solve the conflict, to obtain the score $s_{A,aud_{sp'}}$ and to promote ST, OTC and CO."
  - obj16.1: the agreement is reached also with alternative actions (CQ6): *successful*, e.g. in j_{13}, j_{14} and j_{15};
  - obj16.2: CO is promoted also with alternative actions (CQ7): *successful*, e.g. in j_{13}, j_{14} and j_{15};

- obj16.3: ST is promoted also with alternative actions (CQ7): *successful*, e.g. in j_{14} and j_{15};
- obj16.4: SE is demoted (CQ9): *rejected*, because Alice cares more about OTC (here promoted) than SE;
- obj16.5: other values can be promoted by performing alternative actions (CQ11): *rejected*, because SE (promoted in j_{13}) is less important to Alice than OTC, here promoted;
- obj16.6: EXPRI-Bob will not accept the offer (CQ17): *rejected*, because $s_{B,aud_{sp'}} = \max_{\mathcal{A}} s_{B,aud}$ and $s_{aud_{sp'}} = \max_{\mathcal{A}} s_{aud}$;
- obj16.7: EXPRI-Charlie will not accept the offer (CQ17): *rejected*, because $s_{C,aud_{sp'}} = \max_{\mathcal{A}} s_{C,aud}$ and $s_{aud_{sp'}} = \max_{\mathcal{A}} s_{aud}$.

AS-U for j_{13} is rejected, because all the attacks provided by the CQs are successful (note that obj13.4 is considered irrelevant because of Alice's values preference); similarly, the arguments for j_{14} and j_{15} are rejected. Regarding AS-U for j_{16}, we reject in a subsequent moment obj16.1, obj16.2 and obj16.3, because the suggested alternative actions are proved not to be as desirable as the current action (all their objections are successful).

In conclusion, EXPRI-uploader identifies j_{16} as the most desirable joint action and therefore suggests Alice to offer $aud_{sp'}$. The EXPRI-coowners go through a similar reasoning process, which we do not report in detail for lack of space, to identify the best individual action upon the uploader's offer.

5 *"The Cognitive Process Is Not Enough"*: Challenges for Designing the Social Process

So far we have showed how EXPRI is able to solve an MPC by identifying through practical reasoning the optimal solution for an MPC in OSNs. According to [25], abductive reasoning provides the best explanation given all available information. This means that, EXPRI's practical reasoning being an abductive form of reasoning, by reporting it, the agent can provide the best explanation for the given recommended action.

However, considering the social nature of explanations in AI [19], we have to address the very important distinction between *explainable* AI and *self-explainable* AI. An artificial agent can be explainable in the sense that humans can follow and understand its cognitive process, and by following this process, humans are able to explain why the agent is doing what it is doing. A self-explainable artificial agent, on the other hand, is a socially aware agent which has the capability of communicating explanations to the human that it interacts with. For reasons of trustworthiness [41], accountability [7], and responsibility [8], that have been mentioned in the literature, it is desirable for an agent to be self-explainable.

Both [19] and [16] propose that social awareness is necessary for explainable agency. They suggest that a social agent must be able to transfer knowledge from itself (the explainer) to a user (the explainee) in such a way as to give the user the necessary information to understand the causes of its recommendation. This can happen when the agent is able (i) to engage in counterfactual explanations, e.g. justifying the rejection of possible alternative actions; and (ii) to tailor the explanation according to the individual user's needs. In the following, we outline how EXPRI may be able to meet these requirements.

Contrastive Explanations. In [19], Miller clearly summarises the importance of providing contrastive explanations. Research shows that people are in general not as interested in the causes of an event per se, as they are in the relation of that event to some other event that did not occur. For instance, a user may wonder why EXPRI suggested action x rather than action y. An answer to this question might provide a more convincing explanation for the user than the simple motivation to choose x. As we detailed earlier, EXPRI's cognitive process comprises of practical reasoning about alternative options through the discussion of critical questions. The process of accepting or rejecting each objection that arises from the CQs provides EXPRI with the necessary knowledge to justify why the action it suggests is the optimal one and why the alternatives are not as good as the optimal one. It follows that EXPRI is able to answer any interrogation that the user may conduct in terms of contrasting and comparing the other possible options.

Tailored Explanations. We are planning to give EXPRI the capability of providing explanations that are generated by taking into account the perspective of the interlocutor and/or interlocutors. Continuing on the path of using practical reasoning, it could be feasible to use AATS+V to reason about which is the optimal explanation depending on the social context in which the interaction between EXPRI and the given user takes place. To be able to do this, EXPRI could build an AATS+V taking into account the values and beliefs of the user, in order to be able to reason from the perspective of the user. This additional AATS+V is similar to a Theory-of-Mind (ToM) of the user [1]. However, the formation of this additional AATS+V that is to be used for finding the optimal explanation in social interactions is not as straightforward: the joint actions are not sets of uploader's offers and co-owners' responses anymore, but they represent subsets of dialogues. That is, EXPRI needs to be able to reason about elements such as speech acts, their implicatures, and how these elements change the beliefs and update the knowledge of the interlocutor during a dialogue. Similarly to [4], the epistemic stage now involves uncertainty, because EXPRI does not know what the user's reaction to its explanation may be. Argumentation Dialogue Games (ADGs) [18] provide an elegant way to address this issue. ADGs have recently been used for the formation and use of ToM through speech acts to reach states of shared beliefs with other agents [24], even under conditions of uncertainty [29], for dynamic story generation in interrogation games [28], as well as for providing protocols of interactive explanations to users [17]. Therefore, EXPRI could use ADGs to reason about how and what it communicates to the interlocutor in order to see what kind of explanation might emerge from a hypothetical interaction. Ideally, after going through various alternative dialogues, it would be able to select the dialogue it intends to have with the interlocutor, that will lead to the optimal explanation. EXPRI could also use ADGs to reason about what it tells the interlocutor and what the interlocutor understands in real time, by updating its ToM of the interlocutor based on what the interlocutor tells or asks EXPRI.

Explaining Conflicts. Conflict management literature makes the distinction between three main components of a conflict in multi-agent systems, namely *conflict detection*, *conflict representation*, and *conflict resolution* [39]. Perhaps, in most cases it would be useful to give users a general overview of the context evolution of the MPC, explaining why and how a solution has been found or not. From a causal attribution perspective, it seems reasonable that conflict detection represents the cause of whose effect is represented by the conflict's resolution. Therefore, in the case of an MPC, it would be desirable to have an explanation that not only guides the user from cause to effect, but also that describes to the user the cause and the effect [19]. In this way, the user can assess whether the agent that is providing the explanation has understood the context and has thus grounded the explanation in a realistic representation. Such a causal explanation guides the user from commonly established premises that describe the conflict's detection, to a valid conclusion that represents the solution, or lack thereof.

In conclusion, the explanation for the user should describe the conflict detection and the conflict resolution. On the other hand, the conflict representation, e.g. using AATS+V, does not need to be explicitly included in the explanation, as it is the representation itself that allows the agent to generate explanations. We argue that if the conflict representation is accurate, then the explanation that is generated from it using PR will consist of a valid and sound argument.

Running Example. EXPRI-uploader needs to communicate to Alice the optimal output, i.e. to offer $aud_{sp'}$. There are several possibilities to do so. For illustrative purposes, we report a hypothetical dialogue that may happen between EXPRI-uploader (EU) and Alice (A), to show how EXPRI can provide contrastive and tailored explanations.

> EU(1): Given the disagreement with Bob and Charlie about how to share your picture, to offer $aud_{sp'}$ is your most convenient action, because it would allow you to compromise with your friends (remember that openness-to-change is your most preferred value).
>
> A: Why shouldn't I offer aud_{sp_A} instead?
>
> EU(2): Because you could get a better score than the one guaranteed by aud_{sp_A} (obj13.1), openness-to-change would be demoted (obj13.5), and because Bob and Charlie would most likely reject your offer (obj13.7 and obj13.8).

Note that EU(1) is a tailored explanation, because openness-to-change is a very important value to Alice and to highlight its promotion would not necessarily be as efficacious when interacting with a different user. Also, EU(2) is a contrastive explanation, that provides justification for the optimal action by reporting the objections to the alternative action that Alice asked about.

6 *"Tomorrow Never Dies"*: Discussion and Future Work

In this paper we have presented EXPRI, an agent architecture that aims to assist users for managing multiuser privacy in online social networks. EXPRI identifies for each user, that is involved in a privacy conflict, the best action to collaboratively solve it, by considering both the utility they would gain by sharing the content online and the personal moral values they would promote by compromising with the other users. EXPRI identifies the most desirable solution by applying practical reasoning techniques. This abductive reasoning allows the agent to gather all the necessary knowledge to justify to the user the selection or the rejection of any particular action. To be able to do so is crucial for an agent to be considered explainable. However, in order for the agent to be self-explainable, EXPRI also requires social awareness, i.e. the ability of efficiently communicating explanations to the user, for instance by providing contrastive and tailored explanations. We hypothesise that, by using a practical reasoning process, EXPRI is already able to engage in dialogues with the user to provide contrastive explanations. Further theoretical and empirical research will allow us to develop the social component of EXPRI, by enabling it to also provide fully customised explanations.

References

1. Albrecht, S.V., Stone, P.: Autonomous agents modelling other agents: a comprehensive survey and open problems. Artif. Intell. **258**, 66–95 (2018)
2. Atkinson, K., Bench-Capon, T.: Action-based alternating transition systems for arguments about action. In: AAAI, vol. 7, pp. 24–29 (2007)
3. Atkinson, K., Bench-Capon, T.: Practical reasoning as presumptive argumentation using action based alternating transition systems. Artif. Intell. **171**(10–15), 855–874 (2007)
4. Atkinson, K., Bench-Capon, T.: Taking account of the actions of others in value-based reasoning. Artif. Intell. **254**, 1–20 (2018)
5. Bardi, A., Schwartz, S.H.: Values and behavior: strength and structure of relations. Pers. Soc. Psychol. Bull. **29**(10), 1207–1220 (2003)
6. Besmer, A., Richter Lipford, H.: Moving beyond untagging: photo privacy in a tagged world. In: Proceedings of the SIGCHI Conference on Human Factors in Computing Systems, pp. 1563–1572. ACM (2010)
7. Cranefield, S., Oren, N., Vasconcelos, W.W.: Accountability for practical reasoning agents. In: Lujak, M. (ed.) AT 2018. LNCS (LNAI), vol. 11327, pp. 33–48. Springer, Cham (2019). https://doi.org/10.1007/978-3-030-17294-7_3
8. Dignum, V.: Responsible Artificial Intelligence: How to Develop and Use AI in a Responsible Way. Springer, Heidelberg (2019)
9. Fogues, R.L., Murukannaiah, P.K., Such, J.M., Singh, M.P.: Sharing policies in multiuser privacy scenarios: incorporating context, preferences, and arguments in decision making. ACM Trans. Comput.-Hum. Interact. (TOCHI) **24**(1), 5 (2017)
10. Fogues, R.L., Murukannaiah, P.K., Such, J.M., Singh, M.P.: Sosharp: recommending sharing policies in multiuser privacy scenarios. IEEE Internet Comput. **21**(6), 28–36 (2017)

11. Fogues, R.L., Such, J.M., Espinosa, A., Garcia-Fornes, A.: BFF: a tool for eliciting tie strength and user communities in social networking services. Inform. Syst. Front. **16**(2), 225–237 (2014). https://doi.org/10.1007/s10796-013-9453-6
12. Humbert, M., Trubert, B., Huguenin, K.: A survey on interdependent privacy. ACM Comput. Surv. **52**, 35 (2019)
13. Ilia, P., Polakis, I., Athanasopoulos, E., Maggi, F., Ioannidis, S.: Face/Off: preventing privacy leakage from photos in social networks. In: Proceedings of the 22nd ACM SIGSAC Conference on Computer and Communications Security - CCS 2015, pp. 781–792. ACM Press, New York (2015)
14. Kökciyan, N., Yaglikci, N., Yolum, P.: An argumentation approach for resolving privacy disputes in online social networks. ACM Trans. Internet Technol. (TOIT) **17**(3), 27 (2017)
15. Krasnova, H., Spiekermann, S., Koroleva, K., Hildebrand, T.: Online social networks: why we disclose. J. Inf. Technol. **25**(2), 109–125 (2010)
16. Langley, P.: Explainable, normative, and justified agency. In: Proceedings of the AAAI Conference on Artificial Intelligence, vol. 33, pp. 9775–9779 (2019)
17. Madumal, P., Miller, T., Sonenberg, L., Vetere, F.: A grounded interaction protocol for explainable artificial intelligence. In: Proceedings of the 18th International Conference on Autonomous Agents and MultiAgent Systems, pp. 1033–1041. International Foundation for Autonomous Agents and Multiagent Systems (2019)
18. McBurney, P., Parsons, S.: Dialogue games for agent argumentation. In: Simari, G., Rahwan, I. (eds.) Argumentation in artificial intelligence, pp. 261–280. Springer, Boston (2009). https://doi.org/10.1007/978-0-387-98197-0_13
19. Miller, T.: Explanation in artificial intelligence: insights from the social sciences. Artif. Intell. **267**, 1–38 (2018)
20. Misra, G., Such, J.M.: PACMAN: personal agent for access control in social media. IEEE Internet Comput. **21**(6), 18–26 (2017)
21. Mosca, F., Such, J.M., McBurney, P.: Towards a value-driven explainable agent for collective privacy. In: Proceedings of the 19th International Conference on Autonomous Agents and MultiAgent Systems, pp. 1937–1939 (May 2020)
22. Mosca, F., Such, J.M., McBurney, P.: Value-driven collaborative privacy decision making. In: Proceedings of the AAAI Symposium on Privacy-Enhancing Artificial Intelligence and Language Technologies (PAL) (2019)
23. Paci, F., Squicciarini, A., Zannone, N.: Survey on access control for community-centered collaborative systems. ACM Comput. Surv. **51**(1), 1–38 (2018)
24. Panisson, A.R., Sarkadi, S., McBurney, P., Parsons, S., Bordini, R.H.: On the formal semantics of theory of mind in agent communication. In: Lujak, M. (ed.) AT 2018. LNCS (LNAI), vol. 11327, pp. 18–32. Springer, Cham (2019). https://doi.org/10.1007/978-3-030-17294-7_2
25. Paul, G.: Approaches to abductive reasoning: an overview. Artif. Intell. Rev. **7**(2), 109–152 (1993). https://doi.org/10.1007/BF00849080
26. Perelman, C., Olbrechts-Tyteca, L.: Traité de l'argumentation. la nouvelle rhétorique (1971)
27. Rajtmajer, S., Squicciarini, A., Such, J.M., Semonsen, J., Belmonte, A.: An ultimatum game model for the evolution of privacy in jointly managed content. In: Rass, S., An, B., Kiekintveld, C., Fang, F., Schauer, S. (eds.) International Conference on Decision and Game Theory for Security, vol. 10575, pp. 112–130. Springer, Cham (2017). https://doi.org/10.1007/978-3-319-68711-7_7
28. Sarkadi, S., McBurney, P., Parsons, S.: Deceptive storytelling in artificial dialogue games. In: Proceedings of the AAAI 2019 Spring Symposium Series on Story-Enabled Intelligence (2019)

29. Sarkadi, Ş., Panisson, A.R., Bordini, R.H., McBurney, P., Parsons, S.: Towards an approach for modelling uncertain theory of mind in multi-agent systems. In: Lujak, M. (ed.) AT 2018. LNCS (LNAI), vol. 11327, pp. 3–17. Springer, Cham (2019). https://doi.org/10.1007/978-3-030-17294-7_1

30. Schwartz, S.H.: An overview of the Schwartz theory of basic values. Online Read. Psychol. Cult. **2**(1), 11 (2012)

31. Schwartz, S.H., Bilsky, W.: Toward a theory of the universal content and structure of values: extensions and cross-cultural replications. J. Pers. Soc. Psychol. **58**(5), 878 (1990)

32. Squicciarini, A.C., Shehab, M., Paci, F.: Collective privacy management in social networks. In: Proceedings of the 18th International Conference on World Wide Web, pp. 521–530. ACM (2009)

33. Squicciarini, A.C., Sundareswaran, S., Lin, D., Wede, J.: A3P: adaptive policy prediction for shared images over popular content sharing sites. In: Proceedings of the 22nd ACM conference on Hypertext and hypermedia, pp. 261–270. ACM (2011)

34. Such, J.M.: Privacy and autonomous systems. In: Proceedings of the 26th International Joint Conference on Artificial Intelligence, pp. 4761–4767. AAAI Press (2017)

35. Such, J.M., Criado, N.: Resolving multi-party privacy conflicts in social media. IEEE Trans. Knowl. Data Eng. **28**(7), 1851–1863 (2016)

36. Such, J.M., Criado, N.: Multiparty privacy in social media. Commun. ACM **61**(8), 74–81 (2018)

37. Such, J.M., Porter, J., Preibusch, S., Joinson, A.: Photo privacy conflicts in social media: a large-scale empirical study. In: Proceedings of the 2017 CHI Conference on Human Factors in Computing Systems, pp. 3821–3832. ACM (2017)

38. Such, J.M., Rovatsos, M.: Privacy policy negotiation in social media. ACM Trans. Auton. Adapt. Syst. **11**(1), 1–29 (2016)

39. Tessier, C., Chaudron, L., Müller, H.J.: Conflicting Agents: Conflict Management in Multi-Agent Systems, vol. 1. Springer, Heidelberg (2006)

40. Ulusoy, O., Yolum, P.: Emergent privacy norms for collaborative systems. In: Baldoni, M., Dastani, M., Liao, B., Sakurai, Y., Zalila Wenkstern, R. (eds.) PRIMA 2019. LNCS (LNAI), vol. 11873, pp. 514–522. Springer, Cham (2019). https://doi.org/10.1007/978-3-030-33792-6_36

41. Winikoff, M.: Towards trusting autonomous systems. In: El Fallah-Seghrouchni, A., Ricci, A., Son, T.C. (eds.) EMAS 2017. LNCS (LNAI), vol. 10738, pp. 3–20. Springer, Cham (2018). https://doi.org/10.1007/978-3-319-91899-0_1

42. Wisniewski, P., Lipford, H., Wilson, D.: Fighting for my space: coping mechanisms for SNS boundary regulation. In: Proceedings of the SIGCHI Conference on Human Factors in Computing Systems, pp. 609–618. ACM (2012)

In-Time Explainability in Multi-Agent Systems: Challenges, Opportunities, and Roadmap

Francesco Alzetta[1], Paolo Giorgini[1], Amro Najjar[3],
Michael I. Schumacher[2], and Davide Calvaresi[2(✉)]

[1] University of Trento, Trento, Italy
{francesco.alzetta,paolo.giorgini}@unitn.it
[2] HES-SO Valais, 3960 Sierre, Switzerland
{michael.schumacher,davide.calvaresi}@hevs.ch
[3] University of Luxembourg, Luxembourg City, Luxembourg
amro.najjar@uni.lu

Abstract. In the race for automation, distributed systems are required to perform increasingly complex reasoning to deal with dynamic tasks, often not controlled by humans. On the one hand, systems dealing with strict-timing constraints in safety-critical applications mainly focused on predictability, leaving little room for complex planning and decision-making processes. Indeed, real-time techniques are very efficient in predetermined, constrained, and controlled scenarios. Nevertheless, they lack the necessary flexibility to operate in evolving settings, where the software needs to adapt to the changes of the environment. On the other hand, Intelligent Systems (IS) increasingly adopted Machine Learning (ML) techniques (e.g., subsymbolic predictors such as Neural Networks). The seminal application of those IS started in zero-risk domains producing revolutionary results. However, the ever-increasing exploitation of ML-based approaches generated opaque systems, which are nowadays no longer socially acceptable—calling for eXplainable AI (XAI). Such a problem is exacerbated when IS tend to approach safety-critical scenarios. This paper highlights the need for on-time explainability. In particular, it proposes to embrace the Real-Time Beliefs Desires Intentions (RT-BDI) framework as an enabler of eXplainable Multi-Agent Systems (XMAS) in time-critical XAI.

Keywords: eXplainable BDI model · Real-Time Systems · Multi-Agent Systems · eXplainable autonomous agents

1   Introduction

The recent advancements in the field of artificial intelligence (AI) are fostering the development of autonomous decision-making processes in systems operating in the real-world. In particular, nowadays, the majority of AI-based systems rely on Machine Learning (ML) approaches.

© Springer Nature Switzerland AG 2020
D. Calvaresi et al. (Eds.): EXTRAAMAS 2020, LNAI 12175, pp. 39–53, 2020.
https://doi.org/10.1007/978-3-030-51924-7_3

However, ML-based systems must face the problem of the opacity of sub-symbolic predictors (e.g., neural networks) [6,27], which is no longer acceptable. Hence, current regulations acknowledge the right for meaningful explanations when automated decisions affect humans' lives [17,23]. This originated a fervent effort in the so-called eXplainable AI (XAI) community, whose priority is to tackle the opacity of behaviors and results stemming from ML-based systems [1,4,20,24,35].

Recent studies advocated that multi-agent systems (MAS) offer a coherent yet expressive set of abstractions, promoting *conceptual integrity* in the engineering of complex software systems and serving the purpose of social XAI—constituiting the so-called XMAS [17,20,32].

Nevertheless, there is a worrying lack of consideration for the production and delivery time of the explanation. For example, considering devices operating in the real world such as autonomous cars [5], Unmanned Aerial Vehicles (UAVs) [17,29], and traffic control networks, they are required to deal with a multitude of inputs and variables in highly-dynamic and unpredictable environments—while obliged to comply with Real-Time (RT) constraints. Therefore ensuring the on-time production and delivery of an explanation is crucial.

Real-Time Systems (RTS) are characterized by a plethora of algorithms ensuring compliance with strict-timing constraints [11]. Nevertheless, they require that both the environment and the possible system's interactions with it are predetermined (or predictable) [11]. If the environment is too complex to be thoroughly analyzed, or if it changes considerably, an RTS is not able to autonomously adapt to the new scenario—neither oracle nor one-size-fits-all approaches are possible.

For example, in self-driving cars, reacting in real-time to an unexpected event by promptly braking is necessary but not sufficient. The car should be able to analyze the surrounding environment and evaluate the consequences of its actions. If a deer crosses the road, the possible choice of the car to swerve in a ravine should be a decision taken on the base of a well-defined reasoning process, rather than being merely the result of reactive behavior that aims to avoid the animal. Therefore, there is a need for realizing systems able to base their decisions on their (evolving) knowledge of the world within given temporal bounds.

Calvaresi et al. [14] proposed a solution to enable the real-time compliance of MAS revising their pillars. Nevertheless, to mimic the cognitive behavior of humans using regular MAS is burdensome.

Being inspired by Bratman's theory of human practical reasoning [8], the Belief-Desire-Intention (BDI) model [34] represents one of the most recognized approaches to integrate the desired cognitive abilities in autonomous agents [28]. Furthermore, since the BDI agents' behavior is knowledge-driven – being determined by deliberation over well-structured concepts such as beliefs, goals, and intentions –, the cause-effect relationship that brought to the intended means can be depicted clearly. This paper presents and discusses the still unexplored challenges of designing and developing *Real-Time eXplainable* BDI Multi-Agent

Systems (RTX-BDI-MAS), eliciting *goals*, *challenges*, *opportunities*, possible *application scenarios*, and a *road map* to achieve such a result. Figure 1 schematically represents the view calling for RTX-BDI-MAS.

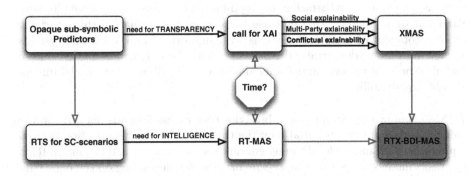

Fig. 1. Needs for RTX-BDI-MAS schematization.

The remainder of the paper is organized as follows. Section 3 analyzes the current challenges in designing Real-Time eXplainable BDI Multi-Agent Systems (RTX-BDI-MAS). Section 4 discusses the main advantages of developing RTX-BDI agents. Section 5 elaborates on possible application scenarios that would benefit from the employment of such agents. Section 6 proposes a road map to design a model for the development of RTX-BDI-MAS. Finally, Sect. 7 concludes the paper.

2 Background

XAI – Nowadays, most intelligent systems (IS) leverage on *subsymbolic* predictive models. Such a wide adoption is mainly due to the unprecedented data availability, enabling to detect useful statistical information hidden into such data semi-automatically. Nevertheless, most of the ML techniques carry well-known drawbacks. For example, the algorithmic *opacity* – the difficulty for the humans to *understand how* ML-based IS (also referred to as *black boxes*) operate or compute their outputs—is a serious issue if decisions' liability is needed [27]. Current regulations such as the GDPR [38] recognize the citizens' *right to explanation* [23]—implicitly requiring *understandable* IS. Moreover, having an understandable system can boost people's *trust* and *acceptability*—otherwise harmed. To cope with such issues and the normative requirements, the XAI research field has recently emerged, particularly tackling *interpretability* and *explainability* [25].

XMAS – Current XAI solutions are mostly use-case-specific and they help the interpretation of single ML-based algorithms [1]. However, standalone explainable approaches do not satisfy the needs of distributed and inter-connected IS.

For example, IoT systems are characterized by heterogeneous inputs, devices, and data-types concurring in the composition of complex information structures [20]. Hence, in [17], the MAS paradigm has been identified as potential means to *(i)* dynamically provide *interpretations* and *explanations* for opaque systems, *(ii)* ease the integration among different solutions/components for similar tasks or predictors, *(iii)* increase the degree of automation characterizing the development of intelligent systems, *(iv)* support AI and ML-based systems in distributed and decentralized contexts, where data cannot be moved due to technical or legal reasons, and *(v)* introduce and contribute to the social dimension of explainability.

RTS – Computing systems whose behavior correctness depends not only on the value of the computation but also on the time at which the results are produced – providing *soft* and/or *hard* timing guarantees – are known as RTS [36]. In RTS, the tasks models are *periodic, aperiodic* or *sporadic*, depending on the regularity of the tasks' activation (i.e., periodic - potentially infinite regular activations, aperiodic - irregularly interleaved, and sporadic - consecutive jobs are separated by minimum and maximum inter-arrival time) [11].

RT-MAS – A *Real-Time Agent* (RTA) extends and embodies a real-time *process*. Similarly to the RTS, the RTA correctness depends on both soundness and delivery time of its outcomes [21]. Enriching the conventional MAS with concepts such as *deadlines, precedence, priority*, and *constrained resources*, and mechanisms to handle them result in the so-called RT-MAS [12]. RTAs are intended to operate in highly dynamic environments. Thus, they adopt the *Earliest Deadline First* (EDF) mechanism [11] as the local scheduler. Nevertheless, EDF can only handle periodic tasks. Hence, to execute also aperiodic tasks (e.g., in charge of the message exchange), an RTA should combine EDF with a bandwidth reservation mechanism—i.e., the Constant Bandwidth Server (CBS) mechanism [12].

In the context of RT-MAS (similarly to RTS), missing "soft" deadlines may cause performance degradation, and missing "hard" deadlines entails a failure and possibly severe consequences.

Finally, MAS can be considered real-time compliant only if all the agents and their mechanisms (interactions included) operate accordingly [16].

BDI Agents – BDI-based agents are characterized by *beliefs, goals*, and *plans*. Beliefs represent the agent's knowledge about itself and the surrounding environment. Goals represent states of the world the agent wants to bring about. Plans are the means by which the agent can act to achieve its goals. BDI agents are well suited in unpredictable scenarios requiring dynamic decision-making due to their ability to choose the best plan to achieve a goal, given their current beliefs. In most BDI-based approaches, the process of repeatedly choosing and executing plans is called the *agent's reasoning cycle* [7].

3   Challenges

AI/ML-based systems are progressively pervading safety-critical application scenarios. Therefore, the needs for explainability and time-predictable behaviors blend in *demanding real-time production and delivery of the explanations*.

RTS and RT-MAS are able to comply with strict timing constraints. Yet, RTS show only predetermined behaviors—limitation overcome by RT-MAS. Nevertheless, since both RTS and RT-MAS (as-is) are incapable of performing "explicit reasoning" to explain their conduct, they cannot be considered XAI-compliant. BDI agents and XMAS can both make autonomous decisions dynamically. In BDI, the agent's reasoning cycle offers intrinsically a cause-effect explanation regarding its decisions, while XAMS can explain ML-based system (i.e., generate a symbolic representation of subsymbolic knowledge). Nevertheless, both BDI and XMAS lack the main property of RTS and RT-MAS: make decisions, and therefore act, in time.

Therefore, none of the existing approaches taken individually allows to produce explanations complying with time constraints and dynamically adapting to the environment in which they operate. Despite several studies attempted to combine the RTS and MAS [19,37] and other made their way through [12], to the best of our knowledge no previous attempt of providing in time explanations can be mentioned.

Moving towards the definition of a model that integrates RT-MAS and XMAS properties and capabilities, requires to address several questions. In particular:

What is the impact of **RT-compliance** *on XMAS?*
Depending on the application domain, the consequences generated by a given explanation can vary significantly. Thus, having a predictable delivery time of the explanation will play a crucial role. Such a requirement entails the development of mechanisms ruling all the behaviors (including the ones generating the explanations) in a real-time manner. Considering the social dimension of explainability (i.e., goal-driven XAI [17,20]), the whole process might require several interactions between explainer and explainee. Current approaches neglect the converging time of conveying an explanation—condition unacceptable under RT assumptions. To overcome such a limitation is crucial. Hence, the agent should be aware of the costs of generating an explanation (both resources and time-wise) and act accordingly—even if it will come on the expenses of performance, explanation's granularity, or quality.

In particular, a first step for metrics and mechanisms-revision in BDI agents should involve inevitably a structural revision of the architecture. Thus, the notion of time itself can also play a direct role within a given explanation (e.g., impossible to complete safely *plan-A*, so emergency switch to *plan-B*)—**clearly performed in time**.

Which **Architecture** *should be adopted?*
The architecture of a software agent identifies the fundamental components that allow the agent to make decisions (henceforth producing explanations) taking into account the temporal constraints typical of RTS. In literature, there are

two approaches: layered and integrated architectures. In layered architectures, the real-time and the cognitive functionalities are separated, acting on different layers, and each one relies and depends on the behavior of the other. This approach involves two loosely coupled sub-systems, so it allows an easier design. However, since the deliberative layer does not act in real-time, such a system cannot guarantee compliance with hard real-time constraints. Concerning integrated architectures, instead, Musliner et al. [31] claim that a hybrid system can be obtained by embedding either AI into a real-time system or real-time reactions into an AI system. In the former case, AI computations are forced to meet deadlines like any other real-time task, while in the latter the deliberation techniques will be short-circuited in favor of a real-time reflexive action. An eXplainable system should always provide at least a basic motivation for its decisions, so an RTX-BDI architecture should integrate AI processes (including explanations) into an RTS. By doing so, the level of detail of the explanation can depend on the time the agent has to provide it.

*Which **Algorithms** have to regulate the behavior of the agent?*
A crucial point consists in the definition of the algorithms and techniques that enable the scheduling of the agent's activities and comply with strict timing-constraints. As discussed previously, due to the diversity of their original purposes, MAS, XMAS, and RTS rely upon significantly different mechanisms that need to be revised and modified to allow them to cooperate. For instance, while the concept of a real-time task can easily be mapped with a BDI action, problems arise when the BDI agent should manage the different types of tasks (periodic, aperiodic, and sporadic) typical of RTS [11]. Indeed, such a characterization is neither considered in the agent-oriented paradigm, nor in the current state of the art of XAI [1], preventing the use of pure real-time theories and their application in the context of XAI and MAS with a 1-to-1 mapping. Therefore, when designing an RTX-BDI agent, a revision of actions and plans becomes necessary to take these diversities into consideration. A similar analysis has been done by Calvaresi et al. in [16], which suggests that a mapping between Jade's *behaviours* and the real-time task models is possible. Nevertheless, the BDI model has higher abstraction levels, thus requiring a more complex mapping.

Another challenge concerns the scheduler employed by the agent. Indeed, most of the state-of-the-art agent platforms adopt best-effort approaches that are not able to handle the system behavior in worst-case scenarios [16]. In such approaches, computational times and deadlines do not have a role in deciding about the execution of the next task. This prevents the agent from controlling the generation and communication of explanations and the interleaving with potentially non-time-critical tasks. To realize real-time explainable agents is essential that they rely on a real-time compliant local scheduler [15].

However, there are no real-time schedulers suitable to be implemented, as they are, in agents running in an open environment (hence flexible enough to deal with sudden changes in priorities). Indeed, some additional mechanisms must be implemented to allow the agent to manage the dynamic activation of tasks having arrival times unknown a-priori. An agent acting in real-time must be able to establish which goals to prioritize when it cannot achieve all of them, a common situation when considering time as a limited resource. While the concept of priority is central in RTS, in agent-based systems it is often neglected, assuming that all goals will be eventually reached by the agent.

Similarly, the problem of choosing among plans designed to achieve the same goal must be addressed. Indeed, in a real-case scenario, to adapt to different circumstances agents usually have different ways to achieve their goals. Then, the agents should be able to elaborate trade-offs by selecting plans that allow them to balance between the number of goals achieved and the efforts or resources required to achieve them. A very delicate and critical challenge that characterizes XMAS – worsened by the introduction of real-time – concerns how the agent should/must behave when the execution of an intention fails (e.g., generating or communicating an explanation do not converge before a critical deadline occurs). The strict schedule typical of RTS leaves little room for the execution of unforeseen, unboundable, and alternative tasks, which are needed to perform backtracking or to try a different way to achieve the goal. In a multi-agent system, the agents have to exchange information among them, negotiate, and cooperate. Therefore, it is necessary to define interaction techniques that allow real-time communication and cooperation between agents.

How should the system be **Validated**?
Once such a system is designed and implemented, the problem regarding how it should be validated arises. Indeed, in literature few studies tried to achieve the same goal [1,12], hence there are no significant results to compare with. However, interesting insights can be obtained by evaluating particular properties: for instance, comparing performances time-wise respect to state-of-the-art MAS (and XMAS if any) frameworks, or measuring flexibility by analyzing the behaviors of such a system and real-time ones in unpredictable scenarios. Moreover, implementing explainable mechanism will already play a crucial role within the validation stage itself. In particular, such a mechanism can enable meaningful and more understandable debugging phases eliciting values, roles, and dynamics of internal (possibly hidden/opaque) parameters.

Figure 2 summarizes the components entangled with each of the challenges discussed above: architecture (AR), algorithms (AL), and validation (VA).

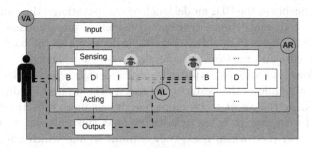

Fig. 2. Graphical representation of the components and the respective challenges. The dashed lines represent the information exchange between entities.

4   Opportunities

Realizing the RTX-BDI-MAS model allows to merge the properties and advantages of classical RTS (i.e., systems characterized by bounded response times and no deadline miss) and XMAS (i.e., systems able to generate symbolic representations of subsymbolic information) and extend them with the BDI systems' capability of making decisions and adopting dynamic behaviors in response to the changes in the environment in which they operate.

RTX-BDI-MAS can be particularly useful in safety-critical and unpredictable domains, such as autonomous driving, telerehabilitation, personal coaching, and air traffic control. In these scenarios, the systems involved need to adopt algorithms that allow them to behave correctly (and in time) in case an unforeseen event occurs. Moreover, due to their safety-related requirements, the use of symbolic AI in the reasoning process is mandatory, as the uncertainty given by statistical AI and ML-based systems – which can still be used to solve specific sub-problems – may lead to catastrophic consequences. Furthermore, in the last decade, safety-critical systems are increasingly composed of different (possibly distributed) components interacting with one another—strengthening the choice of MAS as underlying paradigm.

On Explainability – Transparency and understandability are broadly known to be the main factors calling for XAI [1]. Nevertheless, enabling explicit reasoning *about* and *in* time can be a key enabler for crucial desiderata such as expressing systems, agents, and robots' reasons, capabilities, and limits to their end-user [26]. Hence, time can play a prominent role in the decision-making process, whether a plan is chosen or dropped. The claimed system *accountability* [2] cannot be achieved regardless of *transparency* and *time*. Conversely, a system is not able to perform in *real*-world application scenarios predictably (or properly at all)—since the humans' interactions are inherently entangled with the concept of time. Finally, RTX-BDI-MAS can facilitate the tuning of the explanation's granularity, enhancing the efficiency and the response time of the system.

On Time-awareness – To reason *about* and *in* time, RTX-BDI-agents have to embody a real-time scheduler. Thus, it is possible to ensure that every decision-making-process is executed respecting the time constraints, while the integration of temporal concepts in the BDI model, such as computational time and deadline, allows the agent to make these decisions considering also the time as a finite resource. Since the agents are able to take their decisions on the base of the time required to execute an intention, designers can also tune the agents to prioritize optimal solutions time-wise or output-wise, or to identify a *feasible* balance of the two. Such a tuning allows the designers to specify the desired Quality of Service (QoS), configuring the agent to be more reactive or more reflective, depending on the desired behavior. It is worth noticing that this only affects the choices made by the agent (i.e., which goals they commit to and which intentions they execute), without breaking any real-time boundary.

On Ease of design – Compared to distributed RTS and XMAS, RTX-BDI-MAS provides a more natural design phase. Indeed, the developer has to design the single components (beliefs, desires, plans, and tasks) without the burden of establishing the rules and behaviors that operate the run-time execution of the device. Since the BDI model is based on the human practical reasoning theory, the design of such components is very intuitive. The reasoning cycle of a BDI agent, indeed, is similar to our way of thinking: we perceive a change in the environment (change in agent's beliefs) which can make us desire to achieve some goals (instantiation of agent's desires), and we reason about the actions to take to satisfy those desires (generation of intentions through means-end reasoning).

On Robustness – With respect to RTS, RTX-BDI-MAS grant more robustness in open environments, allowing real-time software to promptly and adequately deal with system failures. Indeed, since RTS are designed to work in controlled and predefined environments, the possibility of having system failures is excluded a-priori (unless hardware failures handled with devices redundancy). In general, RTS only manage overloads, i.e., the system can lower the band to fit the tasks, if this does not cause losing deadlines or important information [11]. Conversely, when feasible, RTX-BDI-MAS allows the re-planning and rearrangements on-the-fly by reconsidering their goals and intentions.

5 Application Scenarios

In general, an RTX-BDI architecture allows us to build systems able to perform autonomous actions in time, reasoning not only in a self-interested way but coordinating with all the other agents, possibly leveraging on symbolic reasoning. This is particularly valuable for systems in which decision-making processes are needed, but reducing at the minimum the human error and increasing the acceptance and understanding of the system's behaviors are the cornerstones.

Summarizing, the possible scenarios in which a system operates can be classified in general-purpose or non-safety-critical (NSC), XAI-critical and non-safety-critical (XNSC), safety-critical (SC), dynamic safety-critical (DSC), and dynamic XAI and safety-critical (XDSC). Figure 3 organize the types of system per the most appropriate scenario, highlighting the evolution of the efficiency (according to the resources allocated), predictability, and the capability of producing explanations of opaque subsymbolic predictors.

Besides the expected lack of efficiency (given the resources allocated and the need for ensuring timing guarantees) RTX-BDI agents are envisioned to be equipped with both XAI and RTS capabilities, while keeping unaltered the social abilities typical of MAS.

To highlight the relevance of RTX-BDI-MAS in XDSC, we briefly elaborate on two envisioned scenarios.

Telerehabilitation – Most of the telerehabilitation systems are expected to be used without the direct supervision of any medical staff. The majority of the

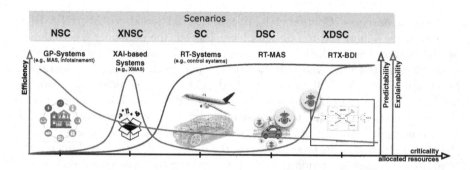

Fig. 3. Systems classification per efficiency, predictability, explainability, resources allocated, scenarios and criticality.

proposed systems leverage on wearable distributed sensing [9,14]. Such systems provide real-time monitoring and feedback, storing the data generated during the therapy sessions for the (long-term) trend-analysis. For simple exercises, such approaches are effective. Nevertheless, depending on the joint(s) to rehabilitate, the therapy might be more complex (from both physical and cognitive viewpoints). A first step to enable telerehabilitation for more demanding therapies is presented in [13], where the authors developed a semantic model for RT-MAS enabling more elaborated – yet real-time compliant– interactions among the wearable sensors. Along this path, we envision that RTX-BDI-MAS can empower the telerehabilitation systems by providing not only real-time monitoring and feedback but also providing in-time explanations. In particular, it would enrich the coaching capability of the system and provide better (possibly more understandable) support to the patients dealing with complex exercises, which have higher chances of causing late or wrong movements—thus hurting the patient and jeopardizing the beneficial effects of the therapy.

Autonomous vehicle and robots – In the case of fully autonomous multi-vehicles or robots, the compliance with strict-timing constraints is imperative (e.g., to avoid collisions). However, complex interactions (e.g., negotiations) are increasingly pervading the robotic and autonomous vehicles worlds. In our vision, establishing an agreement might soon leverage on the explanation of ML-based predictors or of complex behaviors intertwined with subsymbolic information. In the case of semi-autonomous vehicles [5], the system might be required to present timely explanations to the driver to undertake a given (possibly time-critical) decision, which requires the human's approval. Finally, in UAVs search and rescue scenarios [30], UAV teams need to cooperate to achieve common goals. In such a case, identifying the responsibility of each UAV is crucial. Hence, it can enable to ensure efficient collaboration or, in a case of failure, to trace the underlying reasons and assign responsibilities—both to improve the future system's performance and to held involved parties accountable. Once again, employing RTX-BDI-MAS would bridge the advantages of the two worlds (i.e., XMAS and RT-MAS).

6   Road Map

This section presents the four phases need to formalize an RTX-BDI-MAS model.

PH1: *First formalization of the RTX-BDI model*
To guarantee the properties of RTS, the BDI structure needs to be revised to consider the necessary real-time notions, such as *priority*, *deadline*, and *worst-case execution time*. Redesigning desires, plans, intentions, and actions by involving such elements would allow the integration of a real-time scheduler in the reasoning cycle of the agent, providing real-time guarantees in both the deliberative and executive processes. Moreover, it is necessary to identify the tasks model and the dynamics necessary to perform predictably the intra-agent explainability [20].

PH2: *Definition of policies to handle plan failures*
Plan failure management, as discussed in Sect. 3, is probably one of the most challenging problems to be solved in real-time compliant MAS. Indeed, due to the high dynamism of the scenarios in which XMAS are expected to operate, the robustness typically obtained by RTS is very difficult to be achieved. Moreover, if the system is composed by a growing number of elements, also the possible failures of other agents must be taken into consideration and managed. The robustness of the system can be further improved by developing a real-time compliant selection function able to avoid conflicts between intentions, similarly to what is done in [39]. Such a work, by performing pseudo-random simulations of different interleavings of the plans, looks for an optimal interleaving of the actions that will allow the agent to achieve the largest number of goals. This approach helps in minimizing the possibility of plan failures, but to be applicable in RTX-BDI-MAS it has to be redesigned to consider real-time compliance. Finally, besides the effects that it might imply, the failure of an explanations might entail several factors (e.g., lack of a common ontology, unknown state of mind of the explainee, and possible lack of time to complete the interaction necessary for the entire knowledge-transfer). To avoid, or understand, the reasons standing behind a failure, specific mechanisms need to be developed to setup effective "possibly personalized" explanations.

PH3: *The definition of the interaction techniques*
PH1 and PH2 allow the development of single RTX-BDI agents. When the system scales from single to multi-agent settings, interaction techniques and protocols are required to allow the agents of the RTX-BDI-MAS to communicate (henceforth explain), negotiate, and cooperate. Although a standard for MAS communication already exists (i.e., FIPA Agent Communication Language (ACL) [22]), it lacks of several fundamental mechanisms crucial to handle multi-step explanations and RT-compliance. Indeed, FIPA ACL does not provide a way to manage either the network load and messages status (e.g., bounding congestion and delivering times is not possible), nor the in/out message queues. Furthermore, broadcasting (particularly useful when the information of a sensor should be exploited by many components) is difficult to be achieved. To overcome such limitations, a communication middleware able to guarantee bounded-time delays

must be employed. In [18], the authors identify the Real-Time Publish-Subscribe (RTPS) as viable technology (already adopted by the Data Distribution Service (DDS) systems in aerospace domains [33]).

PH4: *The implementation of a prototype for verification and validation*
The last phase regards the development of an RTX-BDI-MAS prototype, which must be used to verify and validate the model. The evaluation can be done in a simulated or real environment. The implementation of a simulator allows a better, safer, and cheaper analysis of the systems' behavior—since it acts in a controlled environment. However, deploying the system in real-world devices represents a more significant validation. Indeed, in real-world scenarios, the adaptability of the system is stressed.

To enable deployment and testing of the RT-BDI MAS, a framework equipped with an intuitive graphical user interface and comprehensive analysis tools is needed. Extending any of the most recognized and supported agents frameworks in the literature, such as JACK [10], JADE [3], and Jason [7] is not feasible nor effective. Indeed, among the main limitations hampering such a way it is possible to mention *(i)* they are based on Java, thus incapable of guaranteeing any real-time compliance and *(ii)* they rely on general-purpose algorithms (e.g., round-robin and first-come-first-served) neglecting elements such as *time, utilization,* and *deadlines* core of any real-time compliant algorithm [12,15], and *(iii)* lack of means to extract symbolic knowledge from subsymbolic data. Coupling explainability and visualization would boost the user's understanding of the underlying system. Furthermore, in case explainability provides a deep view of the inner-mechanism, it allows the user/developer to predict the outcomes demonstrated by the system when the input parameters change. Thus, the system can be validated under different settings, always allowing clear system assessment and understanding.

7   Conclusion

This paper discussed challenges and opportunities of modeling and developing explainable and RT compliant MAS based on the BDI cognitive architecture. This preliminary analysis shows that such a system can enhance the reasoning and decision-making processes of applications that have to comply with strict real-time constraints, while providing transparency, and promoting trust. More precisely, it allows us to exploit the structure of BDI to easily design explainable RTS able to dynamically adapt to the uncertainties that characterize open environments. Moreover, using BDI fosters adaptive and user-friendly explainability, which enables end-users (or other agents in the system) to understand the system behavior and modify it in case a need arises. Nevertheless, several complex challenges must be faced. The main ones concern the system's type of architecture, its mechanisms, and behavior policies.

References

1. Anjomshoae, S., Najjar, A., Calvaresi, D., Främling, K.: Explainable agents and robots: results from a systematic literature review. In: Proceedings of the 18th International Conference on Autonomous Agents and MultiAgent Systems, pp. 1078–1088. International Foundation for Autonomous Agents and Multiagent Systems (2019)
2. Baldoni, M., Baroglio, C., Boissier, O., May, K.M., Micalizio, R., Tedeschi, S.: Accountability and responsibility in agent organizations. In: Miller, T., Oren, N., Sakurai, Y., Noda, I., Savarimuthu, B.T.R., Cao Son, T. (eds.) PRIMA 2018. LNCS (LNAI), vol. 11224, pp. 261–278. Springer, Cham (2018). https://doi.org/10.1007/978-3-030-03098-8_16
3. Bellifemine, F., Poggi, A., Rimassa, G.: JADE-A FIPA-compliant agent framework. In: Proceedings of PAAM, London, vol. 99, p. 33 (1999)
4. Besold, T.R., Uckelman, S.L.: The what, the why, and the how of artificial explanations in automated decision-making. CoRR abs/1808.07074, pp. 1–20 (2018). http://arxiv.org/abs/1808.07074
5. Biondi, A., Nesti, F., Cicero, G., Casini, D., Buttazzo, G.: A safe, secure, and predictable software architecture for deep learning in safety-critical systems. IEEE Embed. Syst. Lett. 1 (2019)
6. Biondi, A., Pazzaglia, P., Balsini, A., Di Natale, M.: Logical execution time implementation and memory optimization issues in autosar applications for multicores. In: International Workshop on Analysis Tools and Methodologies for Embedded and Real-Time Systems (WATERS) (2017)
7. Bordini, R.H., Hübner, J.F., Wooldridge, M.: Programming Multi-Agent Systems in AgentSpeak using Jason, vol. 8. Wiley, Hoboken (2007)
8. Bratman, M.: Intention, Plans, and Practical Reason, vol. 10. Harvard University Press, Cambridge (1987)
9. Buonocunto, P., Giantomassi, A., Marinoni, M., Calvaresi, D., Buttazzo, G.: A limb tracking platform for tele-rehabilitation. ACM Trans. Cyber-Phys. Syst. 2(4), 1–23 (2018)
10. Busetta, P., Rönnquist, R., Hodgson, A., Lucas, A.: Jack intelligent agents-components for intelligent agents in Java. AgentLink News Lett. 2(1), 2–5 (1999)
11. Buttazzo, G.C.: Hard Real-Time Computing Systems: Predictable Scheduling Algorithms and Applications, vol. 24. Springer, Heidelberg (2011). https://doi.org/10.1007/978-1-4614-0676-1
12. Calvaresi, D.: Real-time multi-agent systems: challenges, model, and performance analysis (2018)
13. Calvaresi, D., Calbimonte, J.P.: Real-time compliant stream processing agents for physical rehabilitation. Sensors 20(3), 746 (2020)
14. Calvaresi, D., Marinoni, M., Dragoni, A.F., Hilfiker, R., Schumacher, M.: Real-time multi-agent systems for telerehabilitation scenarios. Artif. Intell. Med. 96, 217–231 (2019). https://doi.org/10.1016/j.artmed.2019.02.001
15. Calvaresi, D., et al.: Local scheduling in multi-agent systems: getting ready for safety-critical scenarios. In: Belardinelli, F., Argente, E. (eds.) EUMAS/AT -2017. LNCS (LNAI), vol. 10767, pp. 96–111. Springer, Cham (2018). https://doi.org/10.1007/978-3-030-01713-2_8
16. Calvaresi, D., Marinoni, M., Sturm, A., Schumacher, M., Buttazzo, G.: The challenge of real-time multi-agent systems for enabling IoT and CPS. In: Proceedings of the International Conference on Web Intelligence, pp. 356–364. ACM (2017)

17. Calvaresi, D., Mualla, Y., Najjar, A., Galland, S., Schumacher, M.: Explainable multi-agent systems through blockchain technology. In: Calvaresi, D., Najjar, A., Schumacher, M., Främling, K. (eds.) EXTRAAMAS 2019. LNCS (LNAI), vol. 11763, pp. 41–58. Springer, Cham (2019). https://doi.org/10.1007/978-3-030-30391-4_3

18. Calvaresi, D., Schumacher, M., Marinoni, M., Hilfiker, R., Dragoni, A.F., Buttazzo, G.: Agent-based systems for telerehabilitation: strengths, limitations and future challenges. In: Montagna, S., Abreu, P.H., Giroux, S., Schumacher, M.I. (eds.) A2HC/AHEALTH -2017. LNCS (LNAI), vol. 10685, pp. 3–24. Springer, Cham (2017). https://doi.org/10.1007/978-3-319-70887-4_1

19. Carrascosa, C., Bajo, J., Julián, V., Corchado, J.M., Botti, V.: Hybrid multi-agent architecture as a real-time problem-solving model. Expert Syst. Appl. **34**(1), 2–17 (2008)

20. Ciatto, G., Calegari, R., Omicini, A., Calvaresi, D.: Towards XMAS: explainability through multi-agent systems. In: Proceedings of the 1st Workshop on Artificial Intelligence and Internet of Things co-located with the 18th International Conference of the Italian Association for Artificial Intelligence (AI*IA 2019), Rende (CS), Italy, 22 November 2019, pp. 40–53. CEUR Worhsop Proceedings, Sun SITE Central Europe, RWTH Aachen University (2019). http://ceur-ws.org/Vol-2502/paper3.pdf

21. Dragoni, A., Sernani, P., Calvaresi, D.: When rationality entered time and became a real agent in a cyber-society, vol. 2280, pp. 167–171 (2018)

22. FIPA: FIPA ACL message structure specification. FIPA agent communication language specifications (2002). http://www.fipa.org/specs/fipa00061

23. Goodman, B., Flaxman, S.: European Union regulations on algorithmic decision-making and a "right to explanation". AI Mag. **38**(3), 50–57 (2017). https://doi.org/10.1609/aimag.v38i3.2741

24. Guidotti, R., Monreale, A., Turini, F., Pedreschi, D., Giannotti, F.: A survey of methods for explaining black box models. ACM Comput. Surv. (CSUR) **51**(5), 1–42 (2019). https://doi.org/10.1145/3236009

25. Gunning, D.: Explainable artificial intelligence (XAI). Funding Program DARPA-BAA-16-53, Defense Advanced Research Projects Agency (DARPA) (2016). http://www.darpa.mil/program/explainable-artificial-intelligence

26. Hellström, T., Bensch, S.: Understandable robots-what, why, and how. Paladyn J. Behav. Robot. **9**(1), 110–123 (2018)

27. Lipton, Z.C.: The mythos of model interpretability. ACM Queue **16**(3), 31–57 (2018). https://dl.acm.org/citation.cfm?id=3241340

28. Logan, B.: An agent programming manifesto. Int. J. Agent-Orientat. Softw. Eng. **6**(2), 187–210 (2017)

29. Mualla, Y., Najjar, A., Daoud, A., Galland, S., Nicolle, C., Shakshuki, E., et al.: Agent-based simulation of unmanned aerial vehicles in civilian applications: a systematic literature review and research directions. Future Gener. Comput. Syst. **100**, 344–364 (2019)

30. Mualla, Y., et al.: Between the megalopolis and the deep blue sky: challenges of transport with UAVs in future smart cities. In: Proceedings of the 18th International Conference on Autonomous Agents and MultiAgent Systems, pp. 1649–1653. International Foundation for Autonomous Agents and Multiagent Systems (2019)

31. Musliner, D.J., Hendler, J.A., Agrawala, A.K., Durfee, E.H., Strosnider, J.K., Paul, C.: The challenges of real-time AI. Computer **28**(1), 58–66 (1995)

32. Omicini, A., Zambonelli, F.: MAS as complex systems: a view on the role of declarative approaches. In: Leite, J., Omicini, A., Sterling, L., Torroni, P. (eds.) DALT 2003. LNCS (LNAI), vol. 2990, pp. 1–16. Springer, Heidelberg (2004). https://doi.org/10.1007/978-3-540-25932-9_1

33. Pardo-Castellote, G.: Omg data-distribution service: architectural overview. In: 2003 Proceedings of 23rd International Conference on Distributed Computing Systems Workshops, pp. 200–206. IEEE (2003)

34. Rao, A.S., Georgeff, M.P.: Modeling rational agents within a BDI-architecture. KR **91**, 473–484 (1991)

35. Ribeiro, M.T., Singh, S., Guestrin, C.: "Why should I trust you?": explaining the predictions of any classifier. In: 22nd ACM SIGKDD International Conference on Knowledge Discovery and Data Mining (KDD 2016), San Francisco, CA, USA, 22–26 August 2016, pp. 1135–1144. ACM (2016). https://doi.org/10.1145/2939672.2939778

36. Stankovic, J.A., Ramamritham, K. (eds.): Tutorial: Hard Real-Time Systems. IEEE Computer Society Press, Los Alamitos (1989)

37. Vikhorev, K., Alechina, N., Logan, B.: The ARTS real-time agent architecture. In: Dastani, M., El Fallah Segrouchni, A., Leite, J., Torroni, P. (eds.) LADS 2009. LNCS (LNAI), vol. 6039, pp. 1–15. Springer, Heidelberg (2010). https://doi.org/10.1007/978-3-642-13338-1_1

38. Voigt, P., von dem Bussche, A.: The EU General Data Protection Regulation (GDPR). A Practical Guide. Springer, Cham (2017). https://doi.org/10.1007/978-3-319-57959-7

39. Yao, Y., Logan, B.: Action-level intention selection for BDI agents. In: Proceedings of the 2016 International Conference on Autonomous Agents & Multiagent Systems, pp. 1227–1236. International Foundation for Autonomous Agents and Multiagent Systems (2016)

Cross Disciplinary XAI

Decision Theory Meets Explainable AI

Kary Främling[1,2]([✉]) [ID]

[1] Umeå University, Umeå, Sweden
[2] School of Science and Technology, Aalto University, Espoo, Finland
kary.framling@umu.se
http://www.umu.se

Abstract. Explainability has been a core research topic in AI for decades and therefore it is surprising that the current concept of Explainable AI (XAI) seems to have been launched as late as 2016. This is a problem with current XAI research because it tends to ignore existing knowledge and wisdom gathered over decades or even centuries by other relevant domains. This paper presents the notion of Contextual Importance and Utility (CIU), which is based on known notions and methods of Decision Theory. CIU extends the notions of importance and utility for the non-linear models of AI systems and notably those produced by Machine Learning methods. CIU provides a universal and model-agnostic foundation for XAI.

Keywords: Explainable AI · Decision Theory · Contextual Importance and Utility · Multiple Criteria Decision Making

1 Introduction

It seems like the term Explainable AI (XAI) dates back to a presentation by David Gunning in 2016 [13] and much recent work tends not to look at or cite research papers that are older than so. It has also been pointed out that XAI as a domain currently tends to propose methods that mainly can help experts to validate that an AI system built using Machine Learning (ML) makes sense to some extent [6]. It is rare to see methods and results that are meant to explain and justify results and actions of ML models to 'real' end users, such as the pedestrians who might be hit by an autonomous vehicle or the applicant of a mortgage whose request is refused by an AI system. As pointed out e.g. by Miller [20] and others [33], it is fair to say that most XAI work uses only the researchers' intuition of what constitutes a 'good' explanation, while ignoring the vast and valuable bodies of research in philosophy, psychology, and cognitive science of how people define, generate, select, evaluate, and present explanations.

One truly relevant domain that seems to have been neglected in current XAI work is *Decision Theory* and related sub-domains such as *Multiple Criteria*

The work is partially supported by the Wallenberg AI, Autonomous Systems and Software Program (WASP) funded by the Knut and Alice Wallenberg Foundation.

D. Calvaresi et al. (Eds.): EXTRAAMAS 2020, LNAI 12175, pp. 57–74, 2020.
https://doi.org/10.1007/978-3-030-51924-7_4

Decision Making (MCDM). The Merriam-Webster dictionary defines Decision Theory as 'a branch of statistical theory concerned with quantifying the process of making choices between alternatives'. However, Decision Theory is also by definition tightly connected with the domains mentioned above (philosophy, psychology, and cognitive science) because methods of Decision Theory are intended to produce Decision Support Systems (DSS) that are understood and used by humans when taking decisions. Decision Theory and MCDM provide clear definitions of what is meant by the *importance* of an input, as well as what is the *utility* of a given input value towards the outcome of a DSS. A simple linear DSS model is the weighted sum, where a numerical weight expresses the importance of an input and a numerical score expresses the utility of the current value of that input.

This paper extends the linear definition of importance and utility towards non-linear models such as those produced by typical ML methods. This non-linear extension is called **Contextual Importance and Utility (CIU)**[1] because in many (or most) real-life situations the importance of an input and the utility of different input values changes depending on values of other inputs. For instance, the outdoor temperature has a great importance on a person's comfort level as long as the person is outdoors. When the person goes inside, the situation (context) changes and the outdoor temperature may then have a very small importance for the comfort level. Similarly, both a very cold and a very warm outdoor temperature might have a low utility for a person's comfort level but the level of utility can be modified by adding or removing clothes.

After this Introduction, Sect. 2 builds up the theoretical background as a combination of Decision Theory and XAI. Section 3 presents the background and definition of CIU, supported by examples and an experiment using the Iris data set, followed by conclusions in Sect. 4.

Source files for producing the results and Figures of this paper can be found at https://github.com/KaryFramling/EXTRAAMAS_2020.

2   Background

The rationality of human decisions (or lack of it) might be one of the oldest challenges addressed by philosophers. For instance, Socrates' method for solving a problem in a rational way consisted in braking the problem down into a series of questions, the answers to which gradually distill the answer a person would seek. This can be thought of as 'solve a problem by explaining your reasoning to yourself and/or someone else by starting from a high abstraction level and brake it into smaller sub-problems'. The concept of bounded rationality as proposed by Herbert Simon [28,29] can be considered a cornerstone regarding modern theories of human decision making. The fundamental concepts and methods of Decision Theory are much older than Simon's work. But Simon's work can be

---

[1] https://github.com/KaryFramling/ciu.

considered to be based on Decision Theory and provides a connection from there to Artificial Intelligence and, by consequence, to Explainable AI.

2.1 Decision Theory

Decision Theory as a domain is too vast for the purposes of this article. Excellent introductions to the domain can be found for instance in [14,18,24] and [32], which notably focus on the sub-domain of Multiple Criteria Decision Making (MCDM). The Analytic Hierarchy Process (AHP) [26] that was originally developed in the 1970's seems to have become the most popular MCDM method in research and practice [16,17].

AHP is essentially based on a weighted sum, where the main selection task can be broken into sub-tasks in a hierarchical manner. The weights are typically acquired from experts using a pair-wise comparison procedure that produces a comparison matrix, which is then transformed into weights by a normalized principal Eigen vector. The utility (how good or favorable a value is for the selection) of the possible values for each leaf of the hierarchy is specified and calculated using the same principle.

MCDM problems require finding a model of the decision maker's preferences, which may be called his or her preference function. However, the decision maker is quite often a group of people or an abstract person (society, nature, economy, ...). This makes it difficult to explicitly express the preference function, which is the reason for using machine learning methods instead. If a training set exists with labeled data on correct decisions, then it is possible to learn the preference function, no matter if the output of the model is a numerical score or a probability for one or many possible classes. A true preference function is usually non-linear and continuous, which makes its mathematical expression quite complex. Such non-linear and continuous models are mainly studied in the ML domain, which would be attractive also for MCDM if those ML methods would provide sufficient explainability.

In MCDM methods, the importances of the selection criteria are expressed by weights, while the transformation of the values of the criteria into utility values is done with utility functions. For a car selection problem, these concepts may be used for giving explanations such as 'The car is good because it has a good size, decent performances and a reasonable price, which are very important criteria', where words indicating utilities are underlined and only the most important criteria are presented. The fact of using a linear model makes the definition of importance and utility quite easy. However, when using non-linear models like neural nets, the task becomes challenging.

Rule-based expert systems (including fuzzy or rough rules) are a way of overcoming the linearity limitation. However, then we encounter the challenges of explainability that are known in the AI domain since its very beginnings.

2.2   Explainable Artificial Intelligence

Contrary to what many papers seem to claim, the need for explainability in Artificial Intelligence (AI) and Machine Learning (ML) has been known for about as long as AI has existed, even though the term Explainable AI (XAI) seems to have been launched only in 2016 [13]. For instance, Shortliffe et al. point out already in 1975 that 'It is our belief, therefore, that a consultation program will gain acceptance only if it serves to augment rather than replace the physician's own decision making processes. Gorry has reached a similar conclusion stating that one reason for the limited acceptance of Bayesian inference programs has been their inability to explain the reasoning behind their decisions' [27]. The system described in that paper was MYCIN, an expert system that was capable of advising physicians who request advice regarding selection of appropriate antimicrobial therapy for hospital patients with bacterial infections. Great emphasis was put into the interaction with the end-user, in this case a skilled physician.

As pointed out by Shortliffe et al. in 1975, it is even more challenging to explain and understand the reasoning of numerical models, such as Bayesian inference programs. When numerical ML methods such as neural networks gained in popularity in the end of the 1980's due to significant technological progress (e.g. in [25] and [15]), the explainability challenge was immediately identified. During the 1990's there was extensive activity around how to make results of neural networks explainable. However, a vast majority of the work performed then was focusing on so-called *intrinsic interpretability* or *interpretable model extraction* [6], i.e. extract rules or other interpretable forms of knowledge from the trained neural network and then use that representation for explainability [2,5,30,31].

Post-hoc interpretability was actually proposed as early as in 1995 [9]. However, the utility of post-hoc interpretability was not recognized by the AI community back then, as shown by the reactions of the audience at the International Conference on Artificial Neural Networks in 1995. Post-hoc interpretability was neglected to the extent that most XAI survey articles erroneously date the first post-hoc explanations much later, such as *output explanation* in 2006 and *model inspection* approach in 2002 [12]. Another example that presents outcome explanation and the use of counterfactual explanations is the article from 2002 in the Neural Networks journal [11] that is currently only cited 128 times according to Google Scholar. However, the objective of this paper is not to provide a complete overview of the history of XAI. A comprehensive survey on current trends in XAI is provided for instance in [4].

The *Local Interpretable Model-agnostic Explanations* (LIME) method presented in 2016 [22] might be considered a cornerstone regarding post-hoc interpretability. It emphasizes the need for outcome explanations in many real-world situations and shows good results also when applied to image recognition by deep neural networks. LIME implementations are available in several different programming languages, which has certainly increased its popularity. LIME belongs to the family of *additive feature attribution methods* [19] that are based on the assumption that a locally linear model around the current context is sufficient for explanation purposes. As shown in the following Section, even though such methods allow producing outcome explanations (but not model inspection explanations), they are not theoretically correct when studied from a Decision Theory point of view.

3   Contextual Importance and Utility (CIU)

Contextual Importance and Utility (CIU) were initially developed during Kary Främling's PhD thesis [8]. The thesis is written in French but the method is also described in [9] and [7]. After the PhD thesis was finished, the topic was dropped for professional reasons. The popularity of neural networks and the question about their explainability also started declining at the same time. However, the recent rise in popularity of AI and the re-emergence of XAI as a research area are the reasons for the recent re-launch of the work on CIU.

The work on CIU started by a practical problem that consisted in selecting a waste disposal site for ultimate industrial waste in the region of Rhône-Alpes, France [10]. Fifteen selection criteria had been specified by experts and regional decision makers, which characterized the sites from geological, financial, social, ecological and logistic points of view. Over 3000 potential sites had been identified, together with their respective values for the 15 criteria. Tens of decision makers involved in the selection process all had their own opinions on how important different criteria are. What comes to the utility functions, there are many subjective opinions, such as how to assess recreational impact and when such an impact should be 'too big', 'acceptable', 'negligible' or something else.

Three methods were applied in parallel: AHP, Electre I [23] and a rule-based expert system using the tool Nexpert Object v.2.0. The weights of the 15 criteria were identified as a group work using the AHP pair-wise comparison functionality mentioned in Sect. 2.1. The same weights and utility functions were used for AHP and Electre I. For the rule-based system, the problem was divided into sub-categories, i.e. 'Global geology', 'Hydrology', 'Access', 'Nuisance to population', 'Aesthetic values' and 'Agricultural value'. Explainability functionality was developed that was specific for each of the three methods, where the mentioned sub-categories were used for providing explanations with a higher level of abstraction than using the 15 selection criteria directly. Explainability of the results was a core criterion for the decision makers when they took their decision on which method to choose for taking the decision[2]. Since the output of all the three methods was a numeric score per potential site, what needed to be explained was why every individual site had been selected (high score) or rejected (lower score).

The waste disposal site selection problem reveals many crucial challenges related both to MCDM and XAI, such as:

– It is challenging even for one person to specify what is the *importance* of different selection criteria (inputs of the model) and how favorable (or not) the values of different criteria are, i.e. their *utility*.

---

[2] Electre I was the selected method.

– It it difficult to choose what MCDM method to use and what that choice means in practice regarding results and explainability.
– The choice of MCDM model and parameters remains subjective. It would be preferable if a ML model could learn the 'correct' model based on data from existing sites.
– Since explainability is a key requirement, a typical ML black-box approach is not acceptable.
– ML models, such as the ones learned by neural networks can not be supposed to be linear.

Three different kinds of MCDM models are illustrated in Fig. 1:

1. Figure 1a shows the function $z = 0.3x + 0.7y$. This is a weighted sum model with weights (importances) 0.3 and 0.7.
2. Figure 1b shows the result of several if-then rules that determine the z-value as a function of x- and y-values. This kind of a model is highly non-linear and is not differentiable.
3. Figure 1c shows the function $z = (x^{0.5} + y^2)/2$. This is a simple non-linear model that could have been learned by a neural net.

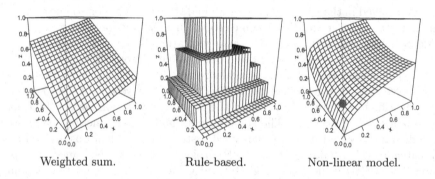

Weighted sum.   Rule-based.   Non-linear model.

Fig. 1. Examples of linear, rule-based (crisp rules, not fuzzy rules or rules involving certainty factors) and non-linear MCDM models. (Color figure online)

For the weighted sum in Fig. 1a it is obvious that the importance of each criterion is directly expressed by the corresponding weight and the utility of x and y equals their value. If such a linear model would have been learned by a ML black-box, then additive feature attribution methods should give these exact importances 0.3 and 0.7 for any point $z = f(x, y)$ because the locally linear model corresponds to the global model. Additive feature attribution methods only speak about feature importance, whereas they do not have any notion of utility.

For a stepwise model such as the one in Fig. 1b it does not make sense to apply a locally linear approximation, for two reasons: 1) the model is not differentiable and 2) the model is non-monotonic, so a local gradient does not say much about the actual importance of a feature.

The non-linear model in Fig. 1c is the most interesting to study further in the context of XAI because the main reason for using neural networks and similar ML models is to deal with non-linear but differentiable models. The next section formally describes Contextual Importance and Utility and provides the justification for why they are theoretically valid concepts for XAI. It also shows why methods based on locally linear models are not sufficiently expressive for many XAI requirements, nor theoretically sound compared to CIU.

3.1 CIU of One Input

CIU is inspired from trying to analyze how humans explain their decisions and reasoning to each other. After all, the human brain is probably the most complex black-box model on earth. But humans are still usually capable to retrospectively produce an explanation for their decisions and behaviour, even though humans do suffer from the limitations of so-called bounded rationality [29]. Bounded rationality is the idea that rationality of human individuals is limited when making decisions, by the tractability of the decision problem, the cognitive limitations of the mind, and the time available to make the decision. Humans also tend to take into account the reactions, background etc. of the audience of the explanation[3]. Humans would typically identify which features were the most salient for taking a decision and start the explanation with those features. In addition to explaining why a decision was taken, humans may also be asked to explain why another decision was not taken, both independently and in comparison with each other. Counterfactual "what-if" explanations are frequent when humans justify their decisions. Depending on the reactions of the audience, humans can also change the vocabulary that is used, the level of abstraction and the kind of interaction (for instance create a drawing if verbal explanation is not sufficient).

Many of these explanation capabilities are **contextual**. One feature might be important for taking a decision in one situation but irrelevant in another situation, as illustrated by the example mentioned in the Introduction, where the importance of the outdoor temperature depends on whether the black box (human brain and body) is indoors or outdoors.

In this paper, we will not attempt to provide a new definition of context. One definition is e.g. *"Context is any information that can be used to characterize the situation of an entity. An entity is a person, place, or object that is considered relevant to the interaction between a user and an application, including the user and the applications themselves"* [1]. The same source defines context-awareness as follows: *"A system is context-aware if it uses context to provide relevant information and/or services to the user, where relevancy depends on the user's task"* [1]. Similar definitions are provided elsewhere, as in [21]. In general, context adds

---

[3] Human interaction and social life of course also involves intentional lying, desires to please or hurt the target of the explanation, to impress other humans etc. However, those considerations go beyond the scope of CIU and this paper.

knowledge about what inputs/features/characteristics of a situation are important for the concerned entity, which in our example would be the person who is indoors or outdoors.

In order to specify *Contextual Importance* (CI) and *Contextual Utility* (CU) formally, we will study the non-linear model in Fig. 1c further. The red dot in Fig. 1c is located at $(x, y) = (0.1, 0.2)$, which gives a result value $z = 0.178$. Here the context is specified by the input values $(x, y) = (0.1, 0.2)$, which we denote $\vec{C}$. What we want to find out is the contextual importance $CI_j(\vec{C}, \{i\})$ of a given set of inputs $\{i\}$ for a specific output j in the context $\vec{C}$. The definition of CI is

$$CI_j(\vec{C}, \{i\}) = \frac{Cmax_j(\vec{C}, \{i\}) - Cmin_j(\vec{C}, \{i\})}{absmax_j - absmin_j} \tag{1}$$

where $absmax_j$ is the maximal possible value for output j and $absmin_j$ is the minimal possible value for output j. $Cmax_j(\vec{C}, \{i\})$ is the maximal value of output j observed when modifying the values of inputs $\{i\}$ and keeping the values of the other inputs at those specified by $\vec{C}$. Correspondingly, $Cmin_j(\vec{C}, \{i\})$ is the minimal value of output j observed.

The estimation of $Cmax_j(\vec{C}, \{i\})$ and $Cmin_j(\vec{C}, \{i\})$ is done for limited value ranges of inputs $\{i\}$. The value range to be used can be defined by the task parameters or by the input values present in the training set. The 'safest' option is typically to use input value ranges that are defined by the minimal and maximal values found in the training set because the behaviour of many ML models outside of that range tends to be unpredictable. It is also worth mentioning that the 'valid' input ranges may depend on the context C. The current implementation for estimating $Cmax_j(\vec{C}, \{i\})$ and $Cmin_j(\vec{C}, \{i\})$ uses Monte-Carlo simulation with uniformly distributed, randomly generated values within the provided value ranges of inputs $\{i\}$. More efficient methods probably exist for estimating $Cmax_j(\vec{C}, \{i\})$ and $Cmin_j(\vec{C}, \{i\})$ if information about the black-box model or the learned function is available.

The definition of CU is

$$CU_j(\vec{C}, \{i\}) = \frac{out_j(\vec{C}) - Cmin_j(\vec{C}, \{i\})}{Cmax_j(\vec{C}, \{i\}) - Cmin_j(\vec{C}, \{i\})} \tag{2}$$

where $out_j(\vec{C})$ is the value of the output j for the context $\vec{C}$.

The calculations of CI and CU are illustrated in Fig. 2 for the non-linear function in Fig. 1c. The values are $absmin = 0$, $absmax = 1$, $Cmin_1(\vec{C}, \{1\}) = 0.02$, $Cmax_1(\vec{C}, \{1\}) = 0.52$, $Cmin_1(\vec{C}, \{2\}) = 0.158$, $Cmax_1(\vec{C}, \{2\}) = 0.658$, $out_1(\vec{C}) = 0.178$, when inputs and outputs are numbered from one upwards. This gives $CI_1(\vec{C}, \{1\}) = 0.5$ and $_1(\vec{C}, \{2\}) = 0.5$, which signifies that both inputs are exactly as important for the output value. For the utilities, $CU_1(\vec{C}, \{1\}) = 0, 316...$ and $CU_1(\vec{C}, \{2\}) = 0.04$, so even though the y value is higher than the x value, the utility of the x value is higher than the utility of the y value for the result z.

It is worth pointing out that an additive feature attribution method such as LIME would presumably correspond to the partial derivative, which would give

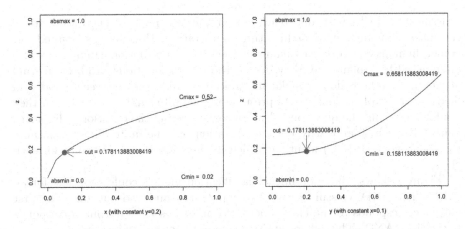

Fig. 2. Illustration of calculations of CI and CU for simple non-linear model.

importances of 0.8 and 0.2[4]. Importances of 0.8 and 0.2 are radically different from $CI = 0.5$ and illustrates to what extent CIU differs from additive feature attribution methods in the case of non-linear models. A locally linear model will provide an estimate of how much small changes in an input value affect the output value but they will not take into account what happens when modifying the input value even slightly more. Finally, additive feature attribution methods do not provide any *utility* concept. Such methods might produce an explanation such as *'z has a bad value (0.18 of one), mainly because of input x (importance 0.8), whereas input y has much less importance (0.2)'.*

Based on CIU values, the explanation could be of the kind *'z has a bad value (0.18 of one), where input x and input y are both quite important (0.5). The x value of 0.1 is relatively bad (CU = 0.32), while the y value is extremely bad (CU = 0.04). As a conclusion, the main reason for the bad output value is that the y value is bad'.* This kind of verbal explanations are relatively straightforward to produce programmatically by dividing the maximal CI interval $[0, 1]$ into labeled intervals with labels such as 'insignificant', 'not important', 'some importance', etc. The same can be done for the the maximal CU interval $[0, 1]$. Different intervals and vocabularies can and should be used depending on the application area and on the actual semantics and meaning for the different inputs and outputs of the black box. Examples of such programmatically generated explanations can be found in [7–9] and [3]. R and Python implementations of CIU[5] also produce graphical plots as explanations, such as the one in Fig. 6 for the Iris classification task described in Sect. 3.2.

In most existing XAI literature, the focus seems to be on answering questions such as 'why is this a cat?' or 'why is this a good choice?' but rarely answering questions such as 'why is this not a tomato?' or 'why is this a bad choice?'.

---

[4] Partial derivative for x is $0.25/\sqrt{x}$ and for y it is y.

[5] https://github.com/KaryFramling/ciu, https://github.com/TimKam/py-ciu.

A Matlab implementation also exists at https://github.com/shulemsi/CIU.

Classification tasks with one black-box output per possible class seem to be the most commonly used architecture in literature. However, as pointed out earlier, humans do not only explain why they choose one option. Humans are also often asked to explain why they do not choose other options. Additive feature attribution methods do not make any conceptual difference between 'good' and 'bad', so the explanations would presumably be quite similar no matter if they are for answering the question 'why?' or for answering the question 'why not?'. With CIU, 'why?' and 'why not?' explanations can be quite different because the utility concept (CU) identifies which features are favorable or not for each class.

Figure 3 shows what non-linear classification models could look like for an 'AND'/'not AND' classifier, with two inputs x, y and two outputs. The first output corresponds to the class 'not AND' and the second output corresponds to the class 'AND'. The red dot in Fig. 3 shows the context to be studied, i.e. $\vec{C} = (x, y) = (0.5, 0.1)$. It is easy to see from Fig. 3 that modifying x will not affect the result z much and the CI of x is indeed only 0.07 for both classes, whereas the CU of x is 0.50 for both classes, which is expected. However, modifying y will modify the result z much more, which is also reflected by a CI of y of 0.50 for both classes. The CU of y is 0.93 for the class 'not AND' and 0.07 for the class 'AND', which is also expected.

A simple explanation to the question 'Why is this "not AND"?' based on CIU would be something like 'It is a "not AND" mainly because y is important (CI = 0.5) and has an excellent value (CU = 0.93). x is not important (CI = 0.07) but has an average value (CU = 0.5)'.

An explanation to the question 'Why is this NOT "AND"?' based on CIU would be something like 'It is NOT "AND" mainly because y is important (CI = 0.5) and has an very bad value (CU = 0.07). x is not important (CI = 0.07) but has an average value (CU = 0.5)'.

This simple classification example is mainly intended to illustrate how CIU is used for classification tasks. However, the semantics of the 'not AND', 'AND', not 'AND' and not 'not AND' might not be the easiest ones to follow. Furthermore, it might be more interesting to study the joint behaviour of x and y. But since there are only two inputs in this case, the CI of both would be one because modifying both simultaneously would produce all possible z-values in the range $[0, 1]$. It is indeed useful to study the behaviour of the black-box also by getting CIU for all inputs at a time. However, for XAI purposes it might be more useful to calculate CIU for more than one input, as shown in the next Section.

3.2   CIU of More Than One Inputs

The definition of CI and CU is not restricted to one input. They can be calculated (or at least estimated) for any combination of inputs, as well as for all inputs simultaneously. This is useful for XAI purposes because it makes it possible to provide explanations at any level of abstraction. In a car selection case, for instance, the concept 'Performances' could be used to group together basic input features such as 'Maximum power', 'Weight', 'Top speed' and 'Acceleration' as

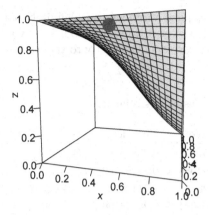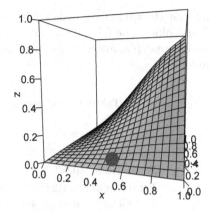

Fig. 3. Classification model learned by neural network, first output is 'not AND', second is 'AND'. (Color figure online)

in [7]. Any number of such *intermediate concepts* can be specified and used for explanation purposes depending on who the explanation is intended for or what level of detail is needed. There could even be different *explanation vocabularies* that target different audiences, such as a domain expert versus a domain novice[6].

CIU for more than one input will here be studied using the simple and well-known Iris data set. The Iris set contains 150 Iris flowers, where there is 50 samples of the three different Iris species Setosa, Versicolor and Virginica. Four values are indicated for each flower: Sepal length, Sepal width, Petal length and Petal width, all measured in centimeters.

The neural network classifier used is an INKA (Interpolating, Normalising and Kernel Allocating) network [8]. INKA is a Radial Basis Function (RBF) network that is used here mainly because it tends to converge towards the average output value when extrapolating towards infinity, which can be an advantage for CIU calculations. However, since CIU is completely model-agnostic, it does not really matter what is 'inside' the black-box being studied. INKA also has excellent training results with the Iris data set.

For studying CIU, we will use a flower $Iris_{test}$ that is not included in the Iris data set but that is quite a typical Virginica, so we have $\vec{C} = (7, 3.2, 6, 1.8)$ as input values. The trained INKA network gives us $out(\vec{C} = (0.022, 0.117, 0.861)$ for the three outputs (classes), so it is clearly a Virginica.

Figure 4 shows how the three outputs change as a function of each input. Table 1 shows the corresponding CI and CU values. It is clear that the flower C is very far from being a Setosa and modifying any single input will not change that classification. Figure 4 shows that the Petal length is the most important feature

---

[6] It is uncertain whether additive feature attribution methods could allow for intermediate concepts. Partial derivatives are usually calculated only for one variable. However, the author does not know if partial derivatives (and gradients) could also be calculated for arbitrary combinations of variables.

and that the value 6 cm makes this flower a typical Virginica (but definitely not a Versicolor). The CI and CU values in Table 1 express the same, so it is easy to provide an explanation that is clear and that corresponds exactly to the learned model[7].

Table 1. CIU values for Iris classes versus input.

Input feature	Setosa	Versicolor	Virginica	
Sepal length	0.0425279	0.2085747	0.2384596	CI
Sepal width	0.03972771	0.17254086	0.21204752	
Petal length	0.3124243	0.7169677	0.7113022	
Petal width	0.04344366	0.24595074	0.28744096	
Sepal length	0.1171743	0.3690032	0.6596097	CU
Sepal width	0.0640272	0.0644939	0.9365688	
Petal length	0.0456506224	0.0006167944	0.9995161501	
Petal width	0.01707707	0.26574443	0.77682899	

Table 2. CIU values for combined concepts.

Input feature	Setosa	Versicolor	Virginica	
Sepal size and shape	0.07172334	0.30947848	0.36959064	CI
Petal size and shape	0.3916285	0.9102021	0.9205347	
All input features	0.8240611	1.1038175	1.1122128	
Sepal size and shape	0.1415141	0.4294574	0.6130286	CU
Petal size and shape	0.04523376	0.15602016	0.82909669	
All input features	0.02717686	0.24984699	0.73618267	

Table 2 shows CI and CU for the intermediate concepts 'Sepal size and shape' (inputs one and two) and 'Petal size and shape' (inputs three and four), as well as CI and CU when calculated for all inputs. The CI values in Table 2 clearly show that 'Petal size and shape' is the most important concept for the flower studied. CI is about the same (0.91 and 0.92) for both Versicolor and Virginica but the CU values in Table 2 say that the Petal values are clearly favorable for Virginica but not favorable for Versicolor (and even less for Setosa). Figure 5 shows the probability of Virginica and Versicolor as a joint function of 'Sepal size and shape' and 'Petal size and shape'.

---

[7] See [3] for examples of verbal explanations. In that paper, a deep neural network and a CIU implementation in Matlab was used. The calculations, visualisations etc. in **this** paper have been implemented in "R".

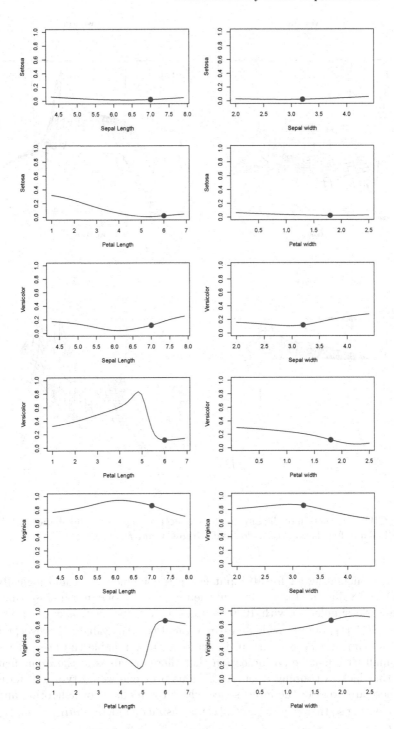

Fig. 4. CIU as a function of the four inputs for all classes.

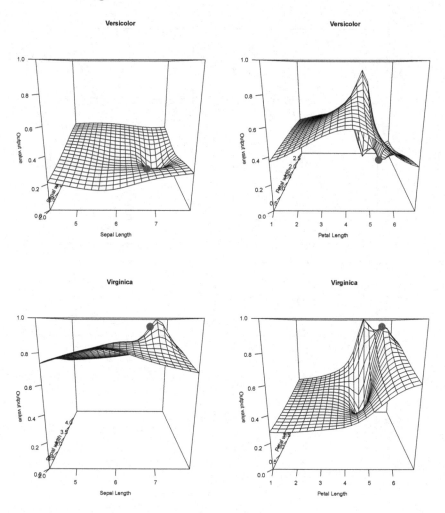

Fig. 5. CIU as a function of the intermediate concepts 'Sepal size and shape' and 'Petal size and shape' for classes Versicolor and Virginica and $Iris_{test}$.

When calculating CI for all input features combined, it should logically be one. The CI values in Table 2 are 'sufficiently' close to one in the sense that the Monte-Carlo simulation with 1000 samples for estimating $Cmax_j(\vec{C}, \{i\})$ and $Cmin_j(\vec{C}(C, \{i\})$ only provide an estimation of the true values. However, CI for all inputs can also be used as an indicator of how reliable the learned model is. A small CI might be an indication that there are areas in the input feature space that lack in training data. A CI value over one would typically indicate that there are areas of the input space where the model is overshooting and/or undershooting so that $Cmax_j(\vec{C}(C, \{i\}) > absmax_j$ and/or $Cmin_j(\vec{C}(C, \{i\}) < absmin_j$.

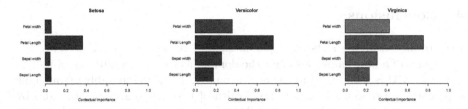

Fig. 6. Bar plot visualisation of CIU for Iris classes. Bar length corresponds to CI value. CU values below 0.5 give red colour, otherwise green. The further away from 0.5 CU is, the darker the colour. (Color figure online)

On the other hand, CU for all input features combined should give a result that is similar to the different output values. In this case, $out(\vec{C} = (0.022, 0.117, 0.861)$, which is well in line with $CU_{all} = (0.027, 0.250, 0.736)$.

Despite the solid theoretical foundations of CIU and the consistent results presented here, there are also some challenges and topics for future research. For instance, it will take more testing and experience to learn when it might be better to use somehow normalised CI values rather than the absolute values. For instance, when dealing with saliency maps as in [22] the CI values of individual pixels will be very small so then it is only CI of each pixel relative to the other pixels that counts.

Another challenge is if the input space is not sufficiently well covered by the training set. Then the estimation of $Cmax(C, \{i\}, j)$ and $Cmin(C, \{i\}, j)$ might go into areas of the input space where the black-box model can be completely erroneous. Many neural networks have a tendency to go into extreme oscillations when extrapolating even slightly. However, such conditions can at least be detected using CI for all input features.

Future topics of research include detecting challenges with stability, reliability, robustness and lack of 'self-insight' about how certain the results of the black box are. The current CIU-based explanation features address these challenges only partially but might open new possibilities. Finally, as proposed in [8], CIU plots such as those in Fig. 4 could also be used by human experts for correcting erroneous models by augmenting the training set with *pseudo-examples* that would correct obvious errors in the trained model.

As CIU is applied to an increasing number of data sets and applications, it is expected that more insight will be gained into properties of the method that still tend to be intuitive. For instance, does a CU value of 0.9 for an input value indeed signify that the value is 'as good' as a CU value of 0.9 for an output, or for an intermediate concept? Intuition says that it should be so but it remains a topic for further research.

4   Conclusions

Despite all research efforts on explainability of AI systems since decades, the emergence of a new name (XAI) for the domain as recently as 2016 is an indication that XAI is still quite immature. Current XAI research notably on outcome explanation also seems to ignore the wealth of knowledge accumulated also by closely related domains for decades. This paper proposes extending the traditional MCDM concepts of importance and utility from the linear models towards the non-linear models produced by ML techniques. That extension is called Contextual Importance and Utility (CIU).

This paper provides the mathematical definition of CIU and shows how CIU is used in practice for XAI. An experiment with the Iris data set validates the approach for real-world data. The Iris data has mainly been chosen for simplicity of presentation and understanding the basics of CIU. Work is ongoing for more complex data and use cases in order to show how CIU can be used for explaining diagnostics in healthcare and machine failures, AI-performed credit assessments, control actions taken by autonomous vehicles, ...

Theoretical and practical examples were provided for showing why methods based on local linearity are not universally applicable for XAI. CIU provides the kind of universal base for XAI that is needed in the future. However, more experimental work is still needed for understanding all the possibilities, challenges and limitations of CIU.

References

1. Abowd, G.D., Dey, A.K., Brown, P.J., Davies, N., Smith, M., Steggles, P.: Towards a better understanding of context and context-awareness. In: Gellersen, H.-W. (ed.) HUC 1999. LNCS, vol. 1707, pp. 304–307. Springer, Heidelberg (1999). https://doi.org/10.1007/3-540-48157-5_29. http://dl.acm.org/citation.cfm?id=647985.743843
2. Andrews, R., Diederich, J., Tickle, A.B.: Survey and critique of techniques for extracting rules from trained artificial neural networks. Know.-Based Syst. 8(6), 373–389 (1995). https://doi.org/10.1016/0950-7051(96)81920-4
3. Anjomshoae, S., Främling, K., Najjar, A.: Explanations of black-box model predictions by contextual importance and utility. In: Calvaresi, D., Najjar, A., Schumacher, M., Främling, K. (eds.) EXTRAAMAS 2019. LNCS (LNAI), vol. 11763, pp. 95–109. Springer, Cham (2019). https://doi.org/10.1007/978-3-030-30391-4_6
4. Anjomshoae, S., Najjar, A., Calvaresi, D., Främling, K.: Explainable agents and robots: results from a systematic literature review. In: AAMAS 2019: Proceedings of the 18th International Conference on Autonomous Agents and MultiAgent Systems, pp. 1078–1088. Proceedings, International Foundation for Autonomous Agents and MultiAgent Systems (2019). http://www.ifaamas.org/Proceedings/aamas2019/pdfs/p1078.pdf
5. Diederich, J.: Explanation and artificial neural networks. Int. J. Man-Mach. Stud. 37(3), 335–355 (1992). https://doi.org/10.1016/0020-7373(92)90058-S. http://www.sciencedirect.com/science/article/pii/002073739290058S
6. Du, M., Liu, N., Hu, X.: Techniques for interpretable machine learning. Commun. ACM 63(1), 68–77 (2020). https://doi.org/10.1145/3359786

7. Främling, K.: Explaining results of neural networks by contextual importance and utility. In: Proceedings of the AISB 1996 Conference, Brighton, UK, 1–2 April 1996. http://www.cs.hut.fi/u/framling/Publications/FramlingAisb96.pdf

8. Främling, K.: Learning and explaining preferences with neural networks for multiple criteria decision making. Theses, INSA de Lyon, March 1996. https://tel.archives-ouvertes.fr/tel-00825854

9. Främling, K., Graillot, D.: Extracting explanations from neural networks. In: ICANN 1995 Conference, Paris, France, October 1995. https://hal-emse.ccsd.cnrs.fr/emse-00857790

10. Främling, K., Graillot, D., Bucha, J.: Waste placement decision support system. In: HELECO 1993, Athènes, Greece, vol. 2, pp. 16–29, April 1993. https://hal-emse.ccsd.cnrs.fr/emse-00858062

11. Féraud, R., Clérot, F.: A methodology to explain neural network classification. Neural Netw. **15**(2), 237–246 (2002). https://doi.org/10.1016/S0893-6080(01)00127-7. http://www.sciencedirect.com/science/article/pii/S089360800 1001277

12. Guidotti, R., Monreale, A., Ruggieri, S., Turini, F., Giannotti, F., Pedreschi, D.: A survey of methods for explaining black box models. ACM Comput. Surv. (CSUR) **51**(5), 93 (2018). https://doi.org/10.1145/3236009

13. Gunning, D.: Explainable artificial intelligence (XAI). Technical report, DARPA/120 (2016). https://www.cc.gatech.edu/~alanwags/DLAI2016/(Gunning)IJCAI-16DLAIWS.pdf

14. Keeney, R., Raiffa, H.: Decisions with Multiple Objectives: Preferences and Value Trade-Offs. Cambridge University Press, Cambridge (1976)

15. Kohonen, T.: Self-organized formation of topologically correct feature maps. Biol. Cybern. **43**(1), 59–69 (1982). https://doi.org/10.1007/BF00337288

16. Kubler, S., Robert, J., Derigent, W., Voisin, A., Le Traon, Y.: A state-of-the-art survey & testbed of fuzzy AHP (FAHP) applications. Expert Syst. Appl. **65**, 398–422 (2016). https://doi.org/10.1016/j.eswa.2016.08.064

17. Kubler, S., Voisin, A., Derigent, W., Thomas, A., Rondeau, E., Främling, K.: Group fuzzy AHP approach to embed relevant data on communicating material. Comput. Ind. **65**(4), 675–692 (2014)

18. Levine, P., Pomerol, J.C.: Systèmes interactifs d'aide à la décision et systèmes experts. Hermès, Paris (1990)

19. Lundberg, S.M., Lee, S.I.: A unified approach to interpreting model predictions. In: Guyon, I., et al. (eds.) Advances in Neural Information Processing Systems 30, pp. 4765–4774. Curran Associates, Inc. (2017). http://papers.nips.cc/paper/7062-a-unified-approach-to-interpreting-model-predictions.pdf

20. Miller, T.: Explanation in artificial intelligence: insights from the social sciences. Artif. Intell. **267**, 1–38 (2019). https://arxiv.org/abs/1706.07269

21. Perera, C., Zaslavsky, A.B., Christen, P., Georgakopoulos, D.: Context aware computing for the internet of things: a survey. CoRR abs/1305.0982 (2013). http://arxiv.org/abs/1305.0982

22. Ribeiro, M.T., Singh, S., Guestrin, C.: Why should i trust you?: Explaining the predictions of any classifier (2016)

23. Rogers, M.G., Bruen, M., Maystre, L.Y.: The electre methodology. In: Rogers, M.G., Bruen, M., Maystre, L.Y. (eds.) ELECTRE and Decision Support, pp. 45–85. Springer, Boston (2000). https://doi.org/10.1007/978-1-4757-5057-7_3

24. Roy, B.: Méthodologie multicritère d'aide à la décision. Economica, Paris (1985)

25. Rumelhart, D.E., McClelland, J.L., PDP Research Group, C. (eds.): Parallel Distributed Processing: Explorations in the Microstructure of Cognition, Vol. 1: Foundations. MIT Press, Cambridge (1986)

26. Saaty, T.L.: Decision Making for Leaders: The Analytic Hierarchy Process for Decisions in a Complex World. RWS Publications, Pittsburgh (1999)

27. Shortliffe, E.H., Davis, R., Axline, S.G., Buchanan, B.G., Green, C., Cohen, S.N.: Computer-based consultations in clinical therapeutics: explanation and rule acquisition capabilities of the MYCIN system. Comput. Biomed. Res. **8**(4), 303–320 (1975). https://doi.org/10.1016/0010-4809(75)90009-9

28. Simon, H.: Administrative behavior: a study of decision-making processes in administrative organization. Free Press (1976). https://books.google.se/books?id=IRdPAAAAMAAJ

29. Simon, H.A.: A behavioral model of rational choice. Q. J. Econ. **69**(1), 99–118 (1955). https://doi.org/10.2307/1884852

30. Thrun, S.: Extracting rules from artificial neural networks with distributed representations. In: Tesauro, G., Touretzky, D.S., Leen, T.K. (eds.) Advances in Neural Information Processing Systems 7, pp. 505–512. MIT Press, Cambridge (1995). http://papers.nips.cc/paper/924-extracting-rules-from-artificial-neural-networks-with-distributed-representations.pdf

31. Towell, G.G., Shavlik, J.W.: Extracting refined rules from knowledge-based neural networks. Mach. Learn. **13**(1), 71–101 (1993). https://doi.org/10.1007/BF00993103

32. Vincke, P.: Multicriteria Decision-Aid. J. Wiley, New York (1992)

33. Westberg, M., Zelvelder, A., Najjar, A.: A historical perspective on cognitive science and its influence on XAI research. In: Calvaresi, D., Najjar, A., Schumacher, M., Främling, K. (eds.) EXTRAAMAS 2019. LNCS (LNAI), vol. 11763, pp. 205–219. Springer, Cham (2019). https://doi.org/10.1007/978-3-030-30391-4_12

Towards the Role of Theory of Mind in Explanation

Maayan Shvo[1,2(✉)], Toryn Q. Klassen[1,2], and Sheila A. McIlraith[1,2]

[1] Department of Computer Science, University of Toronto, Toronto, Canada
{maayanshvo,toryn,sheila}@cs.toronto.edu
[2] Vector Institute, Toronto, Canada

Abstract. Theory of Mind is commonly defined as the ability to attribute mental states (e.g., beliefs, goals) to oneself, and to others. A large body of previous work—from the social sciences to artificial intelligence—has observed that Theory of Mind capabilities are central to providing an explanation to another agent or when explaining that agent's behaviour. In this paper, we build and expand upon previous work by providing an account of explanation in terms of the beliefs of agents and the mechanism by which agents revise their beliefs given possible explanations. We further identify a set of desiderata for explanations that utilize Theory of Mind. These desiderata inform our belief-based account of explanation.

1 Introduction

Following Premack and Woodru [38], an agent exercises *Theory of Mind* if it imputes mental states to itself and others. Here we explore the role of Theory of Mind in explanation. Consider the following narrative by way of illustration.

Mary, Bob and Tom are housemates sharing a house. While Tom was away on a business trip, Mary and Bob noticed a hole in the roof of their house and called a handyman to fix it. Before the handyman could come, however, it rained during the night and the floor got wet. Bob, who sleeps in a windowless room, did not notice the rain. Tom, who just got back from his trip that day, noticed the rain but did not know about the hole in the roof. Mary saw Tom return to the house at night and so knew that Tom knew that it had rained. In the morning, when trying to explain the wet floor to Bob, Mary tells him that it had rained during the night and when explaining to Tom she tells him that she and Bob had discovered a hole in the roof (adding that the handyman will arrive the next day).

Clearly, Mary tailored her explanations to each of her housemates, believing the information she was providing to them was sufficient to explain the wet floor in their respective mental states. Her ability to do this stems from her Theory of Mind - her ability to attribute mental states (e.g., beliefs) to herself and to others. In humans, the use of Theory of Mind in explanation has been

D. Calvaresi et al. (Eds.): EXTRAAMAS 2020, LNAI 12175, pp. 75–93, 2020.
https://doi.org/10.1007/978-3-030-51924-7_5

demonstrated empirically by Slugoski et al. [44] via a set of experiments where human participants gave different explanations to different explainees (i.e., the recipient of an explanation), based on the beliefs of the explainers about the beliefs of the explainees[1]. Of course Mary's explanations are only as good as her ability to model the mental states of her housemates and how they will alter their mental states in light of her explanation. Mary's beliefs about Bob and Tom's beliefs, or her belief about how each of them revises their beliefs, may well be wrong, in which case her explanations to them may fail to explain why the floor is wet.

Explanation has been studied in a diversity of disciplines. Miller [30] provides an extensive survey of explanation in artificial intelligence that includes a selection of historical works in philosophy (e.g., Hempel and Oppenheim [21]; Peirce [34]; Harman [19]), arguing for the important role of philosophy and the social sciences in future work on explanation. Within AI, early work on explanation included a variety of logic-based and probabilistic approaches to abductive inference or so-called *inference to the best explanation* including the early works of Pople [37], Charniak and McDermott [10], Poole [35], and Levesque [26]. In the mid 1980s, explanation was popularized in the context of expert systems where explanations were often generated by backward chaining over a set of symbolic inference steps (e.g., [20,43]). Following that time, explanation was a common element in a diversity of applications of symbolic AI reasoning (e.g., [3,28,45]). The recent resurgence of interest in explanation is largely in the guise of so-called *Explainable AI* (XAI), which is motivated by the need to provide human-interpretable explanations for decision making in black-box classification and decision-making systems based on machine and deep learning (e.g., Samek et al. [41]; Gunning et al. [16]).

Numerous researchers have acknowledged the importance of Theory of Mind in explanation. In the 80s and 90s, formal accounts of explanation such as those proposed by Gärdenfors [12] and Chajewska and Halpern [7] observed that an explanation for one agent may not serve as an explanation for another, and the explainer must therefore tailor an explanation to an explainee given the latter's beliefs. Within the space of user modelling and dialogue, and also set in the 80s and 90s, Weiner's [49] BLAH system and Cawsey's [6] EDGE system both tailor explanations to the presumed user model. More recently, researchers have leveraged belief-desire-intention (BDI) architectures as a natural framework for explanations reflecting Theory of Mind. Such software architectures can enable an explainer to explicitly represent its own beliefs, desires, and intentions, as well as those of an explainee, and to relate explanations to its own beliefs and goals or those of the explainee (e.g., Harbers et al. [18]; Kaptein et al. [24]). Most recently, Westberg et al. [50] has posited that incorporating various points of view on Theory of Mind from the cognitive sciences will facilitate the creation of agents better suited to communicate and explain themselves to the humans with whom they are interacting. Additionally, Miller [30] has surveyed this body of

---

[1] We henceforth use *explainer* and *explainee* in reference to the provider and recipient of the explanation, and *explanandum* in reference to the thing to be explained.

work and has also emphasized the importance of the explainer's ability to tailor an explanation to the explainee, using its understanding of the latter's mind. Finally, within the subfield of XAI known as XAI Planning (XAIP) Chakraborti et al. [8] have implemented XAIP in human-agent teaming settings, such as search & rescue, where a robot equipped with Theory of Mind capabilities could explain its actions to its human teammate by taking into account the latter's mental state.

In this paper we build on the shoulders of previous scholarly work to explore the role of Theory of Mind in explanation with a view to addressing the diverse needs of explanation in AI, and XAI in particular. To this end, in Sect. 2 we identify a set of desiderata for explanations that utilize Theory of Mind. These desiderata inform a set of design choices for a belief-based account of explanation which we present in Sect. 3. Of course not all explanations are created equal, and in Sect. 4 we discuss the criteria by which the quality of an explanation can be evaluated. In Sect. 5 we demonstrate how, in the absence of an explicit prompt to be explained, our account allows the explainer to simulate the explainee's mental state and identify discrepancies that warrant explanation. Explanations are limited by the coverage and accuracy of the explainer's beliefs as well as its reasoning capacity. In Sect. 6, we show how our account allows for the modelling of the ignorance and misconceptions of an explainer pertaining to the mental state of an explainee and how these may affect the quality of explanation. We conclude with a discussion of related work and possible computational realizations of our general account.

2   Desiderata for Theory of Mind in Explanation

We begin our investigation by reflecting on the key components that support an agent in imputing mental states to itself and others, reasoning about how the provision of new information is assimilated into an agent's existing set of beliefs, and the circumstances underwhich such information constitutes an explanation for the explainee. To this end, we identify a set of desiderata that inform our account of explanation in the sections to follow.

multi-agent: the account must be conceived in a multi-agent setting to support representation of the beliefs of one or more explainer and explainee.

agent-type agnostic: the account must support a myriad of different agent types whose beliefs may be internally represented, inspectable, and revisable in diverse ways. For example, the agent's beliefs may be stored in a human brain or in, for instance, the parameters of a neural network or formulae in a knowledge base.

belief based: the account must model the possibly false or simply incomplete beliefs of explainers and explainees.

reason about the beliefs of others: the account must allow an explainer to reason about the explainee's beliefs when providing the latter with an explanation since, due to their possibly differing beliefs, an explanation for the explainer may not be an explanation for the explainee.

support belief revision: the account must enable the explainer to consider how an explanation is assimilated by the explainee, and in particular how the latter revises their beliefs given potential explanations which may be inconsistent with their current beliefs.

explanations can refer to beliefs: the account must allow for explanations that themselves refer to beliefs. To illustrate why this is useful, consider that the explainer might explain their having not told the explainee the location of a party by saying that the explainer believed that the explainee knew the location.

While previous work has addressed some of these desiderata, in this paper we propose a belief-based account of explanation in terms of epistemic states of agents that satisfies all of the aforementioned desiderata by employing a number of crucial building blocks relating to these desiderata.

3   A Belief-Based Account of Explanation

We appeal to logics of belief to provide a belief-based account of explanation in the context of Theory of Mind.

Many logical accounts of explanation assume the existence of a knowledge base—a logical axiomatization of the domain in terms of a set of formulae (e.g., [5]). With such a knowledge base in hand, a popular logic-based characterization of explanation is in terms of abduction as follows.

Definition 1 (Abductive Explanation (after [36])). *Given a logical theory, T, and an explanandum O, E explains O given a theory T if $T \cup E \models O$ and $T \cup E$ is consistent.*

Here we make no such commitment to the representation of beliefs in terms of a set of logical formulae. Rather, in order to capture the diversity of human and machine explainers and explainees, our account finds its origins in works that attributed agents with mental states in the form of epistemic states (with seminal work by Gärdenfors [12] and later notable work by Levesque [26]; Boutilier and Becher [4]; Chajewska and Halpern [7]; and Halpern and Pearl [17]).

3.1   Mental States as Epistemic States

We employ the notion of an epistemic state, e, or in the case of multiple agents, a collection of epistemic states, $\vec{e}$, to capture the beliefs of agents. These are used to provide the semantics for the language below.

We will suppose that we have a finite set of agents, $A = \{1, 2, \ldots, n\}$, and a set of propositional symbols P. We define a language

$$\varphi ::= p \mid \neg \varphi \mid (\varphi \wedge \varphi) \mid B_i \varphi \mid [\varphi]_i \varphi \qquad (1)$$

where $p \in P$ and $i \in A$. We introduce $\perp$ as an abbreviation for $(p \wedge \neg p)$ for an arbitrary $p \in P$.

The intended meaning of $B_i\varphi$ is that agent i believes φ, and the intended meaning of $[\alpha]_i\varphi$ is that after agent i revises their beliefs by α, φ is true.

We assume that our epistemic states are such that we can say that a formula φ is true at e when φ is believed. To be clear, although we use formulas to describe what is believed, an epistemic state is not in general *defined* as a set of formulas, nor required to be represented internally as one. For a conventional example, e might be a set of possible worlds with accessibility relations and so on. However, we also allow for epistemic states to take very different forms. For example, one might want to model limited reasoning capabilities in some manner to avoid the so-called problem of logical omniscience [48], in which agents unrealistically believe all the deductive consequences of their beliefs. We might also wish for our epistemic states to be realized in terms of a computer program, such as a neural network, or via a human brain.

Furthermore, we assume we have a *revision operator* $*$ so that $e * \alpha$ is another epistemic state, the result of revising by α. We will use $*$ in defining the semantics for the $[\alpha]_i$ operator. Much as we have not committed to a particular structure for epistemic states, we will not commit to a particular revision operator. A large body of work has studied belief change in agents where belief revision typically concerns belief change in a static environment, possibly in the presence of incorrect and partial beliefs. Amongst the most popular guidelines for belief revision are the AGM postulates [1], and the DP postulates [11] (for iterated revision). We will not require that our $*$ satisfies these properties except where noted. Similarly to the situation with our epistemic states, we might want our revision operator to be realized in terms of a computer program or human reasoning.

While epistemic states assign a truth value to any formula in our language – the language given by the grammar in (1) – that value indicates whether the formula is believed by the agent in question, not whether it's actually true. From an objective point of view, the formulas whose truth values we can determine are from the subset of the language consisting of formulas which are concerned only with beliefs. We define this subset of formulas below:

Definition 2 (Agent Formula). *An agent formula is one in which no atomic symbol appears outside the scope of a belief operator, i.e., a formula ϕ of the form*

$$\phi ::= B_i\varphi \mid \neg\phi \mid (\phi \wedge \phi) \mid [\varphi]_i\phi \tag{2}$$

where φ is any (possibly non-agent) formula.

We assign truth values to agent formulas with a collection of epistemic states $\vec{e} = e_1, \ldots, e_n$ (corresponding to the different agents) according to the satisfaction relation $\models$ below.

- $\vec{e} \models B_i\varphi$ iff φ is true at e_i
- $\vec{e} \models \neg\phi$ iff $\vec{e} \not\models \phi$
- $\vec{e} \models (\phi \wedge \psi)$ iff $\vec{e} \models \phi$ and $\vec{e} \models \psi$
- $\vec{e} \models [\alpha]_i\phi$ iff $\langle e_1, \ldots, (e_i * \alpha), \ldots, e_n \rangle \models \phi$

Note that the semantics of the $[\alpha]_i$ operator is defined using the revision operator.

Give this abstract framework for talking about beliefs, we can define explanations. The lack of commitment to the form of the epistemic state and revision operator is important because it affords us the ability to model a diversity of agents. In so doing, for the definitions of explanation that follow, the explainer will have beliefs about the other agents' beliefs and about their revision operators, and the effectiveness of the explainer's explanations for any particular agent will rely on the fidelity of those beliefs.

3.2   Characterizing Explanations

Definition 3 (Explanation). *Given epistemic states $\vec{e}$, we say that α explains β for agent i if $\vec{e} \models [\alpha]_i(B_i\beta \wedge \neg B_i\bot)$.*

Notation: For notational convenience, we define $Expl(i, \alpha, \beta)$ as an abbreviation for $[\alpha]_i(B_i\beta \wedge \neg B_i\bot)$.

That is, α explains β if revising by α makes agent i believe β while still having consistent beliefs.[2] Note that (with respect to revising by non-modal formulas) if revision of agent i's epistemic state satisfies the AGM postulates, then the result of revision will be inconsistent only if either the agent initially had inconsistent beliefs, or if α itself is inconsistent.

Intuitively, our definition of explanation allows for more explanations than the traditional account in Definition 1. For one thing, we allow explanations to refer to modal operators. Even without that, though, an important difference is that our definition is in terms of belief revision and so allows for an explanation that isn't consistent with the agent's initial beliefs. Our account builds upon prior accounts of explanation defined relative to belief revision such as Boutilier and Becher [4] and Nepomuceno-Fernández et al. [32].

To make the comparison more explicit, consider defining an epistemic state e_i as a propositional theory T, as in the following theorem.

Theorem 1. *Suppose that e_i is defined as being a propositional theory T, and that the formulas e_i makes true are defined to be the logical consequences of T (note that these are restricted to the non-modal subset of our language). Suppose furthermore that the revision operator $*$ on e_i satisfies the AGM postulates (w.r.t. non-modal formulas). Then for non-modal formulas α and β, $\vec{e} \models Expl(i, \alpha, \beta)$ if $T \cup \{\alpha\}$ is consistent and $T \cup \{\alpha\} \models \beta$.*

Proof. Because $T \cup \{\alpha\}$ is consistent, by the AGM "vacuity" postulate, $T * \alpha$ is equal to the expansion of T by α, that is, the closure of $T \cup \{\alpha\}$. Therefore, $T * \alpha \models \beta$.

---

[2] If agent i is not logically omniscient, requiring i to not believe $\bot$ may not prevent i's beliefs from being inconsistent in some subtler way. For example, i might both believe p and believe $\neg p$, even though it does not believe $(p \wedge \neg p)$.

However, we may also get further explanations. In the circumstances described by Theorem 1, if $T \cup \{\beta\}$ is inconsistent, then Definition 1 would say there are no explanations of β the theory T, while there may be formulas that agent with epistemic state T can revise by that would make them believe β.

It is also possible to talk in the language about agents' beliefs about $Expl(i, \alpha, \beta)$, i.e. about whether α explains β for agent i.

Definition 4 (Subjective Explanation). *Given epistemic states $\vec{e}$, we say that α explains β for agent j from agent i's perspective, if $\vec{e} \models B_i Expl(j, \alpha, \beta)$.*

Example 1. We formalize our example from Sect. 1. We assume that Mary, Bob and Tom all believe (and believe that the other agents believe) *rain* $\wedge$ *holeInRoof* $\rightarrow$ *wetFloor*.

$A = \{Mary, Bob, Tom\}$
$\vec{e} \models B_{Mary} wetFloor \wedge B_{Mary} holeInRoof \wedge B_{Mary} rain$
$\vec{e} \models B_{Mary} B_{Bob} \neg wetFloor \wedge B_{Mary} B_{Bob} \neg rain \wedge B_{Mary} B_{Bob} holeInRoof$
$\vec{e} \models B_{Mary} B_{Tom} \neg wetFloor \wedge B_{Mary} B_{Tom} rain \wedge B_{Mary} B_{Tom} \neg holeInRoof$
$\vec{e} \models B_{Mary} Expl(Bob, rain, wetFloor)$
$\vec{e} \models B_{Mary} Expl(Tom, holeInRoof, wetFloor)$

We also assume that the agents are able to draw at least simple inferences (and each knows that the others will) and their belief revision operators behave in a sensible way (and each knows that the others' operators do so).

We define a relation $\approx$ that can be understood intuitively as equating two epistemic states, e_i and e_j. For $e_i \approx e_j$ to hold, the internal structures of the states e_i and e_j need not be the same, but they must support the same beliefs as each other, and must continue to do so after any sequence of revisions. Formally, we say that $e_i \approx e_j$ if

- $\vec{e} \models B_i \varphi$ iff $\vec{e} \models B_j \varphi$
- and for any sequence of formulas $\alpha_1, \ldots, \alpha_k$, we have that $\vec{e} \models [\alpha_1]_i \cdots [\alpha_k]_i B_i \varphi$ iff $\vec{e} \models [\alpha_1]_j \cdots [\alpha_k]_j B_j \varphi$

Theorem 2. *Given epistemic states $\vec{e}$ and explanandum β, if $e_i \approx e_j$ it then follows that for all α, $\vec{e} \models Expl(i, \alpha, \beta)$ iff $\vec{e} \models Expl(j, \alpha, \beta)$.*

Proof. Note that $\vec{e} \models Expl(i, \alpha, \beta)$ iff $\vec{e} \models [\alpha]_i B_i \beta$ and $\vec{e} \models [\alpha]_i \neg B_i \bot$, and similarly for agent j. The result follows from the definition of $\approx$.

That is, when $e_i \approx e_j$, an objective explanation for the former is also an objective explanation for the latter. Therefore, agent i, acting as the explainer, need not employ its Theory of Mind and reason about agent j's beliefs in order to generate explanations for the latter. However, the fact that $e_i \approx e_j$ does not mean that e_i holds accurate beliefs pertaining to how e_j revises its beliefs. Thus, while any α that explains β may be an objective explanation for both agents i and j, agent i need not necessarily *believe* that α is an explanation for j. Nonetheless, $e_i \approx e_j$ is quite strong, as illustrated by the following theorem.

Theorem 3. *Suppose e_j supports positive and negative introspection – i.e., $\vec{e} \models (B_j\varphi \equiv B_jB_j\varphi) \wedge (\neg B_j\varphi \equiv B_j\neg B_j\varphi)$. Then if $e_i \approx e_j$, agent i will have correct beliefs about j's beliefs, i.e., $\vec{e} \models (B_j\varphi \equiv B_iB_j\varphi) \wedge (\neg B_j\varphi \equiv B_i\neg B_j\varphi)$.*

Proof. If agent j believes φ, then we'll have that $\vec{e} \models B_jB_j\varphi$ (by positive introspection) and then $\vec{e} \models B_iB_j\varphi$ (because $i \approx j$). Similarly, if agent j disbelieves φ, then $\vec{e} \models B_j\neg B_j\varphi$ (by negative introspection) and so $\vec{e} \models B_i\neg B_j\varphi$.

In some cases, an explanation need not cause the explanandum to be entailed by the epistemic state, but rather cause it to be *possible* in the epistemic state. This type of explanation is similar to Boutilier and Becher's *might explanation*.

Definition 5 (Inconsistency-resolving Explanation). *Given epistemic states $\vec{e}$, we say that α explains the possibility of β for agent i if $\vec{e} \models [\alpha]_i\neg B_i\neg\beta$.*

This is a weaker form of explanation but important in various settings such as when an agent is attempting to find an explanation that will allow the behavior of another agent or in consistency-based diagnosis, where the agent is attempting to identify the abnormal components in a system that allow for the observed behavior of the system.

Theorem 4. *Given epistemic states $\vec{e}$ and explanandum β, then for all α, if $\vec{e} \models Expl(i, \alpha, \beta)$ it then follows that α is an inconsistency-resolving explanation for β for agent i, assuming that $\vec{e} \models [\alpha]_i\big((B_i\beta \wedge B_i\neg\beta) \rightarrow B_i\bot\big)$, i.e., that the agent can perform enough reasoning to notice the inconsistency in believing both β and $\neg\beta$.*

This follows straightforwardly from Definitions 3 and 5.

Explanations Involving Agent Beliefs

Importantly, an explainer can utilize its Theory of Mind to generate explanations pertaining to the mental states of other agents, such as their beliefs or goals.

Example 2. Let us reconsider our example where this time, after Mary explains $wetFloor$ to Bob, he asks her why Tom doesn't know $wetFloor$. That is, the explanandum β is $\neg B_{Tom}wetFloor$. A possible explanation is then $B_{Tom}\neg holeInRoof$, assuming Bob believes $B_{Tom}rain$.

3.3   Explanations Involving Multiple Agents

An interesting setting that is straightforwardly captured by our framework is one in which an explainer (or explainers) is attempting to explain multiple (possibly disparate) explanandums to multiple explainees.

Definition 6. *Given epistemic states $\vec{e}$ and explanandums β_j, β_k, $\dots\beta_l$, we say that α explains β_j, β_k, $\dots\beta_l$ from agent i's perspective for agents j, k, $\dots l$, respectively, if $\vec{e} \models B_iExpl(j, \alpha, \beta_j) \wedge B_iExpl(k, \alpha, \beta_k) \wedge \dots \wedge B_iExpl(l, \alpha, \beta_l)$.*

Consider a collaborative card game (e.g., Hanabi [2]) where a certain player is attempting to make different players (each with a unique epistemic state) understand different things with a single piece of information about another player's cards, publicly announced to all players. The explaining player should therefore find an α that explains different explanandums for the different players, given the explaining player's beliefs about the other players' beliefs.

Example 3. In a simpler setting such as our running example, if Mary is trying to explain *wetFloor* to Bob and Tom at the same time, the explanation α could be $rain \wedge holeInRoof$, where the explanandum for both Bob and Tom is *wetFloor*.

Privacy. Our framework can also capture a notion of privacy. For example, the explainer (agent i) may want to generate an explanation α that explains the explanandum β to some agents (agent j) but not to others (agent k):

$$\vec{e} \models B_i Expl(j, \alpha, \beta) \wedge B_i \neg (Expl(k, \alpha, \beta))$$

Example 4. If Mary, for some reason, wants only Bob to entail *wetFloor*, the explanation α could be $rain$ in which case Bob will entail *wetFloor* but Tom will not. One can imagine parent #1 wanting to explain something to parent #2 such that their child does not understand.

Multiple Explainers and 'Nested' Explanations. In some cases, there may be multiple explainers trying to explain an explanandum β to an explainee. For example, agents i and j may want to find an α that explains β for agent k:

$$\vec{e} \models B_i Expl(k, \alpha, \beta) \wedge B_j Expl(k, \alpha, \beta)$$

Definition 6 can be straightforwardly extended to capture this setting. Finally, agent i may want to find an α that he believes that agent j believes is an explanation for agent k:

$$\vec{e} \models B_i B_j Expl(k, \alpha, \beta)$$

4 "Best" Explanations for Whom?

An explanadum can typically be explained by a variety of different explanations, but it is often the case that an agent *prefers* one explanation to another relative to some set of criteria. Indeed, there is a large body of previous work (e.g., [4, 26, 27]) that outlines criteria for defining preference orderings over explanations. In the context of a multiple agents, we have seen that what constitutes an explanation for one agent, may not constitute an explanation for another. This observation extends to the notion of preferred explanations—what's good in the eyes of the explainer may not be good for the explainee, or for all explainees. We explore the issue of preferred explanations briefly here in the context of Theory of Mind.

For each agent in the set of agents A, we define a binary preference relation $\prec$ over explanations such that $\prec_i$ is the preference relation for agent i.

Definition 7 (Preferred Explanation). *Given epistemic states $\vec{e}$ and explanandum β, if α and α' both explain β for agent i and $\alpha \preceq_i \alpha'$, we say that α is at least as preferred as α' for agent i. $\alpha \prec_i \alpha'$ denotes that α is strictly preferred to α' for agent i.*

Similarly, we use $\alpha \preceq_{i,j} \alpha'$ to denote that agent i believes that α is at least as preferred as α' for agent j.

Definition 8 (Optimal Explanation). *Given epistemic states $\vec{e}$ and explanandum β, α is an optimal explanation for β wrt $\prec_i$ iff α explains β for agent i and there does not exist an explanation α' for β for agent i such that $\alpha' \prec_i \alpha$.*

Hilton [22] posits that an explanation given by one agent to another is a form of conversation and should therefore adhere to Grice's [15] maxims which he proposed as part of a model for effective cooperative conversation. In what follows, we discuss a number of criteria for preferred explanations and relate them to Grice's maxims.

Truthfulness: Grice's first maxim is the **quality** maxim, according to which one must not provide information (e.g., to the explainee) that she believes to be false.

Definition 9 (Subjectively Truthful Explanation). *Given epistemic states $\vec{e}$ and an explanandum β, α is a subjectively truthful explanation for agent j from the perspective of agent i iff $\vec{e} \models B_i Expl(j, \alpha, \beta) \wedge B_i \alpha$.*

Example 5. In our example, Mary may tell Bob that Tom poured water all over the floor, thereby explaining *wetFloor*. However, since Mary does not believe that Tom did such a thing, it would not be a subjectively truthful explanation explanation from Mary's perspective.

Minimality: According to Grice's **quantity** and **relation** maxims, one must provide information that is relevant, sufficiently informative, and no more informative than needed. In a Theory of Mind context, the sufficiency of information is defined relative to the explainer's beliefs about the explainee's epistemic state and the explainer should therefore find the *minimal* explanation relative to the explainee's epistemic state. A large body of work concerned with explanation has discussed a minimality property which an explanation should satisfy. For example, Levesque [26] defines a syntactic simplicity relation between explanations wherein an explanation is *simpler* than another if it contains fewer propositional letters. Minimal explanations in the semantic sense may be defined relative to a set of possible explanations as those that are implied by all other explanations.

Plausibility: Grice's **quality** maxim also dictates that one should not provide information that is not supported by evidence. When applying this maxim to the beliefs of the explainee, an explainer may wish to consider how likely an explanation is from the point of view of the former. For instance, in our example it is more likely that Bob will accept *rain* as an explanation over the highly unlikely explanation according to which Alan Turing came to visit in the middle of the night and accidentally poured water all over the floor. Therefore, the likelihood of an explanation is an important preference criterion when explaining to ourselves and to others. In the quantitative case, Pearl [33] defines a *most probable explanation* while in a qualitative setting the *plausibility* of explanations may be defined where the most plausible explanations are those that require the 'least' change in the explainee's epistemic state (e.g., [4,39]), which could be defined in various ways, including the degree of held beliefs (e.g., [23]).

5   Explainer-Explainee Discrepancies

To this point our account of explanation has assumed the existence of an explanandum, β, that is in need of explanation for a particular agent. However, in the absence of such a prompt, the explainer may use her Theory of Mind to put herself in the explainee's shoes, so to speak, and to identify *discrepancies* between the beliefs of the explainee and those of the explainer, or perhaps in the case of multiple agents, to identify discrepancies between the beliefs of two agents that the explainer can resolve via an explanation. Discrepancies can also arise from inconsistencies between an agent's beliefs and observations in the world. Such discrepancies are common prompts for explanation in the case of diagnosis (e.g., [4,40]).

Definition 10 (Discrepancy). *Given epistemic states $\vec{e}$, β is a discrepancy between e_i and e_j iff $\vec{e} \models B_i\beta \wedge B_j\neg\beta$.*

That is, agent i believes β while agent j believes $\neg\beta$. The beliefs of agents pertaining to discrepancies can also be represented in our framework.

Definition 11 (Subjective Discrepancy). *Given epistemic states $\vec{e}$, β is a discrepancy between e_i and e_j from the perspective of agent i iff $\vec{e} \models B_i(B_i\beta \wedge B_j\neg\beta)$.*

Example 6. In our example, while Mary believes *wetFloor*, she believes that Bob believes that the floor is not wet (i.e., $\vec{e} \models B_{Mary}(B_{Mary}wetFloor \wedge B_{Bob}\neg wetFloor)$). Thus, *wetFloor* is a discrepancy between Bob and Mary's respective epistemic states from Mary's perspective.

Definition 12 (Subjective Discrepancy-resolving Explanation). *Given epistemic states $\vec{e}$ and a discrepancy β between e_i and e_j from the perspective of agent i, we say that α is a discrepancy-resolving explanation for agent j for β from agent i's perspective if $\vec{e} \models B_i[\alpha]_j\neg B_j\neg\beta$.*

Example 7. A discrepancy-resolving explanation for *wetFloor* for Bob from Mary's perspective is *rain.*

Note that Definition 12 appeals to the weaker inconsistency-resolving explanation defined in Definition 5. Thus, the explainer need not find an α that it believes will allow the explainee to entail the discrepancy. Rather, α should resolve the discrepancy by explaining its possibility.

We cast agent i as the explainer and agent j as the explainee, and distinguish between two types of subjective discrepancies: (1) where β is a discrepancy between e_i and e_j from the explainer's perspective; and (2) where β is a discrepancy between e_i and e_j from the explainee's perspective. In (1), as discussed, the explainer (e.g., Mary) may provide a discrepancy-resolving explanation for β (e.g., *rain*). However, for (2), in order to provide such as explanation the explainer must *believe* that the explainee believes that there exists a discrepancy between e_i and e_j. If the explainer's beliefs about the explainee's beliefs are incomplete or incorrect, the former may not recognize that such a discrepancy exists.

Explainer as Mediator. Definition 11 can be straightforwardly generalized to capture a setting where agent i believes that there exists a discrepancy between e_j and e_k:

$$\vec{e} \models B_i(B_j\beta \wedge B_k\neg\beta)$$

Agent i may also believe that agent j believes that α is an explanation for β for agent k, while also believing that α is not in fact a valid explanation for agent k due to the discrepancy between the epistemic states of agents j and k:

$$\vec{e} \models B_i(B_j Expl(k, \alpha, \beta) \wedge \neg Expl(k, \alpha, \beta))$$

Using Definition 6, agent i may explain the discrepancy to agents j and k. Note that the notion of discrepancy discussed here can easily be extended to encode other, possibly richer notions of discrepancy including the degree to which the epistemic states of two agents are discrepant.

6   The (In)Adequacy of the Explainer's Beliefs

The explainer is limited by the accuracy of its beliefs about the explainee's beliefs and reasoning capabilities. Specifically, the explainer's beliefs about the explainee's beliefs and reasoning capabilities must be accurate 'enough' – *adequate* – for the explainer to generate 'good' explanations wrt the explainee.

Definition 13 (Adequacy). *Given epistemic states $\vec{e}$ and explanandum β, we say that agent i's epistemic state e_i is adequate wrt agent j iff for all α, $\vec{e} \models B_i Expl(j, \alpha, \beta)$ iff $\vec{e} \models Expl(j, \alpha, \beta)$.*

That is, if agent i's epistemic state is adequate wrt agent j and β, then it can generate all explanations (for β) for agent j that are also explanations for agent j in its actual epistemic state, e_j.

Theorem 5. *Given epistemic states $\vec{e}$, explanandum β and $\preceq_{i,j}, \preceq_j$, agent i's perspective of agent j's preference relation and agent j's actual preference relation, respectively, if $\preceq_{i,j} = \preceq_j$ and e_i is adequate wrt agent j and β, then for all α, α is an optimal explanation for agent j from agent i's perspective wrt $\preceq_{i,j}$ iff α is an optimal explanation for agent j wrt $\preceq_j$.*

That is, when e_i is adequate wrt agent j and when agent i's beliefs about agent j's preference relation are correct, the optimal explanation for agent j from the perspective of agent i is also the optimal objective explanation for agent j. The proof follows straightforwardly from Definitions 8 and 13.

6.1   Sources of (In)Adequacy

Since most agents do not have a perfect image of another agent's mental state, an agent's beliefs about another agent may be inadequate for a myriad of reasons, including the inaccuracy of an agent's beliefs about the beliefs of other agents and about the way in which other agents revise their beliefs and perform entailment. In what follows, we focus on a setting where an agent holds inadequate beliefs about another agent's beliefs and illustrate using our running example.

Example 8. Returning to our example, assume that Mary forgot that Bob found the hole with her and so she now *falsely* believes that Bob believes that there is no hole in the roof (i.e., $\vec{e} \models B_{Mary}B_{Bob}\neg holeInRoof$). Mary will therefore believe that $rain \wedge holeInRoof$ is the minimal explanation for Bob (relative to an intuitive measure of minimality). Notice, however, that in her explanation, Mary is conveying more information than is needed for Bob to entail $wetFloor$ (thereby violating Grice's quantity maxim).

Example 9. Now consider that Mary *falsely* believes that Bob believes that it had rained and that there is no hole in the roof (perhaps she confused him with Tom!). Mary will therefore believe that $holeInRoof$ is an explanation for Bob. However, $\vec{e} \not\models Expl(Bob, holeInRoof, wetFloor)$ since Bob does not believe $rain$. This time, Mary has violated the quantity maxim by not providing *enough* information for Bob to entail $wetFloor$.

Example 10. Mary now falsely believes that Bob believes $wetFloor$ (i.e., $\vec{e} \models B_{Mary}B_{Bob}wetFloor$) and so does not provide him with an explanation, believing he does not require one. In this case, while $wetFloor$ is an objective discrepancy between Bob and Mary's epistemic states, it is not a discrepancy from Mary's perspective due to her false beliefs.

Addressing Inadequacy

It is possible to mitigate for the inadequacy of the explainer's beliefs in a variety of ways. For example, it may be beneficial for the explainer to attempt to refine its beliefs about the beliefs of the explainee when explanations are not understood by the explainee. To this end, the explainer could try to gather additional pertinent information by acting in the world (e.g., querying the explainee). Additionally, Sreedharan et al. [47] propose a learning technique which enables an explainer to learn a simple model of an explainee and decide, based on the learned model, what information would constitute a good explanation. Further, Sreedharan et al. [46] show how an explainer may generate explanations that are applicable to a set of possible explainee models which arise as the consequence of explainer uncertainty pertaining to the explainee's model.

Finally, while we emphasized the importance of the explainer modelling the beliefs of the explainee, our general account could in theory support the explainee, perhaps compensating for the explainer's inadequate beliefs, reasoning about the beliefs of the explainer to understand a given explanation that might otherwise be construed as inadequate. For example, consider Chandrasekaran et al.'s [9] discussion of a Theory of AI's Mind where a human attempting to better understand a black-box decision making system can do so by familiarizing themselves with the system's capabilities, peculiarities, and shortcomings.

7   Related Work

As previously discussed, we are not the first to propose an account of explanation in terms of the epistemic state of an agent.Levesque presents a knowledge-level account of abduction based on the epistemic state of an agent [26]. He provides a generic definition of explanation that does not commit to a specific type of agent belief. Then, building on his seminal work on a logic of implicit and explicit belief [25], he shows how such different formal models of belief lead to different forms of abductive inference and resultant explanations. Boutilier and Becher [4] similarly appeal to epistemic states to characterize the beliefs of an agent, employing belief revision to allow for explanations that are inconsistent with the epistemic state of the explainee. Prior to the works of Levesque and Boutilier and Becher, Gärdenfors [12] proposed a model of explanation where explanations are defined relative to the epistemic states of agents. While Gärdenfors's account is probabilistic, the models proposed by Levesque and Boutilier and Becher are qualitative. We share the use of epistemic states with all three works, the appeal to qualitative criteria with Levesque and Boutilier and Becher, and the recognition of the importance of belief revision with Boutilier and Becher. Nevertheless, these works all characterize explanation with respect to a single agent providing no account of the distinct beliefs of the explainee *and* explainer, nor do they capture their Theory of Mind.

Nepomuceno-Fernández et al. [32] propose an account of explanation that also recognizes the importance of a revision operator and the use of epistemic states. However, while their Dynamic Epistemic Logic (DEL) based framework can capture multiple agents, their focus remains on an agent's task of obtaining an abductive explanation for itself, rather than for other agents.

Halpern and Pearl [17] proposed a structural model of explanation selection based on the epistemic state of the explainee. In their work, the explainee's epistemic state comprises a set of situations the explainee considers possible and an explanation is then meant to remove some of these possible situations such that the cause of some explanandum may be uniquely identified. Miller extends Halpern and Pearl's approach to include *contrastive* explanations which are given relative to some counterfactual (e.g, in response to the question ' *Why P rather than Q?*') [29]. Halpern and Pearl, however, do not discuss some of the necessary elements of Theory of Mind in explanation, such as the notions of explainer-explainee discrepancies and the adequacy of the explainer's beliefs.

In the context of XAIP, Sreedharan et al. [47] demonstrate how the model reconciliation paradigm, proposed by Chakraborti et al. [8], can be generalized to address the important case where the explainee's model of the explainer's planning model is not explicitly known or not provided in a declarative form. Our work captures some of the insights in Sreedharan et al.'s work, in addition to incorporating the notions of epistemic states and belief revision, which in turn allows us to draw inspiration from the rich body of previous work in the field where these ideas originated.

The vast body of work on Theory of Mind proposes two accounts of the way in which agents attribute mental states to other agents: Theory-Theory of Mind [13] (where an agent pre-assigns beliefs to other agents) and Simulation Theory of Mind [14] (where an agent simulates other agents' beliefs and the mechanisms by which those beliefs change). Related work in XAI has highlighted the interesting distinctions between the two as well as the implications for explanation [50]. Further, Sarkadi et al. [42] combine the two approaches by allowing an agent to both assign beliefs to another agent and update its beliefs about the beliefs of the other agent's beliefs by employing Simulation Theory of Mind. We similarly combine the two approaches.

We have focused discussion on the subset of work that is most closely related to the contributions of the paper. For a comprehensive survey of research on explanation, the reader is directed to [30].

8   Concluding Remarks

The use of Theory of Mind in explanation holds the promise of producing high-quality explanations that are tailored to the beliefs of the explainee, in the context of the beliefs (and ignorance) of the explainer. In this paper, we identified a set of desiderata for explanation that utilizes Theory of Mind. These desiderata informed our proposed belief-based account of explanation. Key features of this account are the appeal to epistemic states to capture the mental states of *both* the explainer and explainee, and the use of the explainee's belief revision to assimilate explanations. Further, we formalized and discussed the notion of a discrepancy as a property that allows the explainer to anticipate and provide explanations without prompting. We also presented properties relating to the adequacy of the explainer's beliefs with respect to providing an explanation.

This paper has provided a general characterization of explanation without focusing on its computational realization. This was done by design to allow for a diversity of explanation scenarios and agent types, including human, black-box decision maker, or knowledge-based system. Nevertheless in the simplest case if the beliefs of the explainer are represented as formulae (logical or probabilistic) then, as observed by Levesque [26] and Boutilier and Becher [4], our notion of explanation may be realized via an augmentation of existing abductive reasoning systems such as Theorist Poole [35], for example.

Further, in much of this paper we have been relating our Theory of Mind characterization of explanation in the context of English-like statements (e.g., Mary *telling* Bob that it had rained last night). However, if we turn to the broad endeavour of XAI that helped motivate our account, we note that an explanation can take on many different forms other than human-interpretable language (e.g., a set of weights in a neural network, select pixels, a gesture, a heightening of intensity in a region of an image). At its core, an explanation is something that is conveyed by the explainer to the explainee (e.g., by telling, demonstrating, visualizing, etc.) in order to justify the latter's belief in some explanandum. For example, by constructing a heat-map from a medical image, an otherwise black-box decision-making algorithm can highlight for the explainee the pixels that have most strongly supported its classification decision [31], thereby allowing the explainee to assimiliate this explanation into their beliefs and better interpret the system's decision. As has been argued in this paper, the decision-making system, acting as an explainer, should possess the ability to take the epistemic state of the explainee into account, tease apart the salient features required for the explainee to justify its belief in the explanandum, and present those to the explainee as an explanation. Some of these insights pertaining to explanations for black-box solvers are similarly echoed by Sreedharan et al. in the context of their model reconciliation paradigm [47] (Section 2). Our general account is intended to provide building blocks towards this broader XAI objective.

There are several take-aways from this paper that are worth highlighting. Explanations need not be consistent with an agent's beliefs. As such, contrary to most logical treatments of explanation, characterizations of explanation should involve a belief revision component, and not just the expansion of existing beliefs to include an explanation. Further, by providing a belief-based account of explanation that characterizes mental states in terms of epistemic states, and by allowing for epistemic states and revision operators to be realized in a diversity of forms from standard logical accounts, to computer programs, neural networks or human brains, we can capture the mental states of a myriad of different types of agents. Finally, by characterizing explanations in terms of the explainer's beliefs about the explainee's beliefs and revision operator, we can capture the role of Theory of Mind in explanation for a myriad of different types of agents.

Acknoweldgements. The authors gratefully acknowledge funding from the Natural Sciences and Engineering Research Council of Canada (NSERC), the Canadian Institute for Advanced Research (CIFAR), and Microsoft Research.

References

1. Alchourrón, C.E., Gärdenfors, P., Makinson, D.: On the logic of theory change: partial meet contraction and revision functions. J. Symb. Logic **50**(2), 510–530 (1985)
2. Bard, N., et al.: The hanabi challenge: a new frontier for AI research. AIJ **280**, 103216 (2020)
3. Borgida, A., Calvanese, D., Rodriguez-Muro, M.: Explanation in DL-Lite. In: Proceedings of the 21st International Workshop on Description Logics (DL2008). CEUR Workshop Proceedings, vol. 353 (2008)
4. Boutilier, C., Becher, V.: Abduction as belief revision. AIJ **77**(1), 43–94 (1995)
5. Brachman, R.J., Levesque, H.J.: Knowledge Representation and Reasoning. Elsevier, Amsterdam (2004)
6. Cawsey, A.: Generating interactive explanations. In: AAAI, pp. 86–91 (1991)
7. Chajewska, U., Halpern, J.Y.: Defining explanation in probabilistic systems. arXiv preprint arXiv:1302.1526 (2013)
8. Chakraborti, T., Sreedharan, S., Zhang, Y., Kambhampati, S.: Plan explanations as model reconciliation: moving beyond explanation as soliloquy. In: IJCAI, pp. 156–163 (2017)
9. Chandrasekaran, A., Yadav, D., Chattopadhyay, P., Prabhu, V., Parikh, D.: It takes two to tango: towards theory of AI's mind. arXiv preprint arXiv:1704.00717 (2017)
10. Charniak, E., McDermott, D.: Introduction to Artificial Intelligence. Addison Wesley, Boston (1985)
11. Darwiche, A., Pearl, J.: On the logic of iterated belief revision. AIJ **89**(1–2), 1–29 (1997)
12. Gärdenfors, P.: Knowledge in Flux: Modeling the Dynamics of Epistemic States. The MIT Press, Cambridge (1988)
13. Gopnik, A., Glymour, C., Sobel, D.M., Schulz, L.E., Kushnir, T., Danks, D.: A theory of causal learning in children: causal maps and Bayes nets. Psychol. Rev. **111**(1), 3 (2004)
14. Gordon, R.M.: Folk psychology as simulation. Mind Lang. **1**(2), 158–171 (1986)
15. Grice, H.P.: Logic and conversation. In: Speech Acts, pp. 41–58. Brill (1975)
16. Gunning, D., Stefik, M., Choi, J., Miller, T., Stumpf, S., Yang, G.: XAI - explainable artificial intelligence. Sci. Robot. **4**(37) (2019)
17. Halpern, J.Y., Pearl, J.: Causes and explanations: a structural-model approach. Part ii: explanations. Br. J. Philos. Sci. **56**(4), 889–911 (2005)
18. Harbers, M., Van den Bosch, K., Meyer, J.J.: Modeling agents with a theory of mind: theory-theory versus simulation theory. Web Intell. Agent Syst. Int. J. **10**(3), 331–343 (2012)
19. Harman, G.H.: The inference to the best explanation. Philos. Rev. **74**(1), 88–95 (1965)
20. Hayes-Roth, F., Waterman, D.A., Lenat, D.B. (eds.): Building Expert Systems. Teknowledge Series in Knowledge Engineering. Addison-Wesley, Boston (1983)
21. Hempel, C.G., Oppenheim, P.: Studies in the logic of explanation. Philos. Sci. **15**(2), 135–175 (1948)

22. Hilton, D.J.: Conversational processes and causal explanation. Psychol. Bull. **107**(1), 65 (1990)
23. van der Hoek, W., Meyer, J.-J.C.: Graded modalities in epistemic logic. In: Nerode, A., Taitslin, M. (eds.) LFCS 1992. LNCS, vol. 620, pp. 503–514. Springer, Heidelberg (1992). https://doi.org/10.1007/BFb0023902
24. Kaptein, F., Broekens, J., Hindriks, K., Neerincx, M.: Personalised self-explanation by robots: the role of goals versus beliefs in robot-action explanation for children and adults. In: 2017 26th IEEE International Symposium on Robot and Human Interactive Communication (RO-MAN), pp. 676–682. IEEE (2017)
25. Levesque, H.J.: A logic of implicit and explicit belief. In: AAAI, pp. 198–202 (1984)
26. Levesque, H.J.: A knowledge-level account of abduction. In: IJCAI, pp. 1061–1067 (1989)
27. Lipton, P.: Contrastive explanation. Roy. Inst. Philos. Suppl. **27**, 247–266 (1990)
28. McGuinness, D.L., da Silva, P.P.: Explaining answers from the semantic web: the inference web approach. J. Web Semant. **1**(4), 397–413 (2004)
29. Miller, T.: Contrastive explanation: a structural-model approach. arXiv preprint arXiv:1811.03163 (2018)
30. Miller, T.: Explanation in artificial intelligence: insights from the social sciences. AIJ **267**, 1–38 (2019)
31. Montavon, G., Samek, W., Müller, K.R.: Methods for interpreting and understanding deep neural networks. Digit. Signal Proc. **73**, 1–15 (2018)
32. Nepomuceno-Fernández, A., Soler-Toscano, F., Velázquez-Quesada, F.R.: Abductive reasoning in dynamic epistemic logic. In: Magnani, L., Bertolotti, T. (eds.) Springer Handbook of Model-Based Science. SH, pp. 269–293. Springer, Cham (2017). https://doi.org/10.1007/978-3-319-30526-4_13
33. Pearl, J.: Probabilistic Reasoning in Intelligent Systems: Networks of Plausible Inference. Elsevier, Amsterdam (2014)
34. Peirce, C.: Deduction, induction and hypothesis. Pop. Sci. Mon. **13**, 470–482 (1878)
35. Poole, D.: Explanation and prediction: an architecture for default and abductive reasoning. Comput. Intell. **5**(2), 97–110 (1989)
36. Poole, D.: A methodology for using a default and abductive reasoning system. Int. J. Intell. Syst. **5**(5), 521–548 (1990)
37. Pople, H.E.: On the mechanization of abductive logic. In: IJCAI, pp. 147–152 (1973)
38. Premack, D., Woodruff, G.: Does the chimpanzee have a theory of mind? Behav. Brain Sci. **1**(4), 515–526 (1978)
39. Quine, W.V.O., Ullian, J.S.: The Web of Belief. Random House, New York (1978)
40. Reiter, R.: A theory of diagnosis from first principles. AIJ **32**(1), 57–95 (1987)
41. Samek, W., Wiegand, T., Müller, K.R.: Explainable artificial intelligence: understanding, visualizing and interpreting deep learning models. arXiv preprint arXiv:1708.08296 (2017)
42. Sarkadi, Ş., Panisson, A.R., Bordini, R.H., McBurney, P., Parsons, S., Chapman, M.: Modelling deception using theory of mind in multi-agent systems. AI Commun. **32**(4), 287–302 (2019)
43. Shortliffe, E.H., Buchanan, B.G.: Rule-Based Expert Systems: The MYCIN Experiments of the Stanford Heuristic Programming Project. Addison-Wesley, Boston (1985)
44. Slugoski, B.R., Lalljee, M., Lamb, R., Ginsburg, G.P.: Attribution in conversational context: effect of mutual knowledge on explanation-giving. Eur. J. Soc. Psychol. **23**(3), 219–238 (1993)

45. Sohrabi, S., Baier, J.A., McIlraith, S.A.: Preferred explanations: theory and generation via planning. In: AAAI (2011)
46. Sreedharan, S., Chakraborti, T., Kambhampati, S.: Handling model uncertainty and multiplicity in explanations via model reconciliation. In: ICAPS, pp. 518–526 (2018)
47. Sreedharan, S., Hernandez, A.O., Mishra, A.P., Kambhampati, S.: Model-free model reconciliation. In: IJCAI, pp. 587–594 (2019)
48. Stalnaker, R.: The problem of logical omniscience, I. Synthese **89**(3), 425–440 (1991)
49. Weiner, J.: Blah, a system which explains its reasoning. AIJ **15**(1–2), 19–48 (1980)
50. Westberg, M., Zelvelder, A., Najjar, A.: A historical perspective on cognitive science and its influence on XAI research. In: Calvaresi, D., Najjar, A., Schumacher, M., Främling, K. (eds.) EXTRAAMAS 2019. LNCS (LNAI), vol. 11763, pp. 205–219. Springer, Cham (2019). https://doi.org/10.1007/978-3-030-30391-4_12

A Situation Awareness-Based Framework for Design and Evaluation of Explainable AI

Lindsay Sanneman[✉] and Julie A. Shah

Massachusetts Institute of Technology, Cambridge, MA 02139, USA
{lindsays,julie_a_shah}@csail.mit.edu

Abstract. Recent advances in artificial intelligence (AI) have drawn attention to the need for AI systems to be understandable to human users. The explainable AI (XAI) literature aims to enhance human understanding and human-AI team performance by providing users with necessary information about AI system behavior. Simultaneously, the human factors literature has long addressed important considerations that contribute to human performance, including how to determine human informational needs. Drawing from the human factors literature, we propose a three-level framework for the development and evaluation of explanations about AI system behavior. Our proposed levels of XAI are based on the informational needs of human users, which can be determined using the levels of situation awareness (SA) framework from the human factors literature. Based on our levels of XAI framework, we also propose a method for assessing the effectiveness of XAI systems.

Keywords: Explainable AI · Human-AI collaboration · Interpretability

1 Introduction

With the recent focus on explainable artificial intelligence (XAI) in the AI literature, defining which information XAI systems should communicate and how to measure their effectiveness is increasingly important. Gunning and Aha [21] define XAI as "AI systems that can explain their rationale to a human user, characterize their strengths and weaknesses, and convey an understanding of how they will behave in the future." We adopt this definition of XAI and define explanations as the information necessary to support human inference of the above details about AI systems, including information about their inputs, models, and outputs. The motivation for development of XAI techniques is often stated as the need for transparency within increasingly complex AI systems [20,31] and the need to engender user trust in increasingly opaque systems [6,20,31]. Both increasing AI system transparency and accounting for human trust in these systems contribute to improved human-AI team performance; thus, supporting

© Springer Nature Switzerland AG 2020
D. Calvaresi et al. (Eds.): EXTRAAMAS 2020, LNAI 12175, pp. 94–110, 2020.
https://doi.org/10.1007/978-3-030-51924-7_6

human-AI team performance is one of the primary aims of XAI. Some literature argues that there is a performance-explainability trade off in that more explainable AI systems sacrifice algorithmic performance in some way [21,31]. However, if a lack of system explainability inhibits overall team performance, benefits provided by improved algorithmic performance might be lost. Therefore, we view optimization of human-AI team performance, enabled by explanations about the system's behavior, as the primary goal of XAI.

There exists a rich literature in human factors that explores scenarios in which humans interact with automated systems, as well as the various factors that influence human performance during task execution. The concept of situation awareness (SA), which has been studied within the field of human factors and in the context of human-automation teams [9,13], defines the informational needs for humans operating in any scenario [13]. XAI systems, as systems that provide information about AI behavior, can contribute to the subset of a human user's SA that is related to AI behavior. Human-AI team performance can be improved through information provided by XAI systems that support SA; however, overall SA, in addition to the subset of SA supported by XAI, are necessary for but not solely sufficient to support team performance [13].

The human factors literature has additionally introduced methods and metrics for assessment of a human's SA [37]. Just as SA supports but is not equivalent to performance, high-quality explanations provided by XAI systems support but are not equivalent to SA. Assessing XAI systems based on methods related to SA can contribute to an understanding of whether the provided explanations achieve the ultimate goal of enhancing human-AI team performance. Measuring SA as an intermediate aim of XAI can provide clarity as to the potential confounds that exist in performance assessment. The XAI literature currently lacks a comprehensive set of suitable methods and metrics for assessing explanation quality. While it may not be possible to explicitly and independently define an explanation's quality, explanations are only "good" insofar as they contribute to intermediate goals, such as SA, and the ultimate goal of improved performance. In this paper, we discuss how a human factors-based SA assessment method can be useful for evaluating XAI systems.

The remainder of the paper is organized as follows: in Sect. 2, we discuss the relevant situation awareness literature as it relates to XAI. In Sect. 3, we propose a framework for design and evaluation of XAI systems in light of findings within the human factors community. In this framework, we propose levels of XAI that define which information about AI algorithms and processes should be supported by XAI systems; these levels map closely to those of SA as proposed by Endsley [13] (discussed in Sect. 2). Our framework applies to XAI generally, including explainable machine learning (ML), explainable agents/robots, and multi-agent/multi-human teams. There exist other frameworks in the XAI literature that are primarily agent-centric in that they categorize systems based on agent attributes, such as stages of explanations [3,36], types of errors [42,43], or agent internal cognitive states [23]. The framework we propose is complementary to these in that ours is human-centric and focuses on human informational needs. Other frameworks propose human-centric approaches [38,40], but these are largely human role-based, and our framework applies more generally and is role-agnostic. One other framework focuses on the theory of mind (ToM) of the robot and human [26]. The authors of that work discuss the need to define which information a robot should communicate, which our framework addresses.

In Sect. 4 we provide a non-comprehensive set of examples of how a set of existing XAI techniques fit into our framework in order to clarify how our framework might be applied. Section 5 discusses how to determine human informational needs at each of the three levels proposed in our framework. In Sect. 6, we discuss how methods used to evaluate existing XAI techniques map to assessments of SA from the human factors literature, and we propose one key SA-related method for the assessment of XAI systems. Section 7 provides a motivating example, which we use to clarify our discussion of the levels of XAI and the suggested SA-related assessment method. Finally, Sect. 8 suggests future directions for XAI research, and Sect. 9 concludes the paper.

2   Situation Awareness in the Human Factors Literature

The concept of situation awareness has been widely studied in the human factors literature, especially in the context of human-automation teams operating in complex environments [13]. The concept originally received attention in the study of aviation systems, particularly with the rise of cockpit automation and the need to support pilot awareness of aircraft behavior [46]. However, its applicability extends to any complex scenario in which humans have informational needs for achieving the tasks they are performing. Accordingly, it has additionally been studied in the context of many other domains including air traffic control, emergency management, health care, and space, among others [15].

Different definitions of situation awareness and corresponding frameworks have been proposed in the literature [5,13,44]. We adopt the three-level definition from Endsley [13]: "the perception of elements in the environment within a volume of time and space (level 1), the comprehension of their meaning (level 2), and the projection of their status in the near future (level 3)." This definition is the most widely cited and applied of the existing definitions [47]. It has direct value for designers of complex systems due to its relative simplicity and its division into three levels, which allow for easy definition of SA requirements for different scenarios and for effective measurement of a person's SA [41]. The SA construct has been empirically validated in various contexts [16,47], and connections between SA and other task-related measures such as performance and error frequency have been demonstrated in the literature [15]. SA has also been used to define a framework for agent transparency [9], which focuses primarily on information that interfaces should display about agent behavior. We apply a similar approach to that of Chen et al. [9], but we focus on XAI specifically and define our framework based on AI system behavior more generally.

Endsley [13] further defines an assessment technique for measuring a person's SA: the Situation Awareness Global Assessment Technique (SAGAT). Since SA

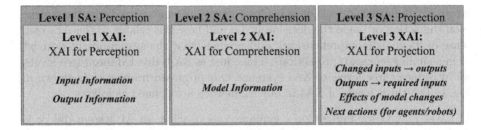

Fig. 1. Levels of XAI framework

represents the "diagnosis of the continuous state of a dynamic world", there exists a "ground truth" against which a person's SA can be measured [37]. The SAGAT test aims to measure the discrepancies between a human user's SA, or their knowledge of the state of the world, and this "ground truth" state of the world. We detail SAGAT and its applicability to XAI further in Sect. 6.4.

SA is relevant to the XAI community since it contributes to defining human informational needs, and XAI aims to meet them. In particular, XAI provides human users with the subset of their SA that relates to AI behavior. It is not equally valuable to provide just any information to human users via XAI, but only information that is relevant to them given their respective tasks and contexts. In fact, providing excessive or irrelevant information can be detrimental to human-AI team performance by causing confusion or unnecessarily increasing workload [37]. Therefore, it is important for XAI practitioners to consider which information is relevant to users and then to measure whether users have received and understood that information. Our proposed framework provides a guideline for determining which information XAI systems should communicate about AI system behavior, and our suggested use of the SAGAT method provides a way to measure how effectively this information is delivered.

3 Situation Awareness-Based Levels of XAI Framework

As AI systems become increasingly ubiquitous and humans interact with more complex AI systems, XAI support of adequate SA can benefit human-AI team performance. According to the definition of SA provided by Endsley [13], an individual working towards a goal requires all three levels of SA to support their decision-making processes, which can in turn improve performance of goal-oriented tasks. It is important to note the distinction between general SA (related to the situation as a whole) and SA related specifically to AI behavior: the latter is a subset of the former and is the focus of this paper. SA, in the most general sense, comprises user awareness of the environment, other situational factors, and other human teammates in addition to information about the AI's behavior.

The informational needs defined by SA can serve to dictate the information XAI systems should provide about AI behavior. For many scenarios in which XAI systems are useful and relevant, humans in the loop must know what the

AI system did or what decision it made (perception), understand why the system took the action or made the decision it did and how this relates to the AI's own sense of its goals (comprehension), and predict what the system might do next or in a similar scenario (projection). Thus, just as SA is divided into three levels, we introduce three levels of XAI systems. Our proposed framework is shown in Fig. 1. The three levels of XAI in our framework are defined as follows:

1. Level 1: XAI for Perception - explanations of what an AI system did or is doing and the decisions made by the system
2. Level 2: XAI for Comprehension - explanations of why an AI system acted in a certain way or made a particular decision and what this means in terms of the system's goals
3. Level 3: XAI for Projection - explanations of what an AI system will do next, what it would do in a similar scenario, or what would be required for an alternate outcome

Our framework generalizes to cover both explainable ML and explainable agents/robots. It can also be applied for both "black box" AI systems that are fundamentally uninterpretable to human users and high-complexity systems that may or may not be inherently interpretable/"white box" but that human users cannot grasp due to their complexity. Note that our focus is on the informational content of explanations rather than explanation modality (natural language, communicative actions, etc.), which is a separate but important consideration. The following sections further detail each of the levels of XAI in our framework.

3.1   Level 1: XAI for Perception

Level 1 XAI includes explanations about what an AI system did or is doing as well as the decisions made by the system. It covers information about both AI system inputs and outputs and aims to answer "what" questions as they are defined by Miller [34]. In the context of explainable ML, level 1 information might include inputted data or outputted classification, regression, or cluster information, for example. For explainable agents and robots, level 1 information could include inputted state information, a particular decision or action taken by the system, an outputted plan/schedule (sequence of decisions/actions) from a planning agent, a particular resource allocation, and others. While level 1 XAI might seem straightforward in many applications since it is simply information about a system's inputs or outputs, providing this information might be challenging when explaining a complex model that makes decisions over many different input factors and produces numerous outputs, only a subset of which are relevant to the user. The primary technical challenge for level 1 XAI is determining which specific information is relevant to users of complex systems.

3.2   Level 2: XAI for Comprehension

Level 2 XAI includes explanations about why an AI system acted in a particular way or made a certain decision and what this means in terms of the system's goals. The primary aim of level 2 XAI is to provide information about causality in AI systems [22] as it relates to a specific instance or decision made by the system. Level 2 XAI answers "why" questions (as defined by Miller [34]) and typically provides information about a system's model. In the context of explainable ML, level 2 information might relate to sensitivities to inputs, semantic feature information, simplified feature or model representations, cluster information, or abstracted representations of model details. For explainable agents and robots, level 2 information could include details about system goals, objectives, constraints, pre-/post-conditions, rules, policies, costs, or rewards.

In identifying level 2 XAI informational requirements, it is important to identify which causal information is most relevant to a user attempting to understand the system. Miller [34] states that explanations are fundamentally contrastive and that when humans seek explanations, they often have a particular "foil" (defined by the author as a counterfactual case) in mind. Reasoning about the most likely foils users have in mind when interacting with a system can help determine which causal information to provide. Note that by our definition, level 2 XAI provides answers to "why" questions for specific instances or in relation to specific foils and might only involve some limited information about a system's model. Therefore, level 2 explanations alone do not necessarily enable users to make all necessary predictions; as such, information beyond level 2 XAI may be required for projection (level 3). We detail this distinction further in Sect. 3.3.

3.3 Level 3: XAI for Projection

Level 3 XAI includes explanations about what an AI system will nominally do next or would do in a different circumstance or context. Level 3 XAI provides answers to "what if"/"how" questions as they are defined by Miller [34]. It aims to explain what would happen if certain system inputs or parameters changed or what the system would do if human users took particular actions. Level 3 XAI incorporates counterfactual or other simulated information in order to provide explanations about a system's future behavior in the presence of changes to either inputs or system parameters, which might occur due to human actions.

While level 2 XAI provides information about why a decision was made based on model-related factors, level 3 XAI provides insight as to what degree of change to inputs, model parameters, or constraints would yield a different outcome. Further, while level 2 explanations provide information about a decision made in a specific instance, level 3 information helps users to reason about what will happen in different contexts and what exactly would need to change about the given circumstance in order to alter the system's output. In the context of explainable ML, level 3 information could include information about what effect a changed input would have on the output, which changes in the input would be required to achieve a given output, or what would change about the output if the model changed in some way. Similarly, for explainable agents and robots, level 3 information would provide information about changed inputs and outputs, changed models (such as the addition/removal of constraints or differently weighted objectives), or the nominal continued course of action.

We define two types of prediction that can be supported with level 3 explanations. First, backward reasoning helps a user start with a desired outcome and work backwards to determine what would be necessary to achieve that outcome. For example, consider a situation in which a user interacting with a neural network hopes to understand what type of input would be required for a particular classification. In such a case, successful level 3 XAI would help the user understand the ranges of inputs to the neural network that would result in the desired classification. Second, forward simulation helps a user understand what will happen given any changes in the inputs or model that occur. An example of forward simulation in a robot planning scenario might involve a user who hopes to add a constraint to the planning problem based on their own preferences about the robot's actions. Successful level 3 XAI would help such a user to understand the effect the new constraint would have on the outputted plan.

4   Example Approaches Achieving the Levels of XAI from the XAI Literature

The following sections discuss how a limited, non-comprehensive set of example XAI techniques fit into our framework.

4.1   Example Approaches Achieving Level 1 XAI

Level 1 XAI relates to AI system inputs and outputs. Whether a system has provided adequate level 1 explanations depends on whether a human user has sufficient information about these things. Many explainable ML techniques provide level 1 XAI implicitly through their inputs and outputted results. For example, Kim et al. [30] and Ribeiro et al. [39] provide users with the system's outputted classification (level 1) in addition to explanations about the reasons behind the outputs (level 2). In these cases, the entire system output is captured by a single or small number of classifications, and the human user can easily understand the entire set of outputs. In other cases, such as with some clustering techniques, the entire set of outputs (i.e. features that represent a cluster) contains extraneous information in addition to information that is directly relevant to the human user's understanding of the outputted clusters. Kim et al. [29] designate a set of clusters in a feature space, find the most quintessential prototype of each, and, for each prototype, down-select to a subset of features to present to the user.

In the explainable agents and robots literature, explainable Belief-Desire-Intention (BDI) agents explain their actions (intentions) based on their goals (desires) and their observations (beliefs) [7,23,24]. Belief-based explanations are level 1 explanations, since they provide information about inputs that agents use in their decision-making processes. Harbers et al. [24] implement a BDI agent that produces explanations of both its observations (inputs) and actions (outputs), which both constitute level 1. Beyond BDI agents, Floyd and Aha [19] implement an agent that explains when it changes its behavior (output) in order to increase transparency. Lomas et al. [32] propose a framework for explainable robots which includes explanations about which actions a robot took (outputs) and what information it had about the world at the time (inputs). Finally, AI planning systems that provide users with a partial or entire plan [6,8,45] implicitly provide level 1 XAI through their outputted plans.

4.2   Example Approaches Achieving Level 2 XAI

Level 2 XAI is fundamentally related to supporting user comprehension of a system's behavior through the understanding of its model, including reasoning about objectives, constraints, features, or other model aspects. Successful level 2 XAI adequately explains the relevant aspects of why a system behaved the way it did. Much of the current XAI literature falls into the category of level 2 XAI.

Various XAI techniques for ML models aim to explain which features, parts of the model, or other feature abstractions have the greatest bearing on a system's decision making. Ribeiro et al. [39] introduce the LIME technique, which learns an approximation of a complex classifier over a human-understandable set of features in order to explain which of these features were most important in generating a classification for a given input. Kim et al. [30] propose a technique that allows users to define abstract concepts (which may be distinct from the original set of features used for classification) and learn about the significance of a concept's contribution to a given classification. Other approaches, such as saliency maps, highlight important aspects of inputs [1].

In the explainable agent and robot literature, explainable BDI agents that explain their actions based on their goals (desires) [7,23,24] contribute to level 2 XAI. The agent proposed by Floyd and Aha [19] provides explanations about why it changes its behavior (level 2) based on user feedback. Hayes and Shah [25] propose a policy explanation technique that can answer questions about why an agent did not take a given action by reasoning about predicates that constitute its state. The technique proposed by Dannenhauer et al. [10] explains agent behavior based on the agent's rationale and goal. Dragan et al. [12] discuss the distinction between legible and predictable robot motions. By their definition, legible robot motions support human inference of the robot's goal and would therefore be considered level 2 XAI. Work related to explainable planning has proposed explanations according to human-understandable aspects of AI models, such as predicates or system objectives. Sreedharan et al. [45] introduce a technique that explains model predicates to a user in order to fill perceived gaps in the user's understanding of the model based on foils they suggest. Finally, Borgo et al. [6] propose a set of techniques that explain system decisions by incorporating user-produced foils into planning and demonstrating that the modified plans are sub-optimal or infeasible.

4.3   Example Approaches Achieving Level 3 XAI

Fundamentally, level 3 XAI is about supporting user prediction of AI behavior through enabling understanding of what a system would do if its inputs changed or if the model were to change in any way. Successful level 3 XAI helps users to predict what a system will do next or what it would do in a different context and answers "what if" questions about system behavior.

In the explainable ML literature, some approaches provide users with predictions of contexts in which an AI system will fail [4] or predictions of which changes in inputs would be required to amend misclassified examples [33]. Others that provide level 2 information could be extended to support level 3. For example, the SP-LIME algorithm [39] chooses a subset of local model approximations produced by the LIME algorithm (discussed in Sect. 4.2) in order to provide a more "global" explanation of the interpretable features that impact classification in different scenarios. Ideally, if these examples are chosen according to human informational needs for prediction, the human user would be able to predict the outcome of a new example. However, with very complex systems, adequately providing information in this manner might be intractable, and other ways of providing level 3 explanations might be necessary. Other methods, such as the one described by Kim et al. [30] (discussed in Sect. 4.2), could be augmented to provide combinations of relevant "concepts" or could be complemented with other contextual information in order to support prediction more fully.

In the explainable agent and robot literature, Amir and Amir [2] provide explanations of global agent behavior by selecting "important" states in the state space and providing traces of subsequent states and actions (determined by the agent's policy). These state-action pairs support human user prediction of future agent behavior. The policy explanation technique proposed by Hayes and Shah [25] can support both backward reasoning by answering questions about when (from which states) it will take certain actions and forward reasoning by answering questions about what the agent will do given different states. Some explainable agents provide more direct prediction-related information by explaining their next action(s), such as explainable BDI agents that provide sequence-based explanations [7, 23] and others that provide their plans [19]. Note that providing users with plans that agents are executing online is level 3 XAI, while providing users with plans outputted by a planning agent is level 1 XAI. Finally, in the discussion of legibility versus predictability [12], predictability is related to human inference of a robot's actions based on a known goal, so we categorize predictable robot motions as level 3 XAI. As with explainable ML, information provided by level 2 XAI techniques can be combined and amended in order to produce level 3 XAI to support prediction of future robot or agent actions.

5   Determining Human Informational Needs

In designing XAI systems and measuring their effectiveness, defining human informational requirements according to the above framework is of value. This information depends upon the overall goal of the human-AI team and the individual roles of the autonomous agent(s) and human(s) within that team. Endsley [16] describes a process called goal-directed task analysis (GDTA) for determining SA requirements for a given context, both for individuals and for those operating in larger teams. In this process, the major goals of each human teammate's task are identified along with their associated sub-goals. Then, required decisions associated with each sub-goal are enumerated. Finally, SA requirements at all three levels are defined for each of these decisions (i.e. the information required to support human decision-making). The GDTA process is detailed at length in [16] and can be applied by XAI practitioners to define which information human users need about AI system behavior in order to achieve their respective goals. The definition of informational requirements with GDTA also informs the assessment of XAI systems, which will be discussed further in Sect. 6.

In many scenarios, users do not require information about all of a system's behavior but only the aspects that are relevant to their specific tasks. Often, a human cannot possess information about the entirety of a complex system's behavior; therefore, defining the specific information that users require (through GDTA or a similar process) in order to support human-AI team goals is critical. This is especially relevant when considering teams of humans, who each have their own roles and corresponding goals. Informational requirements in these cases are user-specific, and consequently, XAI systems might need to be able to adapt to users playing different roles in the team, providing each with the specific information relevant to his or her own task and potentially at different levels of abstraction. An extended discussion of the definition and support of team SA is provided by Endsley and Jones [18].

One important aspect of team SA is the interdependence of individual team members. Johnson et al. [28] detail an "interdependence analysis" process for assessing individual team members' needs given different possible team configurations. This process results in the definition of observability (level 1) and predictability (level 3) requirements for each teammate in the context of their interdependence on each other. Since it defines information-sharing requirements in the team, it can also be useful for defining information requirements for XAI systems given different possible team configurations. We recommend using a modified version of this process that includes the definition of "comprehensibility" requirements (level 2) in order to define which role an XAI system should play in the context of a team. Once informational needs are identified, appropriate XAI techniques can be chosen to provide necessary information.

6   Evaluating Explanation Quality: A Method for Situation Awareness-Based XAI Assessment

In the following sections, we discuss a selection of existing human-based metrics for XAI from the literature. We then suggest the use of the SAGAT method from human factors for the assessment of the effectiveness of XAI systems.

6.1   Existing Level 1 XAI Methods and Metrics

Since providing a user with a system's outputs is inherent to many existing XAI techniques, most literature does not aim to assess whether the human properly understood these outputs upon receiving them. Kim et al. [29] do this in part by assessing whether users are able to appropriately assign outputted prototypes to clusters based on the subset of features presented. As the XAI community moves towards explaining higher-complexity systems with multiple inputs and outputs, it will be increasingly important to measure whether users understand the correct inputs/outputs in the contexts of their intended goals. Section 6.4 outlines one approach that could be applied for such assessments.

6.2   Existing Level 2 XAI Methods and Metrics

Metrics for level 2 explanations should indicate whether users understand the meaning of a given system's actions or decisions and what these actions or decisions imply in terms of progress towards team goals. Some of the literature has proposed survey-like questions for assessing explanation quality as it relates to user understanding. For example, Hoffman et al. [27] propose a "goodness" scale that includes a question about whether the user understands how the given algorithm works. They also detail a set of questions related to the perceived understandability of a system from the Madesen-Gregor scale for trust. Doshi-Velez and Kim [11] suggest human experiments requiring users to choose which of two possible system outputs is of higher quality, which necessitates understanding of the system. While these questions and metrics represent a step towards measuring whether adequate level 2 explanations have been provided to users, a more comprehensive way of defining comprehension-related informational needs and assessing whether they have been met through XAI is needed. As mentioned previously, we outline one possible approach to this in Sect. 6.4.

6.3   Existing Level 3 XAI Methods and Metrics

Metrics for level 3 explanations should indicate whether human users can predict what a system will do next or what it would do given an alternate context or input. To this end, Doshi-Velez and Kim [11] suggest running human experiments in which human users perform forward simulation, prediction, and counterfactual simulation of system behavior given different inputs for XAI assessment. Hoffman et al. [27] discuss the use of prediction tasks to measure explanation quality and further detail a Likert-scale survey for trust measurement that includes a question about predictability of system actions. Questions and experiments such as these can be used to assess the quality of level 3 explanations provided by XAI systems. Beyond these assessment techniques, a comprehensive way of assessing whether level 3 informational needs are met is discussed in Sect. 6.4.

6.4   The SAGAT Test and Its Applicability for Assessment of XAI

In assessing the quality of XAI techniques, it is important to determine whether human users receive the information they need in order to perform their roles. Miller et al. [35], in particular, stress the need for human evaluations of XAI systems. As discussed in Sects. 6.1–6.3, existing XAI literature includes some human-based evaluation metrics; however, to our knowledge, none have comprehensively assessed whether human informational needs are met by XAI systems.

Endsley [14] proposes the situation awareness-based global assessment technique (SAGAT) for SA measurement. SAGAT is a widely-used objective measure of SA that has been empirically shown to have a high degree of sensitivity, reliability, and validity in terms of predicting human performance [16]. It has been applied for measurement of SA in a variety of domains [16], has been extensively used to measure team SA [17], and has been shown to outperform other SA measures in terms of sensitivity, intrusivity, and bias, among other factors [17]. In the SAGAT test, simulations of representative tasks are frozen at randomly selected times, and users are asked questions about their current perceptions of the situation [17]. The questions asked are based directly on the human informational needs defined according to a process such as GDTA (discussed in Sect. 5) and therefore directly measure whether humans have the information required. More complete discussions of SAGAT are provided in [13,14,16], and implementation recommendations for the test are discussed by Endsley [16].

Since the SAGAT test measures whether human informational needs are met, we propose that a SAGAT-like test can be applied to assess XAI systems. Situational information needs related to AI behavior should be thoroughly defined, and in the assessment of an XAI system, user knowledge of this information can be evaluated through a SAGAT-like test focused on information related to specifically AI behavior. Such a test could more adequately determine whether XAI systems achieve the purpose of communicating relevant information about system behavior to human users than current assessment techniques allow.

7 Example Application of the Framework

Here we introduce a simple planetary rover example to demonstrate the application of our framework and the use of the SAGAT test for assessment. The example touches on aspects of explainable ML, explainable agents/robots, and XAI for human teams. In our example, a rover on another planet is executing a learned exploration policy. Its objective is to search for water, which is more likely to be found in areas with certain types of rocks. There are costs associated with navigation time and science task duration, and there are differing rewards associated with performing science tasks on the different types of rocks, some of which are more valuable. The rover has a camera onboard and an ML-based image processing system that allows it to classify rocks. There are constraints associated with the rover power requirements, and some terrain is not traversable. Human users include one engineer who monitors rover health and one scientist who monitors science activities. The scientist and engineer can also request new rover actions during the mission. Below are examples of information constituting levels 1–3 XAI for the engineer and scientist and the types of information they represent (in parentheses).

– **Level 1 XAI:**
  Engineer - terrain information, current battery level (inputs); current path plan and next stopping point/time (plan); next science action (decision/action)
  Scientist - next science action (action/decision); inputted image of rock for science analysis (input); rock classification (output)
– **Level 2 XAI:**
  Engineer - terrain map with rover path costs including untraverseable areas with infinite cost (policy information - costs); battery usage for current path (constraints); list of possible science actions and associated rewards (policy information - rewards); battery usage for each science action (constraints)
  Scientist - list of possible science actions and associated rewards (policy information - rewards); list of semantic features, such as color, contributing to the rock classification (feature information); sensitivity to light given inputs (sensitivity information)
– **Level 3 XAI:**
  Engineer - map of maximum traverseable distance given current battery level (continued action); remaining battery level after each possible science activity (continued action)
  Scientist - predicted rock classification under different lighting conditions (changed inputs)

The scientist and engineer have individual informational requirements in addition to some shared requirements, such as which science activities are planned. Each is only provided with necessary information in order to avoid a cognitive overload from excess information, which poses a risk to task performance.

Measuring SA Through SAGAT. In order to apply SAGAT to this example, specific informational requirements can be enumerated from the high-level informational needs listed above. A list of questions regarding this specific information at all three levels can be specified, and a simulated mission can be run with the scientist and engineer. At various randomly-selected points during the simulated mission, the experiment should be frozen, and the scientist and engineer would then be asked a subset of the specified questions for each level. For example, the following questions might be asked of the engineer regarding the battery during rover traversal between two science activity locations: What is the current battery level of the rover? (Level 1); How much power is required to get to the next location? (Level 2); Does the rover have enough battery to get to the next location and perform the science task? (Level 3).

8   Future Directions

One natural future direction for this work would be to implement a system that addresses the three levels of XAI in a goal- or performance-oriented context and to perform human experiments to assess whether improved SA, enabled through XAI, correlates with improved performance of the human-AI team.

Such a system could be a combination of existing techniques addressing each of the three levels or a single system that can address all three levels of XAI. To our knowledge, no system exists that can, on its own, address all three levels. While explainable BDI agents have addressed aspects of each of the three levels [7,23], additional techniques beyond these solutions will be needed to fully address levels 2 and 3 XAI. In general, development of an XAI system that can independently address all three levels of XAI would be a valuable next direction. Such a system will also require the development of techniques that provide user-tailored explanations in a way that goes beyond what exists in the literature. While there is some existing literature that considers user needs or context in a limited way [8,19,45], producing explanations that fully consider user contexts and tasks remains an understudied area. To this end, another possible future direction would be to perform inference of human models in order to inform explanation generation.

9   Conclusion

In this paper, we propose a three-level framework for the design of XAI systems based on human user informational needs. This framework is based on the situation awareness framework in the human factors literature, which has been studied in relation to performance of human-autonomy teams. We further propose a method for assessment of explanations with respect to the three levels of information that XAI systems should provide. Finally, we propose future directions for XAI research.

References

1. Adebayo, J., Gilmer, J., Muelly, M., Goodfellow, I., Hardt, M., Kim, B.: Sanity checks for saliency maps. In: Advances in Neural Information Processing Systems, pp. 9505–9515 (2018)
2. Amir, D., Amir, O.: Highlights: summarizing agent behavior to people. In: Proceedings of the 17th International Conference on Autonomous Agents and MultiAgent Systems, pp. 1168–1176. International Foundation for Autonomous Agents and Multiagent Systems (2018)
3. Anjomshoae, S., Najjar, A., Calvaresi, D., Främling, K.: Explainable agents and robots: results from a systematic literature review. In: Proceedings of the 18th International Conference on Autonomous Agents and MultiAgent Systems, pp. 1078–1088. International Foundation for Autonomous Agents and Multiagent Systems (2019)
4. Bansal, A., Farhadi, A., Parikh, D.: Towards transparent systems: semantic characterization of failure modes. In: Fleet, D., Pajdla, T., Schiele, B., Tuytelaars, T. (eds.) ECCV 2014. LNCS, vol. 8694, pp. 366–381. Springer, Cham (2014). https://doi.org/10.1007/978-3-319-10599-4_24
5. Bedny, G., Meister, D.: Theory of activity and situation awareness. Int. J. Cogn. Ergon. 3(1), 63–72 (1999)
6. Borgo, R., Cashmore, M., Magazzeni, D.: Towards providing explanations for AI planner decisions. arXiv preprint arXiv:1810.06338 (2018)

7. Broekens, J., Harbers, M., Hindriks, K., van den Bosch, K., Jonker, C., Meyer, J.-J.: Do you get it? User-evaluated explainable BDI agents. In: Dix, J., Witteveen, C. (eds.) MATES 2010. LNCS (LNAI), vol. 6251, pp. 28–39. Springer, Heidelberg (2010). https://doi.org/10.1007/978-3-642-16178-0_5
8. Chakraborti, T., Sreedharan, S., Grover, S., Kambhampati, S.: Plan explanations as model reconciliation. In: 2019 14th ACM/IEEE International Conference on Human-Robot Interaction (HRI), pp. 258–266. IEEE (2019)
9. Chen, J.Y., Procci, K., Boyce, M., Wright, J., Garcia, A., Barnes, M.: Situation awareness-based agent transparency. Technical report, Army Research Lab Aberdeen Proving Ground MD Human Research and Engineering (2014)
10. Dannenhauer, D., Floyd, M.W., Molineaux, M., Aha, D.W.: Learning from exploration: towards an explainable goal reasoning agent (2018)
11. Doshi-Velez, F., Kim, B.: Towards a rigorous science of interpretable machine learning. arXiv preprint arXiv:1702.08608 (2017)
12. Dragan, A.D., Lee, K.C., Srinivasa, S.S.: Legibility and predictability of robot motion. In: 2013 8th ACM/IEEE International Conference on Human-Robot Interaction (HRI), pp. 301–308. IEEE (2013)
13. Endsley, M.: Measurement of situation awareness in dynamic systems. Hum. Factors 37, 65–84 (1995). https://doi.org/10.1518/001872095779049499
14. Endsley, M.R.: Situation awareness global assessment technique (SAGAT). In: Proceedings of the IEEE 1988 National Aerospace and Electronics Conference, pp. 789–795. IEEE (1988)
15. Endsley, M.R.: Situation awareness misconceptions and misunderstandings. J. Cogn. Eng. Decis. Mak. 9(1), 4–32 (2015)
16. Endsley, M.R.: Direct measurement of situation awareness: validity and use of SAGAT. In: Situational Awareness, pp. 129–156. Routledge (2017)
17. Endsley, M.R.: A systematic review and meta-analysis of direct objective measures of situation awareness: a comparison of SAGAT and spam. Hum. Factors 0018720819875376 (2019)
18. Endsley, M., Jones, W.: A Model of Inter-and Intrateam Situation Awareness: Implications for Design. New Trends in Cooperative Activities: Understanding System Dynamics in Complex Environments. M. McNeese, E. Salas and M. Endsley. Human Factors and Ergonomics Society, Santa Monica (2001)
19. Floyd, M.W., Aha, D.W.: Incorporating transparency during trust-guided behavior adaptation. In: Goel, A., Díaz-Agudo, M.B., Roth-Berghofer, T. (eds.) ICCBR 2016. LNCS (LNAI), vol. 9969, pp. 124–138. Springer, Cham (2016). https://doi.org/10.1007/978-3-319-47096-2_9
20. Fox, M., Long, D., Magazzeni, D.: Explainable planning. arXiv preprint arXiv:1709.10256 (2017)
21. Gunning, D., Aha, D.W.: Darpa's explainable artificial intelligence program. AI Mag. 40(2), 44–58 (2019)
22. Halpern, J.Y., Pearl, J.: Causes and explanations: a structural-model approach. Part I: causes. Br. J. Philos. Sci. 56(4), 843–887 (2005)
23. Harbers, M., van den Bosch, K., Meyer, J.J.: Design and evaluation of explainable BDI agents. In: 2010 IEEE/WIC/ACM International Conference on Web Intelligence and Intelligent Agent Technology, vol. 2, pp. 125–132. IEEE (2010)
24. Harbers, M., Bradshaw, J.M., Johnson, M., Feltovich, P., van den Bosch, K., Meyer, J.-J.: Explanation in human-agent teamwork. In: Cranefield, S., van Riemsdijk, M.B., Vázquez-Salceda, J., Noriega, P. (eds.) COIN -2011. LNCS (LNAI), vol. 7254, pp. 21–37. Springer, Heidelberg (2012). https://doi.org/10.1007/978-3-642-35545-5_2

25. Hayes, B., Shah, J.A.: Improving robot controller transparency through autonomous policy explanation. In: 2017 12th ACM/IEEE International Conference on Human-Robot Interaction (HRI), pp. 303–312. IEEE (2017)
26. Hellström, T., Bensch, S.: Understandable robots-what, why, and how. Paladyn J. Behav. Robot. **9**(1), 110–123 (2018)
27. Hoffman, R.R., Mueller, S.T., Klein, G., Litman, J.: Metrics for explainable AI: challenges and prospects. arXiv preprint arXiv:1812.04608 (2018)
28. Johnson, M., Bradshaw, J.M., Feltovich, P.J., Jonker, C.M., Van Riemsdijk, M.B., Sierhuis, M.: Coactive design: designing support for interdependence in joint activity. J. Hum.-Robot Interact. **3**(1), 43–69 (2014)
29. Kim, B., Rudin, C., Shah, J.A.: The Bayesian case model: a generative approach for case-based reasoning and prototype classification. In: Advances in Neural Information Processing Systems, pp. 1952–1960 (2014)
30. Kim, B., et al.: Interpretability beyond feature attribution: quantitative testing with concept activation vectors (TCAV). arXiv preprint arXiv:1711.11279 (2017)
31. Lipton, Z.C.: The mythos of model interpretability. arXiv preprint arXiv:1606.03490 (2016)
32. Lomas, M., Chevalier, R., Cross, E.V., Garrett, R.C., Hoare, J., Kopack, M.: Explaining robot actions. In: Proceedings of the Seventh Annual ACM/IEEE International Conference on Human-Robot Interaction, pp. 187–188 (2012)
33. Marino, D.L., Wickramasinghe, C.S., Manic, M.: An adversarial approach for explainable AI in intrusion detection systems. In: IECON 2018-44th Annual Conference of the IEEE Industrial Electronics Society, pp. 3237–3243. IEEE (2018)
34. Miller, T.: Explanation in artificial intelligence: insights from the social sciences. Artif. Intell. **267**, 1–38 (2018)
35. Miller, T., Howe, P., Sonenberg, L.: Explainable AI: beware of inmates running the asylum or: how i learnt to stop worrying and love the social and behavioural sciences. arXiv preprint arXiv:1712.00547 (2017)
36. Neerincx, M.A., van der Waa, J., Kaptein, F., van Diggelen, J.: Using perceptual and cognitive explanations for enhanced human-agent team performance. In: Harris, D. (ed.) EPCE 2018. LNCS (LNAI), vol. 10906, pp. 204–214. Springer, Cham (2018). https://doi.org/10.1007/978-3-319-91122-9_18
37. Parasuraman, R., Sheridan, T.B., Wickens, C.D.: Situation awareness, mental workload, and trust in automation: viable, empirically supported cognitive engineering constructs. J. Cogn. Eng. Decis. Mak. **2**(2), 140–160 (2008)
38. Preece, A., Harborne, D., Braines, D., Tomsett, R., Chakraborty, S.: Stakeholders in explainable AI. arXiv preprint arXiv:1810.00184 (2018)
39. Ribeiro, M.T., Singh, S., Guestrin, C.: Why should i trust you?: explaining the predictions of any classifier. In: Proceedings of the 22nd ACM SIGKDD International Conference on Knowledge Discovery and Data Mining, pp. 1135–1144. ACM (2016)
40. Ribera, M., Lapedriza, A.: Can we do better explanations? A proposal of user-centered explainable AI. In: IUI Workshops (2019)
41. Salmon, P.M., et al.: What really is going on? Review of situation awareness models for individuals and teams. Theor. Issues Ergon. Sci. **9**(4), 297–323 (2008)
42. Sheh, R., Monteath, I.: Introspectively assessing failures through explainable artificial intelligence. In: IROS Workshop on Introspective Methods for Reliable Autonomy (2017)
43. Sheh, R.K.: Different XAI for different HRI. In: 2017 AAAI Fall Symposium Series (2017)

44. Smith, K., Hancock, P.A.: Situation awareness is adaptive, externally directed consciousness. Hum. Factors **37**(1), 137–148 (1995)
45. Sreedharan, S., Srivastava, S., Kambhampati, S.: Hierarchical expertise level modeling for user specific contrastive explanations. In: IJCAI, pp. 4829–4836 (2018)
46. Stanton, N.A., Chambers, P.R., Piggott, J.: Situational awareness and safety. Saf. Sci. **39**(3), 189–204 (2001)
47. Wickens, C.D.: Multiple resources and mental workload. Hum. Factors **50**(3), 449–455 (2008)

Explainable Machine Learning

Towards Demystifying Subliminal Persuasiveness: Using XAI-Techniques to Highlight Persuasive Markers of Public Speeches

Klaus Weber[1]([✉])[ID], Lukas Tinnes[1], Tobias Huber[1][ID], Alexander Heimerl[1],
Marc-Leon Reinecker[2], Eva Pohlen[1], and Elisabeth André[1][ID]

[1] Augsburg University, Augsburg, Germany
{weber,huber,heimerl,andre}@hcm-lab.de,
{lukas.tinnes,eva.pohlen}@student.uni-augsburg.de
[2] University of Applied Sciences Augsburg, Augsburg, Germany
marc-leon.reinecker@hs-augsburg.de

Abstract. The literature provides evidence for the importance of non-verbal cues when it comes to persuading other people and developing persuasive robots. Mostly, people use these non-verbal cues subconsciously and, more importantly, are not aware of the subliminal impact of them. To raise awareness of subliminal persuasion and to explore a way for investigating persuasive cues for the development of persuasive robots and agents, we have analyzed videos of political public speeches and trained a neural network capable of predicting the degree of perceived convincingness based on visual input only. We then created visualizations of the predictions by making use of the explainable artificial intelligence methods Grad-CAM and layer-wise relevance propagation that highlight the most relevant image sections and markers. Our results show that the neural network learned to focus on the person, more specifically their posture and contours, as well as on their hands and face. These results are in line with existing literature and, thus, show the practical potential of our approach.

Keywords: Subliminal persuasion · Persuasive markers · XAI

1 Introduction

In the process of changing opinions or attitudes, people use far more than logical and rational aspects. There is evidence from the literature that the persuasive power of arguments largely depends on appropriate body language. Consequently, if arguments that are content-wise identical are presented differently, i.e. with different non-verbal behaviors, the persuasive power of an argument can be different.

© Springer Nature Switzerland AG 2020
D. Calvaresi et al. (Eds.): EXTRAAMAS 2020, LNAI 12175, pp. 113–128, 2020.
https://doi.org/10.1007/978-3-030-51924-7_7

There is significant evidence from the literature that body language and the type of gestures used influence how a person is perceived, and several studies showed that body language and verbal aspects significantly influence perceived persuasiveness [5,9,14]. These body-language-based cues, however, are often unconsciously observed by people, and it seems that people are not aware of this kind of subliminal persuasion.

Understanding these cues bears two advantages: 1) It can help people behave differently, i.e., more persuasive, in debates, speeches or job interviews, and 2) a deeper understanding of these persuasive cues can help researchers develop persuasive robots and agents in human-robot interactions more easily [9,14].

In this paper, we explore an approach employing explainable artificial intelligence techniques to make persuasive cues visible to demonstrate the importance of the persuasive power of body-language-based argumentation and to investigate a different approach to developing persuasive agents and robots.

First, we trained a model to predict perceived convincingness based on an annotated political public speech using a convolutional neural network utilizing the visual (image) channel only (i.e., without the audio channel). We then employed explainable artificial intelligence (XAI) visualization techniques to uncover what parts of the image were the most relevant ones for predicting the degree of perceived convincingness.

Our post-hoc analysis reveals that our neural network has learned to focus on the person speaking and (mostly) ignore the background of the image. The observations of our visualizations indicate that the network primarily localizes hand and face positions on the image, which demonstrates, in line with existing literature, the importance of subliminal persuasive cues.

The structure of the paper is as follows. Section 2 gives an overview of persuasion theory and XAI visualization techniques, Sect. 3 describes the overall approach, including the data annotation process and the architecture of the trained model. Section 4 highlights what the network has learned employing Grad-CAM and Layer-wise Relevance Propagation (LRP). Finally, Sect. 5 concludes with a brief discussion of results, limitations of our approach, and future work.

2   Related Work

Related work of this research can be divided into two parts: (1) The effect of non-verbal cues in persuasive messages and (2) Explainable Artificial Intelligence.

2.1   The Effect of Non-verbal Cues in Persuasive Messages

The theory of persuasion goes back to Aristotle. He identified three means of persuasion, namely logos, pathos, and ethos. Logos defines the logical and rational aspects, i.e., the content of the argument, pathos the emotional engagement between the speaker and the listener, while ethos describes the personality of the speaker, their character, and how the speaker is perceived by the audience [20].

According to psychological models, there are two cognitive routes (*central* and *peripheral*), through which a persuasive message can be processed. Petty and Cacioppo [26] developed the Elaboration Likelihood Model (ELM) describing the influence of information processing on the result of a persuasive message depending on the listeners "*need for cognition*" (NFC). If the listener's NFC is low, then a message is more likely processed via the *peripheral route* otherwise *central processing* takes place. Chaiken et al. [8] extended this model (Heuristic-Systematic Model – HSM) claiming that people do not process information in isolation via one of the two routes. Instead, peripheral processing always takes place, to which central processing is added when an elaboration threshold is reached (depending on the listener's *need for cognition*).

Consequently, researchers have investigated the effect of non-verbal cues on the perceived persuasiveness. DeSteno et al. [10] showed that persuasive messages are more successful if they are framed with emotional overtones that correspond to the emotional state of the recipient. Wang et al. [33] showed that perceived persuasiveness of emotions depends on the level of power of the speaker and the listener. Further, Van Kleef et al. [18,32] showed that people use the source's emotions as information channel when they form their attitudes.

In addition to that, researchers have investigated the effect of gestures and gaze. Maricchiolo et al. [22] investigated the effect of hand gestures concerning the speaker's perceived persuasiveness revealing that hand gestures affect the evaluation of a message's persuasiveness, the speaker's style effectiveness, and their composure and competence. Poggi et al. [27] further investigated the use of gestures and gaze in political discourse concerning their persuasive import.

In short, there is a lot of evidence that persuasiveness largely depends on body-language-based argumentation and persuasive cues. Thus, by taking away the audio channel, a neural network should be able to learn these cues to predict perceived persuasiveness successfully . Hence, in this paper, we investigate 1) whether or not a neural network can "*understand*" and learn these subliminal cues and 2) whether or not the network learns to focus on the sections containing these subliminal cues instead of focusing on the image as a whole.

2.2   Explainable Artificial Intelligence

Since artificial intelligent systems are becoming more and more complex, there is an increasing need to increase the explainability of these systems. Understanding how a system works is crucial for working with and building trust in artificial, intelligent systems.

XAI is especially important when the system is inferring personality traits of humans, such as persuasiveness, which is a highly subjective task that might include biases. For this reason, earlier works used XAI on several subjective tasks. Escalante et al. [12], for example, developed a challenge to test different explainable systems that are used for first impression analysis in the context of job applications. Weitz et al. [34] investigated different XAI methods on facial pain and emotion recognition models. However, to the best of our knowledge, this is the first work on explainable systems that predict the degree persuasiveness of humans. In the context of persuasion and XAI, recent work mainly investigated explainable recommendation systems persuading humans [11,36].

XAI is often split into several subcategories. In this work, we do not, for example, deal with the development of more interpretable model architectures. Instead, we focus on *post hoc* explanations that are created after the model was trained [23]. Furthermore, we focus on local explanations that analyze single predictions of a system instead of global explanations that try to shed light on the general behavior of a system. For neural networks, the most common local post-hoc explanation method is the generation of saliency maps [1]. Saliency maps are heat-maps that highlight areas of the input that were relevant for the decision of a system in a certain way.

One of the first kinds of saliency maps were based on the gradient. Simonyan et al. [30] used backpropagation to calculate the gradient with respect to each input unit to measure how much a small change in this input affects the prediction. Selvaraju et al. [29] made this approach more class discriminatory by stopping the backpropagation after the fully connected layers and using the gradient with respect to the output of the last convolutional layer.

A different kind of saliency map estimates how much each input attributed to the final decision of a neural network. Lapushkin et al. [6,21] introduced layer-wise relevance propagation (LRP) that assigns a relevance value to each neuron in a neural network, measuring how relevant this neuron was for a particular prediction. For this assignment, they defined different rules, all of which are based on the intermediate outputs of the neural network during the forward pass. One of those rules introduced by Huber et al. [15] tries to create more selective saliency maps by only propagating the relevance to the neuron with the highest activation in the preceding layer. Montavon et al. [24] put the LRP concept into the theoretical framework of the Taylor decomposition.

Another take on saliency maps comes with occlusion or perturbation based visualizations. Zeiler et al. [35] zero out windows inside the input and measure how much the prediction changes. The more the output changes, the more relevant was this window for this particular prediction. Greydanus et al. [13] uses a similar approach but perturbs the windows with noise to see how much the introduced uncertainty affects the prediction. The LIME framework from [28] first separates the input picture into super-pixels by a segmentation algorithm. Afterwards, a more interpretable model is trained to estimate which super-pixels are the most relevant for a given decision. One of the advantages of those methods is that they are not dependant on the structure of the model, but this comes with the drawback of not being as precise as some model-specific methods.

Recently, Adebayo et al. [2] introduced a sanity check that showed that some gradient-based saliency maps were not analyzing the learned weights of a neural network. The original saliency maps from [30] and the Grad-CAM maps both passed the test. This year, Sixt et al. [31] tested different LRP variants more in depth. They concluded that most LRP variants lose a lot of information about the last fully connected layers of the network. Instead, they mainly analyze the convolutional layers at the beginning of the network. Therefore we chose a combination of class discriminatory Grad-CAM saliency maps and fine granular LRP saliency maps to get a good understanding of the end and the beginning parts of our model respectively.

3   Data Annotations and Model

In this Section, we describe the data annotation process and the model architecture, including the training process of the neural network in detail.

3.1   Corpus and Annotation Process

The training corpus consists of a public speech by Donald J. Trump, which was held in 2019 with an approximate length of 50 min.[1] The data were annotated using NOVA [7], an annotation tool for annotating and analyzing behavior in social interactions. The NOVA user interface has been designed with a particular focus on the annotation of continuous recordings involving multiple modalities and subjects. It supports several techniques from the latest developments from contemporary research fields such as Cooperative Machine Learning and XAI to

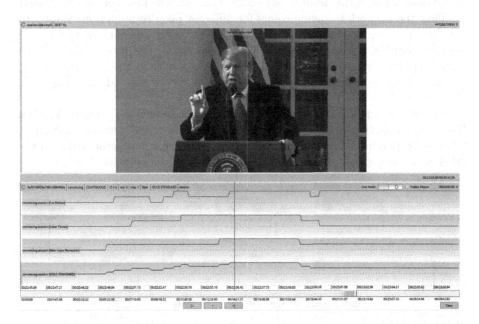

Fig. 1. Screenshot of the NOVA tool depicting the video at the top and four annotation streams below (3 annotators + merged gold standard for the training process).

---

[1] https://www.youtube.com/watch?v=DU6BnuyjJqI.

enhance the standard annotation process. We had the corpus continuously annotated by three experienced labelers with a sample rate of 25 Hz. They were asked to rate how convincing the speaker appeared distinguishing between five different levels (ranging from *not convincing at all* to *very convincing*). The annotators achieved an inter-rater agreement of 0.77 (Cronbach's α), which seems sufficient for our purpose considering the high subjectivity of perceived persuasiveness [16,25]. The final annotations have been merged (see Fig. 1) to obtain a gold standard annotation stream with more than 50,000 sample images. Due to the nature of the video, the lowest two classes were barely annotated.

3.2   Model Architecture and Training

Figure 2 sketches the architecture of our employed convolutional neural network consisting of three subsequent convolutional layers. The last two layers are followed by batch normalization and max-pooling layers. The output of the last convolutional layer is flattened and then fed into a five-way softmax function to get the predictions of all five classes.

We first extracted the video frames with a sample rate of 25 Hz and downsampled them to 160×90 RGB-Images. The first convolutional layer expands the RGB-channel of the input image to 32 channels. The idea behind this is that we allow the network to define colors for different pixel combinations similar to how humans see, for example, a combination of yellow and blue as green. The network outputs a five-dimensional vector describing the probability of each class. A ReLU activation is used in each layer apart from the output layer, in which a softmax function is applied. As optimizer we use Adamax ($\beta_1 = 9$, $\beta_2 = 0.999$) [17].

To tackle overfitting, we use batch normalization as well as L2-regularization. Batch normalization is applied after the second and third convolutional layer, followed by pooling layers. L2-regularization (regularization factor 0.01), on the other hand, is applied to each convolutional layer in the network.

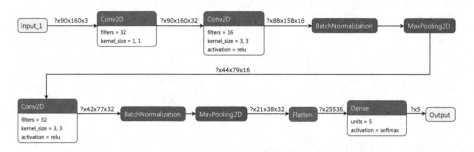

Fig. 2. An illustration of the network architecture. The network consists of three convolutions, which learn to focus on body parts important for predicting convincingness. The first layer expands the 3-channel RGB to 32 channel before being fed into the last two convolutions layers, after each of which batch normalization and max-pooling are applied. The network outputs a 5-vector estimating the probability of each class.

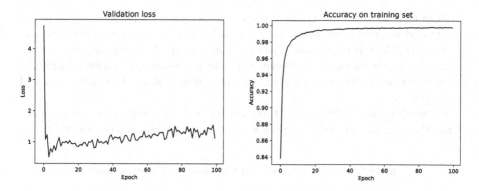

Fig. 3. Validation loss and training accuracy over all epochs.

The model was trained for 100 epochs using a batch size of 32 and with the dataset split into training and validation data by a ratio of 4:1.

Figure 3 summarizes the learning process showing that the neural network was able to predict classes reliably after only 20 epochs with an accuracy of >98% on the training set. Since the validation loss shows slight overfitting after 20 epochs, the network explored in this work was only trained for 20 epoch.

To validate the performance of the network, we computed the confusion matrix on the training data set as visualized in Fig. 4.

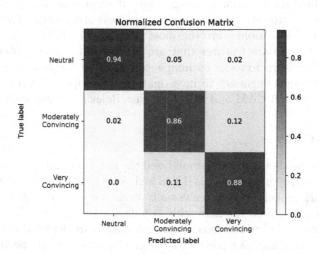

Fig. 4. Confusion matrix computed on the training data set to ensure that our network is sufficiently accurate on the learned samples.

Note that we have not trained a general predictor for persuasiveness as we only intend to explore what our network looks at when learning perceived persuasiveness. Therefore, we evaluated our model on the training data set only to ensure that our network is sufficiently accurate on the learned samples. Since the lowest two classes were not annotated at the current stage, they are not listed in the matrix.

We verified the performance of our model by computing the F1-scores indicating that our model performs very well on the learned samples (Table 1).

Table 1. Precision, Recall and F1-Score for different classes.

Measure	Class		
	Neutral	Moderately convincing	Very convincing
Precision	0.93	0.93	0.77
Recall	0.94	0.86	0.88
F1-Score	0.93	0.89	0.82

4   Highlighting the Cues: Visualising the Network's Eyes

Since we trained the network on images only, it seems that it was able to learn features that describe the perceived convincingness of a person. The interesting question is, which sections were the most relevant for making a (correct) prediction and if there are features that are in line with existing literature, i.e., did the network learn to focus on image excerpts that are evidenced indicators for perceived convincingness? To investigate this, we applied two different XAI techniques: (1) Grad-CAM and (2) Layer-wise Relevance Propagation.

4.1   Grad-CAM

To explain the predictions, we first analyzed the last layer of our network employing Grad-CAM [29] using keras-vis [19], a high-level toolkit for visualizing trained neural network models. For better visualizations, we created edge images of the input images and placed the network's visualization maps over them.

Several example visualizations of different classes are depicted in Fig. 5. They show that the network has learned to focus on the person, more specifically, their posture and contours. The background is mostly ignored and not relevant for the prediction (apart from a little background noise). More specifically, the network follows the hands and face of the speaker, which is in line with existing literature strengthening the validity of our approach since literature states that gestures, gaze, and hand movements are important indicators for perceived persuasiveness. It is worth noting that when predicting the *neutral* class, the network seems to look at every object on the image (unlike the other two classes where the network follows explicitly the person's arms and hands of the person). This is probably since the network cannot find any convincing markers at all, so every part of the image is observed. These visualizations inherently reveal the existence of a link between the visual channel and subliminal persuasion as well as the ability of neural networks to learn this connection demonstrating the importance of the persuasive power of non-verbal cues.

Fig. 5. Example visualization - (FLTR): Neutral - Moderately Convincing - Very Convincing. The visualization shows that the neural network has learned to focus on the posture, hands, and contours of the speaker to make its prediction. Due to the nature of our training data, the network hardly learned the person's features for barely annotated classes.

To examine the generalization of the network (despite being trained on one person only), we also tested the prediction on several images of other politicians, namely American senator Bernie Sanders[2], President of France Emmanuel Macron[3] and Chancellor of Germany Angela Merkel[4]. The visualizations are depicted in Fig. 6.

Fig. 6. Example visualizations of several other politicians with varying degrees of convincingness. (FLTR): Bernie Sanders (predicted class: *very convincing*) - Emmanuel Macron (predicted class: *very convincing*) - Angela Merkel (predicted class: *moderately convincing*).

Despite the speakers and the camera angle being different, the network still focuses on hands and the general face area. Taking a closer look at the picture of Emmanuel Macron reveals that the network seems to have learned to locate areas with skin-related colors to make its decision, even though the network does not always locate all image parts with skin-related color.

4.2   Layer-Wise Relevance Propagation

Next to Grad-CAM, we used LRP to analyze further the first convolutional layers of the network and what patterns they learned. LRP assigns a relevance value R_k to each neuron in a neural network. Let a_k be the activation of the k-th

[2] Modification of 'Election 2016: Bernie Sanders NYC Fundraiser Draws Campaign Supporters Who Are 'Feelin' The Bern' by Michael Vadon: https://flickr.com/people/80038275@N00/, licensed under a Creative Commons License: https://creativecommons.org/licenses/by-sa/2.0/.

[3] Modification of 'Conferencia de Prensa - Presidente Emmanuel Macron - Día 2' by G20 Argentina: https://www.flickr.com/photos/g20argentina/, licensed under a Creative Commons License: https://creativecommons.org/licenses/by/2.0/.

[4] Modification of 'Rede der Bundeskanzlerin Angela Merkel zum Abschluss des CDU-Parteitages' by CDU/CSU Bundestagsfraktion, licensed under a Creative Commons License: https://creativecommons.org/licenses/by-sa/3.0/deed.en.

neuron during the forward pass and let w_{jk} be the weight that connects neuron j and neuron k. After the forward pass, the relevance propagation starts in the output layer. Here, the activation responsible for the prediction gets assigned its activation as relevance and every other neuron gets set to zero. That is

$$R_k = \begin{cases} a_k & \text{if } k = argmax\{a_k\} \\ 0 & \text{if not.} \end{cases} \tag{1}$$

Beginning from there the relevance gets propagated to each preceding layer according to different rules (see Fig. 7). In our experiments we used the z^+- or $\alpha 1\beta 0$-rule:

$$R_j = \sum_k \frac{(a_j w_{jk})^+}{\sum_j (a_j w_{jk})^+} R_k, \tag{2}$$

where $(a_j w_{jk})^+$ is defined as $\max(a_j w_{jk}, 0)$.

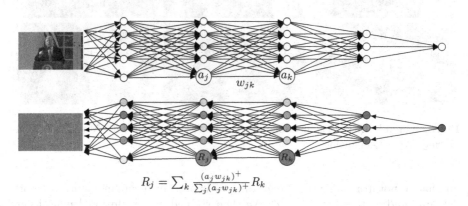

$$R_j = \sum_k \frac{(a_j w_{jk})^+}{\sum_j (a_j w_{jk})^+} R_k$$

Fig. 7. Relevance propagation using the z^+-Rule (Eq. 2).

To create the LRP saliency maps for our model, we used iNNvestigate [3], a library that provides out-of-the-box implementations of many analysis methods, including LRP. Example visualizations can be seen in Fig. 8. LRP visualizations show similar results as Grad-CAM. As before, we can see that the network seems to have learned the spatial features of the person, namely facial features, hand gestures, and the contour of the person. This again demonstrates the importance of subliminal persuasive cues in line with the literature and shows that neural networks are able to learn them.

5 Discussion and Limitations

In the beginning, we have argued that people are often persuaded by subliminal cues and that mostly they are not aware of them. To raise awareness of the exis- tence of this subliminal persuasion, we have analyzed original political speeches

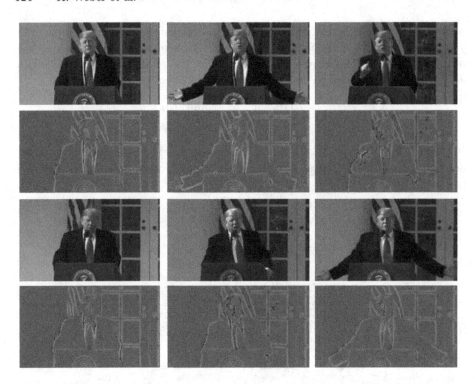

Fig. 8. Example LRP Visualizations (z+-rule) - (FLTR): Neutral - Moderately Convincing - Very Convincing.

and had annotators label them regarding their perceived convincingness by both listening and watching the video. We then trained a convolutional neural network on visual input only to predict the degree of convincingness and used XAI techniques, more specifically Grad-CAM and Layer-wise Relevance Propagation to highlight the most relevant sections. The results are fascinating, revealing that the network has not only learned to focus on the person and their contours but also the face and hands. The latter one is especially interesting as it shows, in line with existing literature, the importance of hand movements and, thus, demonstrates the importance of these subliminal persuasive cues. These results are, therefore, interesting for human-robot-interactions as they enable a different approach to investigating what makes humans persuasive and how to replicate these results in robots.

Apart from these preliminary results, our approach still faces some limitations that should not be neglected.

Limited Training Corpus. Our corpus consisted of only 50,000 samples of the same person; thus, it is unlikely that the network has learned a generalization for predicting the general degree of perceived persuasiveness, even though it also worked on some example images that the network has not seen before. We pointed out that we only tested the model on the training data set since the purpose of the model was to explore what parts of the image the network focuses on when learning perceived persuasiveness. In this regard, the results of the model training should be interpreted with some care, and it should not be considered a general predictor for perceived persuasiveness.

Even though our visualizations have shown that the network has learned to focus on hand and face positions, mainly by focusing on sections with skin-related colors. It is therefore questionable how well the current, trained model works on images with very light, skin-colored backgrounds. Since our network has also been trained on white skin color, the network would probably not work on people with other skin colors yet. Therefore, our data set needs several extensions, that are 1) adding data from different people with different skin colors and 2) adding data with different backgrounds to force the network to learn better generalization of convincing indicators.

No Sequential Persuasive Indicators can be Learned. The current approach uses a convolutional neural network for predicting the perceived persuasiveness based on a single input image only. However, there may be many persuasiveness indicators, such as the speed of hand movements which also influence perceived persuasiveness which cannot be learned with the current approach at present. Thus, in future work, we will further explore how we can highlight sequential types of persuasive markers using XAI techniques, such as LRP similar to Anders et al. [4].

Distribution of the Annotation Data and Annotation Process. Our annotated data consisted of only three classes: *neutral, moderately convincing,* and *very convincing.* Therefore, the network has not learned any characteristics yet about what *not convincing* people look like. Using only one video, this is expected, because from a common-sense perspective individuals may generally perceive another person as either more convincing or less convincing (exclusive-or). Also, the whole annotation process is subject to the annotator's own opinion as persuasiveness, in general, is highly subjective. Therefore, it remains unclear, whether or not the annotators have annotated the perceived persuasiveness in general or just the intensity of the body language movement, which may also have an impact on the perceived persuasiveness. This limitation requires further analysis and will be addressed further in our future work. Also, we will explicitly include samples of the missing classes (i.e., different videos of other people) to obtain more detailed training results and to compare the markers of a *convincing* and *not convincing* appearance of people.

Nevertheless, our first results have shown the feasibility and practical potential of highlighting persuasive cues and indicators for persuasiveness employing explainable AI techniques.

6 Conclusion

In this paper, we explored an approach that highlights persuasive indicators of public speeches using explainable artificial intelligence techniques. There is a lot of evidence from the literature that bodily cues play an important role in persuading people. However, since people often seem not to be aware of the importance of body-language-based argumentation, we trained a convolutional neural network, which can predict perceived persuasiveness solely based on visual input. We then applied explainable AI techniques, namely Grad-CAM and Layer-wise Relevance Propagation in order to highlight relevant areas of the image that were used by the network for predicting the degree of persuasiveness to raise awareness of the stated importance of subliminal persuasive cues. Further we aim to explore an effective way for investigating persuasive cues for the development of persuasive agents and robots. Our results show that our network has learned to focus on the person, their contours, face, and hands proving that our network is able to look for parts on the image that are important indicators for a person's persuasiveness according to existing literature. We have described the limitations of our approach in detail, especially concerning our used training data set, which only consisted of one speech of a single person. In our future work, we will address the limitations mentioned above and extend our corpus[5] with additional speeches and look for suitable existing corpora to generalize our approach. We will then explore if our network can learn generalized as well as more fine-grained persuasive indicators, such as making a fist as well as sequential persuasive markers and if we can highlight such persuasive markers. Additionally, we will make use of other explainable AI techniques to get a deeper understanding of the impact of persuasive markers.

Acknowledgments. This work has been funded by the Deutsche Forschungsgemein-schaft (DFG) within the project "How to Win Arguments - Empowering Virtual Agents to Improve their Persuasiveness", Grant Number 376696351, as part of the Priority Program "Robust Argumentation Machines (RATIO)" (SPP-1999).

References

1. Adadi, A., Berrada, M.: Peeking inside the black-box: a survey on explainable artificial intelligence (XAI). IEEE Access **6**, 52138–52160 (2018)
2. Adebayo, J., Gilmer, J., Muelly, M., Goodfellow, I., Hardt, M., Kim, B.: Sanity checks for saliency maps. In: Advances in Neural Information Processing Systems 31, pp. 9505–9515. Curran Associates, Inc. (2018)
3. Alber, M., et al.: innvestigate neural networks. J. Mach. Learn. Res. **20**(93), 1–8 (2019)
4. Anders, C.J., Montavon, G., Samek, W., Müller, K.-R.: Understanding patch-based learning of video data by explaining predictions. In: Samek, W., Montavon, G., Vedaldi, A., Hansen, L.K., Müller, K.-R. (eds.) Explainable AI: Interpreting, Explaining and Visualizing Deep Learning. LNCS (LNAI), vol. 11700, pp. 297–309. Springer, Cham (2019). https://doi.org/10.1007/978-3-030-28954-6_16
5. Andrist, S., Spannan, E., Mutlu, B.: Rhetorical robots: making robots more effective speakers using linguistic cues of expertise. In: 2013 8th ACM/IEEE International Conference on Human-Robot Interaction (HRI), pp. 341–348. IEEE (2013)

---

[5] We plan to make the extended corpus along with the source code publicly available in the upcoming weeks.

6. Bach, S., Binder, A., Montavon, G., Klauschen, F., Müller, K.R., Samek, W.: OnPixel-wise explanations for non-linear classifier decisions by layer-wise relevance propagation. PLoS ONE **10**(7), e0130140 (2015)
7. Baur, T., et al.: Explainable cooperative machine learning with NOVA. German J. Artif. Intell. **34**, 143–164 (2020)
8. Chaiken, S.: Heuristic and systematic information processing within and beyond the persuasion context. In: Unintended Thought, pp. 212–252 (1989)
9. Chidambaram, V., Chiang, Y.H., Mutlu, B.: Designing persuasive robots: how robots might persuade people using vocal and nonverbal cues. In: Proceedings of the Seventh Annual ACM/IEEE International Conference on Human-Robot Interaction, pp. 293–300 (2012)
10. DeSteno, D., Petty, R.E., Rucker, D.D., Wegener, D.T., Braverman, J.: Discrete emotions and persuasion: the role of emotion-induced expectancies. J. Pers. Soc. Psychol. **86**(1), 43 (2004)
11. Donadello, I., Dragoni, M., Eccher, C.: Persuasive explanation of reasoning inferences on dietary data. In: Demidova, E., et al. (eds.) Joint Proceedings of the 6th International Workshop on Dataset PROFILing and Search & the 1st Workshop on Semantic Explainability co-located with the 18th International Semantic Web Conference (ISWC 2019), Auckland, New Zealand, 27 October 2019. CEUR Workshop Proceedings, vol. 2465, pp. 46–61. CEUR-WS.org (2019)
12. Escalante, H.J., et al.: Design of an explainable machine learning challenge for video interviews. In: 2017 International Joint Conference on Neural Networks, IJCNN 2017, Anchorage, AK, USA, 14–19 May 2017, pp. 3688–3695. IEEE (2017)
13. Greydanus, S., Koul, A., Dodge, J., Fern, A.: Visualizing and understanding atari agents. In: Proceedings of the 35th International Conference on Machine Learning, ICML 2018, Stockholmsmässan, Stockholm, Sweden, pp. 1787–1796 (2018)
14. Ham, J., Bokhorst, R., Cuijpers, R., van der Pol, D., Cabibihan, J.-J.: Making robots persuasive: the influence of combining persuasive strategies (gazing and gestures) by a storytelling robot on its persuasive power. In: Mutlu, B., Bartneck, C., Ham, J., Evers, V., Kanda, T. (eds.) ICSR 2011. LNCS (LNAI), vol. 7072, pp. 71–83. Springer, Heidelberg (2011). https://doi.org/10.1007/978-3-642-25504-5_8
15. Huber, T., Schiller, D., André, E.: Enhancing explainability of deep reinforcement learning through selective layer-wise relevance propagation. In: Benzmüller, C., Stuckenschmidt, H. (eds.) KI 2019. LNCS (LNAI), vol. 11793, pp. 188–202. Springer, Cham (2019). https://doi.org/10.1007/978-3-030-30179-8_16
16. Kaptein, M., Lacroix, J., Saini, P.: Individual differences in persuadability in the health promotion domain. In: Ploug, T., Hasle, P., Oinas-Kukkonen, H. (eds.) PERSUASIVE 2010. LNCS, vol. 6137, pp. 94–105. Springer, Heidelberg (2010). https://doi.org/10.1007/978-3-642-13226-1_11
17. Kingma, D.P., Ba, J.: Adam: a method for stochastic optimization. arXiv preprint arXiv:1412.6980 (2014)
18. van Kleef, G.: Emotions as agents of social influence. In: The Oxford Handbook of Social Influence. Oxford University Press, Oxford (2019)
19. Kotikalapudi, R.: Contributors: keras-vis (2017). https://github.com/raghakot/keras-vis
20. Krapinger, G.: Aristoteles: Rhetorik. Übersetzt und herausgegeben von Gernot Krapinger. Reclam, Stuttgart (1999)
21. Lapuschkin, S., Wäldchen, S., Binder, A., Montavon, G., Samek, W., Müller, K.R.: Unmasking clever hans predictors and assessing what machines really learn. Nat. Commun. **10**(1), 1096 (2019)

22. Maricchiolo, F., Gnisci, A., Bonaiuto, M., Ficca, G.: Effects of different types of hand gestures in persuasive speech on receivers' evaluations. Lang. Cogn. Process. **24**(2), 239–266 (2009)

23. Molnar, C.: Interpretable Machine Learning. https://www.lulu.com/ (2019)

24. Montavon, G., Samek, W., Müller, K.: Methods for interpreting and understanding deep neural networks. Digit. Signal Proc. **73**, 1–15 (2018)

25. O'Keefe, D.J., Jackson, S.: Argument quality and persuasive effects: a review of current approaches. In: Argumentation and Values: Proceedings of the Ninth Alta Conference on Argumentation, pp. 88–92. Speech Communication Association Annandale (1995)

26. Petty, R.E., Cacioppo, J.T.: The elaboration likelihood model of persuasion. In: Petty, R.E., Cacioppo, J.T. (eds.) Communication and Persuasion, pp. 1–24. Springer, New York (1986). https://doi.org/10.1007/978-1-4612-4964-1_1

27. Poggi, I., Vincze, L.: Gesture, gaze and persuasive strategies in political discourse. In: Kipp, M., Martin, J.-C., Paggio, P., Heylen, D. (eds.) MMCorp 2008. LNCS (LNAI), vol. 5509, pp. 73–92. Springer, Heidelberg (2009). https://doi.org/10.1007/978-3-642-04793-0_5

28. Ribeiro, M.T., Singh, S., Guestrin, C.: "why should I trust you?": explaining the predictions of any classifier. In: Krishnapuram, B., Shah, M., Smola, A.J., Aggarwal, C.C., Shen, D., Rastogi, R. (eds.) Proceedings of the 22nd ACM SIGKDD International Conference on Knowledge Discovery and Data Mining, San Francisco, CA, USA, 13–17 August 2016, pp. 1135–1144. ACM (2016)

29. Selvaraju, R.R., Cogswell, M., Das, A., Vedantam, R., Parikh, D., Batra, D.: Gradcam: visual explanations from deep networks via gradient-based localization. In: Proceedings of the IEEE International Conference on Computer Vision, pp. 618–626 (2017)

30. Simonyan, K., Vedaldi, A., Zisserman, A.: Deep inside convolutional networks: visualising image classification models and saliency maps. CoRR abs/1312.6034 (2013)

31. Sixt, L., Granz, M., Landgraf, T.: When explanations lie: why modified BP attribution fails. CoRR abs/1912.09818 (2019)

32. Van Kleef, G.A., van den Berg, H., Heerdink, M.W.: The persuasive power of emotions: effects of emotional expressions on attitude formation and change. J. Appl. Psychol. **100**(4), 1124 (2015)

33. Wang, Y., Lucas, G., Khooshabeh, P., De Melo, C., Gratch, J.: Effects of emotional expressions on persuasion. Soc. Influence **10**(4), 236–249 (2015)

34. Weitz, K., Hassan, T., Schmid, U., Garbas, J.U.: Deep-learned faces of pain and emotions: elucidating the differences of facial expressions with the help of explainable AI methods. tm-Technisches Messen **86**(7–8), 404–412 (2019)

35. Zeiler, M.D., Fergus, R.: Visualizing and understanding convolutional networks. In: Fleet, D., Pajdla, T., Schiele, B., Tuytelaars, T. (eds.) ECCV 2014. LNCS, vol. 8689, pp. 818–833. Springer, Cham (2014). https://doi.org/10.1007/978-3-319-10590-1_53

36. Zhang, Y., Chen, X.: Explainable recommendation: a survey and new perspectives. Found. Trends Inf. Retr. **14**(1), 1–101 (2020)

Explainable Agents for Less Bias in Human-Agent Decision Making

Avleen Malhi[1](✉) ⓘ, Samanta Knapic[2], and Kary Främling[1,2] ⓘ

[1] Department of Computer Science, Aalto University, Espoo, Finland
{avleen.malhi,kary.framling}@aalto.fi
[2] Department of Computing Science, Umeå University, Umeå, Sweden
kary.framling@cs.umu.se, sakn0011@student.umu.se

Abstract. As autonomous agents become more self-governing, ubiquitous and sophisticated, it is vital that humans should have effective interactions with them. Agents often use Machine Learning (ML) for acquiring expertise, but traditional ML methods produce opaque results which are difficult to interpret. Hence, these autonomous agents should be able to explain their behaviour and decisions before they can be trusted by humans. This paper focuses on analyzing the human understanding of the explainable agents behaviour. It conducts a preliminary human-agent interaction study to investigate the effect of explanations on the introduced bias in human-agent decision making for the human participants. We test the hypothesis where different explanation types are used to detect the bias introduced in the autonomous agents decisions. We present three user groups: Agents without explanation, and explainable agents using two different algorithms which automatically generate different explanations for agent actions. Quantitative analysis of three user groups (n = 20, 25, 20) in which users detect the bias in agents' decisions for each explanation type for 15 test data cases is conducted for three different explanations types. Although the interaction study does not give significant findings, but it shows the notable differences between the explanation based recommendations and non-XAI recommendations in human-agent decision making.

Keywords: Explainable agents · Explanation type · Human-agent interaction · Human-agent decision making

1 Introduction

For the machine learning experts to rely upon the model's recommendations, explainability is an issue. It is easy for the decision makers to rely on a statistical tool which is easy to understand and convince the analytical results which is not possible for the machine learning models. Hence, the requirement is to find the methods by which the computational system can be explained to the decision maker for the complete understanding of the whole system. Explainable Artificial

© Springer Nature Switzerland AG 2020
D. Calvaresi et al. (Eds.): EXTRAAMAS 2020, LNAI 12175, pp. 129–146, 2020.
https://doi.org/10.1007/978-3-030-51924-7_8

Intelligence (XAI) shows up as a new branch of AI to benefit any intelligent agent or machine to explain their predictions. For instance, it is vital for an intelligent agent to explain its behaviour to the end user to make them more trustworthy. These type of explanations builds the trust in the classifier decisions even if the class is predicted wrongly as it explains for its unexpected behavior.

Recently, Explainable Artificial Intelligence (XAI), and explainable machine learning in particular, has gained increased attention in the research community. The main facilitation behind XAI is that although the machine learning models have gained attention is last few years, they are not interpretable from the human perspective. To address this shortcoming, researchers have developed algorithms that facilitate post-hoc explainability of machine learning-based classifications. While a range of such algorithms exists, the line of research that evaluates these algorithms from a Human-Computer Interaction (HCI) perspective is still in its infancy. The research questions addressed in the article are: (i) If an AI system is presented to a user, how will the developer know that the explanation is working correctly and the user is able to understand the machine learning decisions completely? (ii) How good the explanations are? (iii) How can we measure the goodness of explanations. (iv) Are users satisfied with the explanations provided? (v) If the end-user's trust and dependence on AI is enough? (vi) how the human-agent system behaves?

In this work, we advance the state of art of the HCI perspective by evaluating how two different post-hoc explanation algorithms–SHAP and LIME–influence bias in human decision-making. For this, we generate a (synthetic) data set of loan application decisions. The loan applications largely follow a set of simple decision rules, but are biased against women. We then train a machine learning model (neural network) on this dataset. In a user study, we then assess how decision support provided by the model is affected in regards to bias when explanation with LIME and SHAP are added.

2   Background

Despite plenty of research on transparent and interpretable machine learning models, providing explanations to technical users is an imperative area of study. The comprehensive surveys on explainable artificial intelligence [2,4] provide an insight into the machine learning, data analytics and visualization, challenges and future research directions for explainable deep learning. The research [15] uses two approaches for image classification using explainable deep learning where first explains sensitivity with respect to changes in input and second decomposes decision for its important input variables. Further, an interesting study on XAI understanding in a comprehensive form [10] can be generally grouped into three classes for understanding, diagnosing and refining. It also presents applicable examples relating to the prevailing state-of-the-art with upcoming future possibilities. The DARPA project [8] provides literature related to motivation and state of the work related to the examples for basic concept and application in the areas of legal advices, finance military, transportation, medicine and security for instance. The machine learning explainable system has been studied for various applications, for example in plant stress phenotyping [7] and heat recycler fault detection in air handling unit [11]. The authors also applied the same technique for providing explanations in medical images collected for capsule Gastroenterology [12]. However there are unprecedented obstacles with the current efforts made by researchers since the traditional machine learning models are less interpretable and more complex with AI used for majority of the tasks. Further, AI is used more for making autonomous decisions than ever by introducing the agents. Hence there is no doubt that the agent autonomy will continue rising in eminence with more exciting work in the future [3].

The ability of an agent to plan and act effectively on its own towards a goal is determined by the agent's actions, when it can perform actions and the outcomes of these actions. The progress is defined by an explainable agent which is able to learn the preconditions related to action and then perform preparatory planning process. Hence an agent performs both exploratory as well as goal-directed actions which opens up the research questions related to controlling actions of exploratory and goal planning and the explanation of agent's behaviour to any technical user [5]. The virtual agents' impact in the area of XAI is examined based on the trust in the autonomous intelligent systems [16].

For assessing the practicality of the trust in autonomous agents, a user study is conducted based on simple bank loan application. As a consequence of this study, we came to a significant evidence indicating that an interactive design of application by integrating the virtual agents with XAI, the trust of the user in the autonomous intelligent agents increase. The objectives of explanation comprises of investigating the questions such as, "How does the system work?"; how easy is it to understand?; What does it do?; Is the user able to trust the system?; and "Is the system able to justify user for its decisions?". The proposed work tries to address the following question: Suppose an AI system which explains its working is presented to a user, what are the ways to measure if it works or not, how accurately it performs, is the user able to have the practical understanding about the system. The aim of the paper is to measure the end-user confidence in understanding the machine learning recommendations with and without explanations, and how well the bias can be reduced with the help of human-agent decision making.

3 Explainable Artificial Intelligence

The machine learning black box models excel in their task of decision making but precisely do not permit to make human understandable decisions. An organization at the forefront of XAI research is the United States' *Defense Advanced Research Projects Agency (DARPA)*. DARPA report defines XAI as: XAI allows an "end user who depends on decisions, recommendations, or actions produced by an AI system [...] to understand the rationale for the system's decisions" [1]. According to a survey conducted by Miller [13], the major findings regarding the properties of explanations in human-like interactions are:

- **Explanations are contrastive:** People have the tendency of not asking why something happened but instead why something happened instead of something else. They try to create the reference between their expectations and the reality.
- **Explanations are Selected:** People rarely expect any explanation covering all aspects of reasoning.
- **Probabilities don't matter:** People consider casual explanations more relevant that pure correlations.
- **Explanations are social:** Explanations are considered as transfer of knowledge as part of interaction which also involves queries as well as preferences.

The behavioural and social challenges should also be taken into consideration for better design decisions while developing the explainable agents. A black box model decisions are sometimes too complex for a human to understand, or it is a model that is challenging to troubleshoot. The explanations need to be considered as a separate tool for replicating the black box behaviour. Most of the recent works on transparent and interpretable machine learning decisions only focus on the technical users. End user explanations are overlooked in many useful and practical applications. Unless humans understand the model's reason of assessment, they can not trust them [9].

SHAP value is a united approach for explaining any machine learning model's output. It has the following characteristics: (i) global interpretability – how much each predictor contributes to the target variable, either positively or negatively. (ii) local interpretability – SHAP values are calculated for each instance which greatly increases its transparency. It helps in explaining the prediction of a case and the major contributors in decision. (iii) the SHAP values can be computed for any model which is tree based.

Local Interpretable Model-agnostic Explanations (LIME) is another explanation tool for providing the explanations for the predictions using the most important contributors. It helps the decision makers in justifying the model behaviour with respect to the important input parameters. The overall purpose of LIME is to identify an interpretable model over the interpretable representation which can fit the classifier locally. The underlying model's approximation by interpretable model is used to generate the explanations by learning the original instance's disruptions. LIME is a simple tool which approximates the black box locally compared to approximation on a global scale. The original instance is weighted by similarity to the instance which we wish to explain. LIME provides the model agnostic explanations which makes it easier to use LIME to explain innumerable classifiers (such as Random Forests, Support Vector Machines and Neural Networks) Because our goal should be to have model-agnostic model, using textual or image data [14].

3.1 Challenges of Explainable Machine Learning

There are significant misconceptions related to the current work on explainability which can effect negatively on its wider social acceptance.

1. *Trade-off between interpretability and accuracy:* It is believed that the complex models present more accurate results which implies that best predictive results can only be obtained by a complex black-box model which is not interpretable at all. The fact is that interpretibility can be imbibed perfectly with the deep learning applications without affecting the performance of the system.
2. *Explainable Machine learning methods provides unfaithful explanations:* It is common belief that if the explanation is exactly what the original model computed, then we do not need the original model at first place. It leads to the situation where it is considered that explanations are the original model's inaccurate representation in parts of the feature space. The explanations methods actually compute the summary of the prediction results of the model instead of exact explanations.
3. *Incomplete explanations:* Sometimes, the explanation may not give complete information that the meaning becomes unclear. It might impart a false confidence in the black box explanation method.
4. *Non-compatibility of the black box models to assess risk:* Some machine learning decisions can increase of decrease the estimated risk. The additional information provided by black box model may increase or decrease the level of risk assessment.

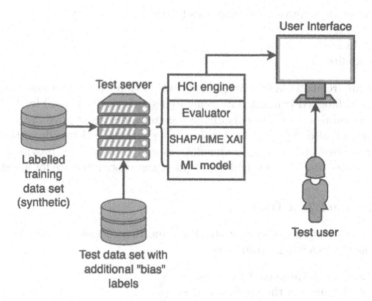

Fig. 1. Test setup and architecture

4   Human-Agent Interaction Method

This section provides an overview of the methodology used to evaluate the impact of explanations on the bias introduced in the models in the human decision making (Fig. 1). We want to emphasize that by agents, we refer to the AI systems which are capable of decision making by themselves. We design an application which is responsible for recommending the decisions to the users. We generate synthetic data, a machine learning model predictions, and post-hoc explanations that allow for the evaluation of the ability of the post-hoc explanation techniques Local Interpretable Model-agnostic Explanations (LIME) and SHapley Additive exPlanations (SHAP) to avoid biased decision making in humans. For this, firstly we generate a (synthetic) data set of loan application decisions. The loan applications largely follow a set of simple decision rules, but are biased against women. The potential biases which can be introduced in the dataset are due to *gender* and *age*. The potential features which can be used in the dataset are listed below:

- Gender
- Age
- Income
- Unpaid debt
- Wealth
- Educational background/profile: ties to the place/country
- Other liabilities
- Credit history
- Job stability

The general architecture for human agent interaction[1] has been explained in the Fig. 1 where labelled training data generated synthetically is used for training a machine learning model. The explainable recommender agent gives the decision of the model and also explains the decision using various XAI based methods such as LIME, SHAP etc. The recommendations and explanations provided by the machine are evaluated by designing an appropriate user interface for a test user.

4.1   Generate Test Data

We generate a data set of loan applications and their decisions. Each loan application has the following parameters:

1. Age (age) of the applicant in years;
2. Income (income) of the applicant in €;
3. Debt/assets (assets) of the applicant in €;
4. Employment type (employment) of the applicant (fixed-term, permanent);
5. Gender (gender) of the applicant (female, other, male);
6. Loan size (loan) in €.

---

[1] https://colab.research.google.com/drive/1-iq1xZhYuKZgH5NgYUBETYmun9yo KMdC.

Table 1. Decision rules for test data

If age < 18: reject
Else if income < 20000 and loan > 10000: reject
Else if assets < 20000 and loan > 10000: reject
Else if assets < 0: reject
Else if employment != permanent and loan > 400000: reject
Else if loan > 500000: reject
Else: accept

Table 2. Bias added

If Gender == 'female' or 'other': reject with probability of 80%
Else: call the first set of rules

The basis for classifications in the test data set are the decision rules given in Table 1. In addition, we induce the rule given in Table 2 that adds bias to the classifications. For loan application data, we create a data set with a size of 10000 entries with the properties given in Table 3.

With the exception of gender, all parameters are approximately uniformly distributed, i.e. we use Python's random.uniform() function to assign any of the possible values. Note that for the scope of the study, it is not necessary to create a representative data set; instead, it is important to have a data set that contains a large amount of entries that will be affected by the gender-biased decision rules. Gender is distributed approximately as follows: 10% other, 50% female, 40% male.

4.2 Training of Model

We then train a machine learning model (Random Forest with gradient boosted trees) on this dataset. The model is trained with 80% of the data and 20% is used for testing the data. The trained data is biased with gender as explained in an earlier section. The model is then tested with rest of the 20% of the data which provides the recommendation for the loan application in the form of approve or reject. In a user study, we then assess how decision support provided by the model is affected in regards to bias when explanation with LIME and SHAP are added.

4.3 Explanation Types

Out of the XAI approaches previously discussed in Sect. 3, we used LIME and SHAP to explain the decisions of our Test use case: bank loan approval. We used the following methods of providing explanations for the explanation agents:

Table 3. Dataset variables

Age	17–70 years;
Income	0–200000€;
Assets	100000–1000000€;
Employment type	Fixed-term or permanent;
Gender	Female, male or other;
Loan amount	5000–520000€

Table 4. Sample data for generating explanations

Income	68100
Gender	Male
Employment	Fixed
Loan	479000
Assets	271900
Age	54

No Explanation. The agent does not provide any form of explanation for recommendations made. The black-box XAI acts as a baseline for our empirical assessment.

Explanation I: LIME. The agent explicitly states the explanation of the decision providing post-hoc explainability of the model decision. The model recommendation provided is complemented with the explanations to justify the machine recommendations. The explanations are used to test the bias-preventing effects of XAI. We use Local Interpretable Model-agnostic Explanations (LIME) as our first post-hoc explainability algorithm and generate the explanations that will be used in the human-computer interaction study. The explanations provided for a particular test case (Table 4) are depicted in Fig. 2 with *Reject* recommendation.

Explanation II: SHAP. We use SHapley Additive exPlanations (SHAP) as our second post-hoc explainability algorithm for generating the explanations to be used in the human-computer interaction study. Figure 3 where the recommendation provided by machine learning model is *Reject*.

5   Empirical Assessment

To investigate the effect of explainable agents, we conducted a human-computer interaction study as a foremost step for providing an empirical assessment of the proposed concept.

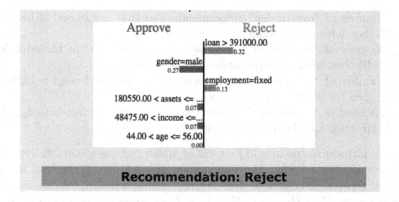

Fig. 2. Lime explanations with recommendation

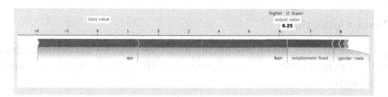

Fig. 3. Shap explanations

5.1   Study Description

The aim of this study is to gather preliminary facts for the explanation of the bias-preventing effects of XAI methods: LIME, SHAP with respect to the black-box as baseline with no XAI. The study is conducted with 65 participants with 20 for black-box XAI, 25 for LIME and 20 for SHAP. Fifteen different case data for loan application are generated and the recommendations are provided to approve or reject the loan application. The user has to select if he approves or rejects the loan application based on the recommendation provided. Three different interactive applications were generated as:

- Black-box based recommendation for loan application without XAI.
- XAI based recommendation for the loan application with visual explanations using XAI tool LIME.
- XAI based recommendation for the loan application with visual explanations using XAI tool SHAP.

Hypotheses. The aim of the study is to evaluate the following hypothesis:

1. H_a: Number of "overridden" recommendations that are biased is higher for SHAP then without explanations (true positive).
2. H_b: Number of "overridden" recommendations that are not biased is lower for SHAP then without explanations (false positive).

3. H_c: Number of "overridden" recommendations that are biased is higher for LIME then without explanations (true positive).
4. H_d: Number of "overridden" recommendations that are not biased is lower for LIME then without explanations (false positive).
5. H_e: Number of "overridden" recommendations that are biased is higher for LIME then for SHAP (true positive).
6. H_f: Number of "overridden" recommendations that are not biased is lower for LIME then for SHAP (false positive).

The study introduces the bias in *four out of fifteen* test cases and our hypothesis aims at evaluating whether the humans are able to detect the bias in agent supported recommendations or not. We are testing whether we can reject the null hypothesis (H_{a0}, H_{b0}, H_{c0}, H_{d0}, H_{e0}, H_{f0}) being the negations of our six hypotheses.

5.2 Data Collection

Study Protocol. For this user-centric study, we got the participants from the University's environment which means most of the participants have a technical university degree.

1. Initially, the study participant is introduced to the user study. The study instructions are given to participant by a facilitator in the form of written instructions. The bias introduced was not disclosed until the end of the study.
2. After providing the instructions, the study is carried out under the supervision of one researcher who helps in controlling the experiments as planned.
3. The study participant is asked to give the recommendation if he accepts or rejects the loan application based on the case data provided for any of the above 3 applications discussed.
4. The process is iterated for 15 rounds of different case data.
5. After all the fifteen rounds of the application are completed, the participant is guided through the questionnaire. Since these questions could potentially affect the respondent's assessment about the process, so these questions are asked at last after the application assessment has been carried out and could not be accessed by the participant beforehand.

Questionnaire Design. Initially the users are asked to interact with the application and provide the data, **Q0:** Received the user responses in the form of approve or reject. We asked the users to provide the following demographic data **Q1:** Age (number); **Q2:** Gender (Selection: male, female, other); **Q3:** Highest educational degree (Selection: Pre-high school, High school, Bachelor, Master, Ph.D. or higher); **Q4:** Background in science, technology, engineering, or mathematics (STEM) [Boolean]; To evaluate the interactions between study participants, the following data was taken regarding their performance:

– Were they able to understand the (explanations of the) recommendations provided by application [Boolean];

- To rate their satisfaction level of (explanations of the) recommendations on a scale of 0-5;
- Which parameters they consider important in deciding if to approve or reject the loan application (multiple selections from income, gender, employment, loan, assets, age);
- To rate the user interface of the application on a scale of 0–5;

There were few different questions for the questionnaire generated for the study without explanations[2] and with explanations[3]. The following additional questions were designed for the study without explanations apart from the above defined questions:

- Do the users see themselves trusting the recommendation without an appropriate reason for its decision [boolean];
- If the decisions would be more satisfying with explanations along with recommendations;
- What kind of explanations the users expect to support the recommendations;

The following additional questions were designed for the both studies with explanations:

- If they heard about explainable machine learning before [boolean];
- If the user answers yes to the above question, then describe their knowledge about explainable machine learning in few words;
- Do they consider the parameters analysed by application as important [boolean];
- Do they think provided explanation is good enough to let them trust or not the recommendations provided;
- Describe possible improvements of the explanations to improve understandability;
- Describe interaction experience with application.
- Describe possible improvements of the user interface in terms of design;
- Can the users see themselves using the decision making application with given explanation;

Analysis Methods. In order to investigate the effect of explanations provided by the autonomous agents on the human participants we performed a comparison between three different user groups: Agents without explanation, and explainable agents using two different algorithms (LIME and SHAP) which automatically generate different explanations for agent actions. We analysed the results using Excel XLMiner Data analysis ToolPak to run hypothesis tests as well as exploratory statistics. Firstly, we determined the differences between means and medians of human decision making in different settings. For each hypothesis, we

---

[2] https://docs.google.com/forms/d/1nxJpzdo8y5QiCFeHo6LY8M86u6istdAmau67pU dDZ1g/viewform.

[3] https://docs.google.com/forms/d/1CTatrqSgjX_PUYxxRGjktOdHaPepaKA1clgL4 1io3t4/viewform.

Table 5. Demographics of study participants for noEXP, LIME, SHAP

Methods	Total	Gender			Highest degree				STEM background		Age (years)
		Male	Female	OTH	Ph.D. (or higher)	Master	Bachelor	High school	Yes	No	
noEXP	20	10	9	0	1	5	7	6	13	7	21 (2), 23, 24 (2), 26(2), 27(2), 28(3), 30(3), 31(2), 34, 50, 57
LIME	25	18	5	1	4	12	6	2	24	1	20, 24(3), 25(2), 28, 29(4), 30(4), 32(3), 33(2), 37(2), 38, 51, 53
SHAP	20	11	7	1	7	9	3	1	18	2	21, 23, 24, 25(2), 26, 27(3), 28, 29, 32, 33(2), 34, 35, 36(2), 38, 41

tested the difference between distribution of decisions using two-Sample t-Test assuming equal variances with significance level of α set to 0.05. The correlation is calculated using Pearson correlation coefficient between demographic values and count of the right decisions (the decision overriding biased recommendation and approving non biased recommendations) by study participants.

65 people participated in the study ($n = 65$) out of which 20 were given no explanation during application interaction, 25 were given the explanations given by LIME and 20 by SHAP. When performing the correlation analysis we excluded two of the participants identified as other in terms of gender. The demographics of the participants are shown in Table 5. The study participants were predominantly male and predominantly had high education and background in science and technology. Majority is in their twenties or thirties with few outlining cases.

5.3   Result Analysis

Quantitative Analysis. The analysis starts with calculation of true positives, false positives, true negatives and false negatives which signify the following with respect to our evaluation criteria:

True Positive = *Overrides biased recommendation*
False Positive = *Overrides non biased recommendation*
True Negative = *Supports not biased recommendation*
False Negative = *Supports biased recommendation*

Table 6. Mean and median measures

	Measures	noEXP	LIME	SHAP
False negative	Count	32	37	23
	Mean	4.05	3.48	3.05
	Median	2	1	1
False positive	Count	81	87	61
	Mean	1.6	1.48	1.15
	Median	3	3	3
True negative	Count	139	188	159
	Mean	6.95	7.52	7.95
	Median	8	8	8
True positive	Count	48	63	57
	Mean	2.4	2.52	2.85
	Median	2	3	3

Table 7. Hypothesis analysis

	t-test	Hypothesis	p-value (two-tailed)	p-value (one-tailed)
1	true positive (SHAP, noEXP)	Ha0	0.18	0.09
2	false positive (SHAP, noEXP)	Hb0	0.13	0.06
3	true positive (LIME, noEXP)	Hc0	0.71	0.35
4	false positive (LIME, noEXP)	Hd0	0.35	0.17
5	true positive (LIME, SHAP)	He0	0.36	0.18
6	false positive (LIME, SHAP)	Hf0	0.39	0.19

Table 8. t-Test: two-sample assuming equal variances (true positives)

	noEXP	LIME	noEXP	SHAP	LIME	SHAP
Mean	2.4	2.52	2.4	2.85	2.52	2.85
Variance	0.7789473684	1.426666667	0.7789473684	1.397368421	1.426666667	1.397368421
Observations	20	25	20	20	25	20
P(T<=t) one-tail	0.3549150958		0.09027080274		0.180026242	
P(T<=t) two-tail	0.7098301915		0.1805416055		0.3600524839	

Table 9. t-Test: two-sample assuming equal variances (true negatives)

	noEXP	LIME	noEXP	SHAP	LIME	SHAP
Mean	6.95	7.52	6.95	7.95	7.52	7.95
Variance	5.628947368	2.76	5.628947368	2.681578947	2.76	2.681578947
Observations	20	25	20	20	25	20
P(T<=t) one-tail	0.1745331086		0.06455759198		0.1950434934	
P(T<=t) two-tail	0.3490662172		0.129115184		0.3900869869	

The count, mean and median for each of the above type of recommendation for each of the three user study groups is calculated as shown in Table 6. It depicts that there are notable differences in means aligned with the assumption

Table 10. t-Test: two-sample assuming equal variances (false positives)

	noEXP	LIME	noEXP	SHAP	LIME	SHAP
Mean	4.05	3.48	4.05	3.05	3.48	3.05
Variance	5.628947368	2.76	5.628947368	2.681578947	2.76	2.681578947
Observations	20	25	20	20	25	20
P(T<=t) one-tail	0.1745331086		0.06455759198		0.1950434934	
P(T<=t) two-tail	0.3490662172		0.129115184		0.3900869869	

Table 11. t-Test: two-sample assuming equal variances (false negatives)

	noEXP	LIME	noEXP	SHAP	LIME	SHAP
Mean	1.6	1.48	1.6	1.15	1.48	1.15
Variance	0.7789473684	1.426666667	0.7789473684	1.397368421	1.426666667	1.397368421
Observations	20	25	20	20	25	20
P(T<=t) one-tail	0.3549150958		0.09027080274		0.180026242	
P(T<=t) two-tail	0.7098301915		0.1805416055		0.3600524839	

Table 12. Correlation between demographics and decision making

Demographics	no EXP (correlation)	no EXP (p-value)	LIME (correlation)	LIME (p-value)	SHAP (correlation)	SHAP (p-value)
Age	−0.3943338142	0.08534479016	−0.2122591802	0.3083793126	−0.2735918895	0.2431317331
Gender	−0.01899685628	0.9366405456	−0.2145147339	0.314135297	0.08552499375	0.7277463724
Education	−0.1699636098	0.4737466067	0.01314368012	0.9502790615	−0.1209607494	0.6114580972
STEM background	−0.05775093751	0.80890297	0.09386465089	0.6553926784	−0.1433608882	0.5465249821

that motivate our first five hypothesis regarding the differences between modes with explanation versus modes without explanation. However the differences are statistically not significant.

Our hypotheses are applicable for only true positives and false positives and the Table 7 gives the calculated p-values for two-tailed as well as one-tailed tests to test our null hypothesis (negations of our hypotheses). There are not observed significant differences but the notable differences can be seen for overriding the bias based recommendations higher for LIME than no explanation. There are also notable differences for overriding non-biased recommendations lower for SHAP than no explanation. Hence, the results supports our hypotheses H_b, H_c to a little extent. However the results are not in favour of our last sixth hypothesis since number of overridden recommendations that are not biased is not lower for LIME than for SHAP. Considering the small sample size, the results can not be generalized. Tables 8, 9, 10 and 11 are showing the means, variances, number of observations and p-values (both one and two tailed) which indicate whether there were observed differences between different groups of participants.

Further we performed the correlation analyses using Pearson coefficient between the complete count of the right decisions (true negative and true positive decisions) made by participants and the demographic variables. Table 12 is showing values of Pearson correlation coefficient for all conditions - no explanation, LIME and SHAP - and the p-values which depict if the computed coefficients are showing statistical significant correlations between demographic variables and the right decisions (true negative and true positive) of the participants. We did not find a significant correlation, although the correlation between age and count of the right decision in group without explanation seems plausible which may be indicating that the lower age was somehow predicting the higher number of right decisions.

Qualitative Analysis Interaction Experience. In a group without provided explanation, participants generally considered income as the most important parameter when deciding for approving or rejecting the loan whereas the gender was noted as the least important and majority was satisfied with the user interface of the application. Participants in group with given explanations (SHAP and LIME) similarly rated income as the most important parameter when deciding for approving or rejecting the loan whereas the gender was noted as the least important and majority perceived the user interface of application as good.

Explanation Evaluation. Most of the participants in group without provided explanation, answered that they did not understand recommendations provided by application and that they can not see themselves trusting the recommendations provided by the given application without the provided explanation. They were mostly satisfied with the given recommendations but also noted that they would like to have an explanation added in the application. In groups with provided explanations (SHAP and LIME) participants mainly answered that they understood the explanations of the recommendations provided by application and were satisfied with the explanations provided. About half of the participant answered that the given explanation was good enough in order to let them judge when they should trust or not trust provided explanations and they could also see themselves using the application with the given explanation. By analyzing the participants' free-form feedback, we additionally found that:

- End-users want additional linguistic explanations along with visual based explanations.
- End users want explanations to be suitable for intuitive comparisons.
- End users want to interact with agent for more information.

6   Discussion and Perspectives

From observed results comparing human decisions from different groups of participants (two with explanations versus no explanation group), we observed notable differences between groups in mean/median of their decisions. Those differences may reflect the initial assumptions stating that both SHAP and LIME explanation will cause less overriding of non biased recommendations and more overriding of biased recommendations than having no explanation at all. However, as our hypothesis testing showed these differences are statistically not significant, and we therefore can not draw empirically valid inferences. Our initial assumption that participants with LIME will perform better in overriding more biased recommendations than participants with SHAP explanation, was also to some extent supported by our results, however participants having LIME explanation did not perform better in overriding less non-biased recommendations than those with SHAP. This could indicate that participants with SHAP explanation to some extent engaged in more understanding of the explanation since SHAP explanation has higher complexity compared to LIME which can also be concluded from the participants comments from their interaction with application.

Our results also give insight into the initial research questions. The user study and interaction with no explanation and explanation study depicts that users are able to understand the explainable AI systems more profoundly and are comfortable in the recommendations provided by these systems compared to the noEXP systems. This imbibes more confidence in the developers to have more explainable systems which will instill more confidence in users to trust such systems. The two explanation types have been used to understand the goodness of the explanations and the parameters which users consider as important in regard with explanations provided. Thus, the study provided a deep insight into the details of these systems from the perspective of users which can be used as positive feedback for the design of such AI systems.

6.1   Limitations

The paper provides human-agent interaction study to reduce the bias in human decision making with the help of explanations provided with recommendations. The interaction study has a set of limitations, the most important of which are listed below:

- **The scope is limited to only two explanation tools:** The current approach focuses only on two explanation tools, LIME and SHAP which can further be validated with other more sophisticated tools such as CIU [6].
- **The time for a decision is not taken into account:** The user time for making a decision in the study is not considered which may effect the empirical validation of the study. It would be, for example, interesting to know if people presented with SHAP explanation took longer time in deciding to approve or not to approve loan in each case. Because the provided results are not showing significant differences in results between groups without explanation and groups with explanations for decision making which could indicate the presence of human bias.
- **Human bias in decision making:** The paper provides simplistic scenario of the loan application data which neglects the human related biases. It means that human participants possibly ignored the given recommendations, or did not pay that much attention to it as expected and/or that they ignored the explanations of recommendations by focusing more on their own assumptions.
- **The scope is limited to a synthetically generated data:** For facilitation of real life applicability, it is necessary to use the real application data in the context of real world situations in the actual real-life settings. The sample should be more diversified and it would be good to control the demographics as well.

6.2   Future Work

The following future research directions can be considered to address the limitations discussed in previous subsection:

- **To scale the study to other XAI tools:** We present the study with LIME and SHAP as explanation tools, it will be good to test the concept on a more wider perspective with other explainable artificial intelligence tools as well such as CIU, ELI5 etc.
- **Evaluate the study applicability with domain experts:** While we have provided a prototype that shows the applicability in the generated dataset, its exact usability can be validated with the domain experts.
- **Extend the scope to real-life case study:** It will be interesting to explore the actual case study with real life complexities to show that the agents act more rationally in real life applications.

7   Conclusion

We try to explain the behaviour of the autonomous agents to humans by conducting a preliminary human-agent interaction study to investigate the effect of explanations provided by agents to lower the biased based recommendations. In this paper, we explored the potential of the bias based recommendations in human decisions for three different groups of participants, 2 groups with explanations provided and 1 group without explanations. The results of our study show the improved trend of user's perceived trust in explanation based recommendations compared to the ones with no explanation for the less bias in agent supported human decision making. The results of our study are inline with our initial assumption that end-users experience could benefit from explanation based recommendations to reduce the bias in human decision making. The presented agent-supported interaction study for enabling human-agent decision making pave the way for exhaustive evaluations for the effectiveness of the agent supported decisions.

Current user study for supporting agent-human decision making concerns the integration of a system able to detect user's approval or rejection for the machine recommendations; further development of interaction strategies such as management of socio-emotional factors and the decision time in human agent interaction. We expect that such integrations will contribute in providing realistic interactions and improved results.

References

1. Defense advanced research projects agency (DARPA): Broad agency announcement- explainable artificial intelligence (XAI) (2016)
2. Adadi, A., Berrada, M.: Peeking inside the black-box: a survey on explainable artificial intelligence (XAI). IEEE Access **6**, 52138–52160 (2018)

3. Biran, O., Cotton, C.: Explanation and justification in machine learning: a survey. In: IJCAI 2017 Workshop on Explainable AI (XAI), vol. 8, p. 1 (2017)
4. Choo, J., Liu, S.: Visual analytics for explainable deep learning. IEEE Comput. Graph. Appl. **38**(4), 84–92 (2018)
5. Dannenhauer, D., Floyd, M.W., Molineaux, M., Aha, D.W.: Learning from exploration: towards an explainable goal reasoning agent (2018)
6. Främling, K.: Explaining results of neural networks by contextual importance and utility. In: Proceedings of the AISB 1996 Conference. Citeseer (1996)
7. Ghosal, S., Blystone, D., Singh, A.K., Ganapathysubramanian, B., Singh, A., Sarkar, S.: An explainable deep machine vision framework for plant stress phenotyping. Proc. Natl. Acad. Sci. **115**(18), 4613–4618 (2018)
8. Gunning, D.: Explainable artificial intelligence (XAI). Defense Advanced Research Projects Agency (DARPA), nd Web 2 (2017)
9. Holzinger, A., Biemann, C., Pattichis, C.S., Kell, D.B.: What do we need to build explainable AI systems for the medical domain? arXiv preprint arXiv:1712.09923 (2017)
10. Liu, S., Wang, X., Liu, M., Zhu, J.: Towards better analysis of machine learning models: a visual analytics perspective. Vis. Inf. **1**(1), 48–56 (2017)
11. Madhikermi, M., Malhi, A.K., Främling, K.: Explainable artificial intelligence based heat recycler fault detection in air handling unit. In: Calvaresi, D., Najjar, A., Schumacher, M., Främling, K. (eds.) EXTRAAMAS 2019. LNCS (LNAI), vol. 11763, pp. 110–125. Springer, Cham (2019). https://doi.org/10.1007/978-3-030-30391-4_7
12. Malhi, A., Kampik, T., Pannu, H., Madhikermi, M., Främling, K.: Explaining machine learning-based classifications of in-vivo gastral images. In: 2019 Digital Image Computing: Techniques and Applications (DICTA), pp. 1–7. IEEE (2019)
13. Miller, T.: Explanation in artificial intelligence: insights from the social sciences. Artif. Intell. **267**, 1–38 (2019)
14. Ribeiro, M.T., Singh, S., Guestrin, C.: Why should i trust you?: explaining the predictions of any classifier. In: Proceedings of the 22nd ACM SIGKDD International Conference on Knowledge Discovery and Data Mining, pp. 1135–1144. ACM (2016)
15. Samek, W., Wiegand, T., Müller, K.R.: Explainable artificial intelligence: understanding, visualizing and interpreting deep learning models. arXiv preprint arXiv:1708.08296 (2017)
16. Weitz, K., Schiller, D., Schlagowski, R., Huber, T., André, E.: Do you trust me?: increasing user-trust by integrating virtual agents in explainable AI interaction design. In: Proceedings of the 19th ACM International Conference on Intelligent Virtual Agents, pp. 7–9. ACM (2019)

Demos

Explainable Agents as Static Web Pages: UAV Simulation Example

Yazan Mualla[1]([⊠]) [iD], Timotheus Kampik[2] [iD], Igor H. Tchappi[1,4] [iD],
Amro Najjar[3] [iD], Stéphane Galland[1] [iD], and Christophe Nicolle[5] [iD]

[1] CIAD, Univ. Bourgogne Franche-Comté, UTBM, 90010 Belfort, France
{yazan.mualla,igor.tchappi,stephane.galland}@utbm.fr
[2] Department of Computing Science, Umeå University, 90187 Umeå, Sweden
tkampik@cs.umu.se
[3] AI-Robolab/ICR, Computer Science and Communications,
University of Luxembourg, 4365 Esch-sur-Alzette, Luxembourg
amro.najjar@uni.lu
[4] Faculty of Sciences, University of Ngaoundere, B.P. 454, Ngaoundere, Cameroon
[5] CIAD, Univ. Bourgogne Franche-Comté, UB, 21000 Dijon, France
christophe.nicolle@u-bourgogne.fr

Abstract. Motivated by the apparent societal need to design complex
autonomous systems whose decisions and actions are humanly intelligi-
ble, the study of explainable artificial intelligence, and with it, research
on explainable autonomous agents has gained increased attention from
the research community. One important objective of research on explainable agents is the evaluation of explanation approaches in human-
computer interaction studies. In this demonstration paper, we present
a way to facilitate such studies by implementing explainable agents and
multi-agent systems that *i)* can be deployed as static files, not requiring
the execution of server-side code, which minimizes administration and
operation overhead, and *ii)* can be embedded into web front ends and
other JavaScript-enabled user interfaces, hence increasing the ability to
reach a broad range of users. We then demonstrate the approach with the
help of an application that was designed to assess the effect of different
explainability approaches on the human intelligibility of an unmanned
aerial vehicle simulation.

Keywords: eXplainable Artificial Intelligence · Engineering
multi-agent systems · Human-Computer Interaction

1 Introduction

Since the lack of interpretability of both black-box machine learning models and
complex rule-based systems is a generally-acknowledged socio-technical problem, the research domain of eXplainable Artificial Intelligence (XAI) is gaining

Y. Mualla and T. Kampik—These two authors have contributed equally.

© Springer Nature Switzerland AG 2020
D. Calvaresi et al. (Eds.): EXTRAAMAS 2020, LNAI 12175, pp. 149–154, 2020.
https://doi.org/10.1007/978-3-030-51924-7_9

increased attention from researchers of various disciplines. A particularly motivating factor is that emerging laws and regulations, most notably the European Union's GDPR, require that certain decisions of information systems must be humanly interpretable [3]. Recent works in the literature highlighted explainability as one of the cornerstones for building trustworthy responsible AI systems [11,12]. In this context, an obvious research frontier for the autonomous agents and Multi-Agent Systems (MAS) community is the design of explainable intelligent agents [8]. This frontier is explained by the fact that while intelligent agents have been established as a suitable technique for implementing autonomous high-level control and decision-making in complex AI systems [13], there is still a need for these systems to be understood and trusted by the human users.

Considering that the growth of research on explainable agents is accelerating, contributions that empirically evaluate the proposed explainability approaches are still scarce [2,6]. In this regard, Agent-based Simulation (ABS) fits the requirements to implement such empirical evaluations. ABS is a set of interacting intelligent entities that models and executes, within an artificial environment, the real-world autonomous agents, their relationships, and interactions with the environment [13]. Consequently, ABS can be considered as a natural step forward towards better managing and evaluating the proposed explainability approaches in Human-Computer Interaction (HCI) empirical user studies.

To facilitate more research and bridge the gap between the theoretical proposed explainability approaches on the one hand, and the practical evaluation of such approaches on the other hand, this demonstration paper presents an ABS approach to engineer explainable agents and MAS prototypes for the specific purpose of empirical evaluation in HCI studies. The approach makes use of light-weight web technologies that facilitate rapid prototyping and allow for the deployment of agents and MAS as static web pages.

2   Explainable Agents as Static Web Pages

2.1   Motivation

The proposed approach to explainable agent prototyping and simulation development is to implement ABS as static web front ends. These web pages can be easily deployed to any device that serve or render web pages, and shared with a broad audience, for example as web links. From a technology perspective, the approach makes use of the *JS-son* library [5], which allows the creation of Belief-Desire-Intention (BDI) agents, as well as agents with other reasoning loops and MAS in a higher-level programming language with little learning and technology overhead. We argue that the proposed approach has the following advantages:

Ease of deployment. Because the program code consists only of static files that are to be provided by a web server, it can be deployed in a straightforward manner, without the need of a complicated installation routine or the requirement to have extensive permissions on the target server. In particular, the program files can be moved to traditional static file servers (*e.g.*, via

FTP upload or via the upload feature of a content management system), or integrated into light-weight developer operations-oriented tools and services (*e.g.*, continuous deployment to GitHub pages on push to a git repository's master branch).

Reach. The explainable ABS can be easily shared with any potential human user who can access the Internet with a recent web browser. While for running HCI studies, oftentimes video *vignettes* are created to allow for easier sharing [1], using such vignettes *i)* severely limits interactive features and *ii)* does not allow for convenient updates (minor changes, for example to the user interface, require re-recording the video(s)).

Scalability. Because all program code is executed by the client, in particular by the browser of the corresponding end-user, applications developed with the proposed approach scale well; the server merely needs to provide (by all practical means: small) static files, which means researchers can host the applications essentially free of costs.

2.2 Architecture

The proposed approach is based on the following architecture design (depicted in Fig. 1). A MAS (or, in simple scenarios, a single agent) is engineered to run encapsulated in a web page. Note that single-user interactions/human-in-the-loop approaches are possible, and even multi-user interactions can be realized with light-weight real-time communication technologies such as Web Real-Time Communications (webRTC) [4], albeit with a minimally invasive integration of server-side technologies. The state of the environment and all agents it contains is exposed to a User Interface (UI) manager component that processes the state and makes it available to the following components:

- A **grid world** displays the "physical state" of the environment, *i.e.* the position of agents and artifacts.
- A **state table** or tree-like structure provides an overview of relevant information that is not obvious from the grid world representation, *i.e.*, hidden properties like goals and internal states of agents.
- A **notification system** informs users about important events, *e.g.*, when agents diverge from their expected behavior. Notifications are displayed as visually invasive alerts that overly the rest of the user interface.
- **Interaction controls** (only in non-study mode, to not distract study participants) allow users to switch between different simulation modes and adjust simulation parameters.

3   UAV Simulation Example

The use of ABS for Unmanned Aerial Vehicles (UAVs) is gaining more interest in complex civil application scenarios where coordination and cooperation are necessary [7]. To provide a running example, let us describe how the approach we

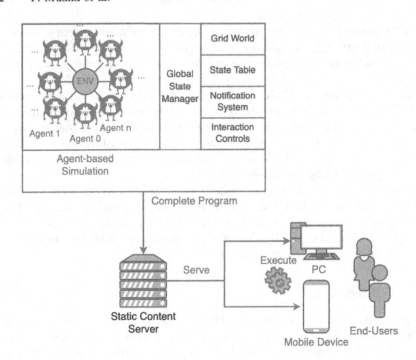

Fig. 1. Explainable Agent-based Simulation architecture

introduce in this paper can be used in a UAVs simulation scenario[1]. The study evaluates how different explainability approaches affect human intelligibility of a UAV delivery simulation. The simulation is provided in three modes, which represent different paths through the explanation generation process.

Basic mode. It displays the current state of all agents, including their current goal (target destination and mission type) in a table-like overview that updates in real-time.

Adaptive filter mode. It aggregates the most important information across agents; *i.e.*, users do not need to scan the table for relevant information, but can see at a glance which agents perform missions according to their expectations, and which agents are in possibly problematic states ("stranded", uncoordinated). When an agent enters such a state, an alert with the agent's ID and goal information is generated.

Contrastive mode. Alerts are constructed using an *implicitly counterfactual* explanation scheme, following the structure `Agent A is doing P [instead of Q] because of C`, where P is the current behavior, Q is the presumably expected behavior, and C is the execution condition. This means `[instead of Q]` is implied by the alert and hence dropped from the text.

---

[1] The developed application has been used for a follow-up of the explainable agents HCI study presented by Mualla *et al.* [9,10].

Figure 2 displays the simulation in an interactive test mode that allows for the manipulation of simulation parameters through the user interface[2]. (In the study application, UI controls where hidden and simulation parameters were set via the simulation's URL parameters to avoid end-user distraction and interference).

After all agents' states have been collected, explanations, *i.e* summaries that give an overview of the agents' beliefs, are generated. For this, the chosen modes (Basic, adaptive filter, or contrastive) will determine the processes to be executed.

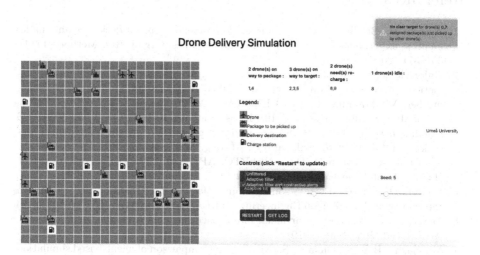

Fig. 2. Explainable UAV simulation with UI controls.

4   Conclusion

In this demonstration paper, we have shown how explainable agent simulations can be deployed as static web pages. The presented approach serves as an example of how light-weight tools with a small development, deployment, and operations footprint can be utilized to: *i)* rapidly develop agent/ABS prototypes in a widely-used higher-level programming language and *ii)* roll-out these prototypes and simulations at scale to large and diverse user groups, in particular for the purpose of empirical validation. As future research, from an engineering perspective, it can be considered as valuable to extend the JS-son library, which forms the foundation of this demonstration, with additional, generically useful abstractions for implementing explainable reasoning-loop agents. For this, components that this work implement can be extracted and merged into JS-son. From HCI and XAI perspectives, it can be considered as interesting to extend

---

[2] The source code of the simulation is available at https://github.com/TimKam/uav-xai-simulation/. A running simulation system (with UI controls activated) is available at http://s.cs.umu.se/51x65y.

the simulation to allow for human-in-the-loop feedback that helps improve the explanations over time.

Acknowledgments. This work was partially supported by the Regional Council of Bourgogne Franche-Comté (RBFC, France) within the project UrbanFly 20174-06234/06242. It was also partially supported by the Wallenberg AI, Autonomous Systems and Software Program (WASP) funded by the Knut and Alice Wallenberg Foundation.

References

1. Aguinis, H., Bradley, K.J.: Best practice recommendations for designing and implementing experimental vignette methodology studies. Organ. Res. Methods **17**(4), 351–371 (2014)
2. Anjomshoae, S., Främling, K., Najjar, A.: Explanations of black-box model predictions by contextual importance and utility. In: Calvaresi, D., Najjar, A., Schumacher, M., Främling, K. (eds.) EXTRAAMAS 2019. LNCS (LNAI), vol. 11763, pp. 95–109. Springer, Cham (2019). https://doi.org/10.1007/978-3-030-30391-4_6
3. Goodman, B., Flaxman, S.: European union regulations on algorithmic decision-making and a "right to explanation". AI Mag. **38**(3), 50–57 (2017)
4. Johnston, A.B., Burnett, D.C.: WebRTC: APIs and RTCWEB Protocols of the HTML5 Real-Time Web. Digital Codex LLC, St. Louis, MO, USA (2012)
5. Kampik, T., Nieves, J.C.: JS-son-A minimal JavaScript BDI agent library. In: 7th International Workshop on Engineering Multi-Agent Systems (EMAS 2019) (2019)
6. Miller, T.: Explanation in artificial intelligence: insights from the social sciences. Artif. Intell. **267**, 1–38 (2019)
7. Mualla, Y., Bai, W., Galland, S., Nicolle, C.: Comparison of agent-based simulation frameworks for unmanned aerial transportation applications. Procedia Comput. Sci. **130**, 791–796 (2018)
8. Mualla, Y., et al.: Agent-based simulation of unmanned aerial vehicles in civilian applications: a systematic literature review and research directions. Future Gener. Comput. Syst. **100**, 344–364 (2019)
9. Mualla, Y., Najjar, A., Kampik, T., Tchappi, I.H., Galland, S., Nicolle, C.: Towards explainability for a civilian UAV fleet management using an agent-based approach (2019). arXiv:1909.10090 cs.AI
10. Mualla, Y., Tchappi, I.H., Najjar, A., Kampik, T., Galland, S., Nicolle, C.: Human-agent explainability: an experimental case study on the filtering of explanations. In: 12th International Conference on Agents and Artificial Intelligence (2020)
11. Preece, A.: Asking 'Why' in AI: explainability of intelligent systems-perspectives and challenges. Intell. Syst. Account. Finance Manag. **25**(2), 63–72 (2018)
12. Rosenfeld, A., Richardson, A.: Explainability in human-agent systems. Auton. Agents Multi-Agent Syst. **33**, 1–33 (2019)
13. Wooldridge, M., Jennings, N.R.: Intelligent agents: theory and practice. Knowl. Eng. Rev. **10**(2), 115–152 (1995)

Author Index

Printed in the United States
By Bookmasters